About The Cover

The view here is from the eyes of One who is seated between the cherubim on the Ark of the Covenant in the Most Holy Place of the Tabernacle of Moses. The veil has been rent. A ripened harvest of the nations of the earth stands without in the courts of the Lord. This scene was received in a vision of the Lord while attending the recent prophetic roundtable at Destiny Image in Shippensburg, Pennsylvania. Several attractive cover designs had been submitted, but all from the perspective of looking into the Holy of Holies. The Lord inspired the cover design to portray the Christ-centered vision of The More Excellent Ministry! This is how the Man in the throne with a ministry sees all things.

Acknowledgments

To Scott Jaynes, for transcribing the original messages.

To Tony LeQuire, for the use of his personal computer to produce the manuscript.

To Don Nori, for his encouragement and trust to go ahead with the impossible.

To the members of the Body of Christ, for their prayerful and financial support from the beginning of this project.

To my family, for allowing me the time to write this book.

To the Holy Ghost, Who is my teacher.

The

More Excellent

Ministry

By Kelley Varner

Destiny Image Publishers
P.O. Box 351
Shippensburg, PA 17257

"We Publish the Prophets"

ISBN 0-914903-60-8

For Worldwide Distribution
Printed in the U.S.A.

Dedication

I lovingly dedicate this book to one who has been called to share His Mercy-seat. No one has influenced and changed my life more than this one. No one has ministered His grace to help me in time of need more than this one. No one has taught me to love and appreciate people more than this one. No one has shown more patience and unselfishness than this one.

This one is April's mother, Jonathan's mom, Joy Beth's and David's momma. This one is my companion, my lover, and my closest friend.

Joann, I love you.

Foreword

When I "discovered" Kelley Varner's teaching through reading his book, *Prevail*, I took comfort in knowing that another preacher was hearing the same spiritual sound as I. The greatest and worst thing that can happen to a man who is seeking God's perspective is for God to speak to him. Spiritual understanding is worth everything — which is precisely what it costs.

Kelley Varner is a man who hears from the Lord, and he has paid the price of that trust with humility and endurance. As a result he speaks with tremendous prophetic insight to give direction to this generation. *The More Excellent Ministry* opens the dynamics of Jesus' ministry to Church leaders at a time when the trumpet of the Lord is sounding an alarm and a call to action. Christians know that they must do something, but what? Kelley Varner has the answers.

That trumpet blasts across the land in a day of

confusion, purging and challenge. The call is clear, "Unity, maturity, and reconciliation yield true Kingdom righteousness, peace and joy." We have entered a new reformation led by the Holy Spirit. Meanwhile, Kelley Varner continues as a called forerunner, speaking direction to the Church on the cutting edge where Christianity is interesting and people have ears to hear the Word of the Lord.

The More Excellent Ministry will challenge, excite and ignite your own ministry. When a true prophet speaks, God requires that people make choices. If you shun accountability to God, don't read this book because spiritual insights are costly. But if you want the kind of spiritual food that is nourishing, strengthening and satisfying, you have come to a table spread with a feast.

Enjoy! Hear! Then, do!

Our King Cometh!

Bishop Earl Paulk
Chapel Hill Harvester Church
Atlanta, Georgia

Contents

Preface

"I am going to deliver My creation by forgiving it!"
God had spoken. Beginning as a whisper in the depths of my spirit, these words of light have become ever-widening. So simple, and yet so profound.

The principles of truth which you are about to learn have changed my life, and have revolutionized the thinking of many shepherds and sheep in the Body of Christ.

The Day of the Lord has dawned, and men in every nation are beginning to hear the Gospel of the Kingdom for the first time. The present reality of the Most Holy Place is truth that is being worked into the inward parts. The realm of His life and love is available to those who now come into His Presence boldly by His blood. An overcoming Church is beginning to sit down with Him in His throne. A throne-room people is the heart-throb of our Heavenly Father. We are becoming

His throne of grace in the earth, for as He is, so are we in the now.

The messages in this volume were preached at the House of Prayer in Springfield, Missouri, in March of 1981. Bro. Bill Britton was the host pastor of that gathering. There was a sovereign move of God in that meeting as Jesus opened our hearts to understand His ways. I have desired to share this Word with you, and now is the time.

We have been given the word and ministry of reconciliation. Every wall must come down in the Name of the Lord! Our King is answering the cry of a groaning creation by sending His army out of Zion. A people with the nature and the ministry of Jesus. A people with the more excellent ministry.

Kelley Varner
April, 1988

Chapter One

The More Excellent Ministry

This is not a sermon. It is a message, and the Word of the Lord to this generation. He is unveiling this mystery by revelation, which in other ages was not made known unto the sons of men as it is now revealed unto His holy apostles and prophets by the Spirit (Eph. 3:5).

This is that day of unveiling and we must come with a right spirit. We cannot afford to be burdened with a top-heavy theology that is not relevant. Just as the City of Rev. 21 descends from the realm of the invisible to the realm of the visible, so the truth about His Kingdom and Lordship must descend from the heights of our intellect to be birthed in our hearts. Once the logos, or the written Word, has become the rhema, or the living Word, in our spirits, it must continue its descent to our feet. We must walk out these principles in shoe leather, or the light that is in us will be but darkness (Matt. 6:22-23). We must not lust after knowledge for its own sake, or we will be thrust from paradise (Gen. 3). There was a walk with God in that garden, and out of that relationship God speaks to man

(II Cor. 12:1-4). We cannot allow ourselves to have the indulgent spirit of the Athenians, who wallowed in the sensuality of always wanting to hear something new, ever learning and never coming to the knowledge of the truth (Acts 17:21). Our life must now match our lip. There has been too much rhetoric. We cry for reality!

It is with this attitude that we approach the truths of the more excellent ministry. I long to impart to you these life-changing concepts, the very heart and soul of the king-priest ministry which is after the order or arrangement of Melchisedec. Our study will be focused in the epistle to the Hebrews, especially chapters four through ten.

This message is intensely practical. In these days of shaking and transition, God is bringing a great balance to all His servants and His Body. He is the great Filter through which we all must pass (Rom. 11:36). None of us is going to carry our mess into His Kingdom. God is concerned about the condition of the Church. On the one hand, the abuses and extremes of sonship and deeper life teaching have caused many godly people to look elsewhere for light. On the other hand, many of the saints are not being fed. They are tired of peanuts, popcorn, and candy. Like the younger prodigal (or "waster") of Luke 15, these have been eating husks, the empty shell of yesterday's leftovers, the fading flower of a former day, the lifeless traditions of men which make the Word of no effect (Isa. 28:1; Mk. 7:13). The land is filled with churches that have either the wineskin or the wine, either good governmental order and structure or the present truths of the Kingdom and the Most Holy Place; but few of the brethren have a sensible passion for both. There are good, solid churches who have yet to hear what the Head of the Church is saying now, or there are those with revelation knowledge without a receptacle or a dispenser (Prov. 29:18). Understanding that the home and the local church are the vehicles for the Kingdom, the arenas in which these principles must be lived out day by day, let us now proceed to lay the foundation for these truths.

Excellent Things

God's purposes are revealed in three dimensions.

Deut. 16:16 KJV:

> *Three times in a year shall all thy males appear before the Lord thy God in the place which he shall choose; in the feast of unleavened bread, and in the feast of weeks, and in the feast of tabernacles: and they shall not appear before the Lord empty: ...*

This refers to the Feast of Passover, the Feast of Pentecost, and the Feast of Tabernacles. Compare the three dimensions of the Tabernacle of Moses: the Outer Court, the Holy Place, and the Most Holy Place. This principle of three-fold things is consistent throughout the Bible. I listed forty examples of these threes on pages 84-85 of the book *Prevail: a Handbook for the Overcomer*. Consider the following examples from that reference:

Passover	Pentecost	Tabernacles
Outer Court	Holy Place	Most Holy Place
New Birth	Holy Ghost Baptism	Maturity
Jesus (Saviour)	Christ (Anointing)	The Lord
Milk	Bread	Meat
The Way	The Truth	The Life
Faith	Hope	Love

Water Baptism	Spirit Baptism	Fire Baptism
Babes	Youth	Men

Prov. 22:20-21 KJV:

Have not I written to thee excellent things in counsels and knowledge, That I might make thee know the certainty of the words of truth; that thou mightest answer the words of truth to them that send unto thee?

Young's Literal Translation says, "Have I not written to thee three times ...?" *The Jerusalem Bible* adds, "Have I not written for you thirty chapters ...?" Keep in mind that the number thirty reveals the principle of coming to maturity or coming to the throne. It is also a number denoting priesthood. The patriarch Joseph and the monarch David were thirty years old when they ascended to their places of rulership. The priests began to minister at the age of thirty. The heavens opened over the head of the prophet Ezekiel when he was thirty. The Pattern Son Jesus came to the river Jordan and began his public ministry at the age of thirty. The Child was born at Bethlehem, but the Son was given at the Jordan (Isa. 9:6-7).

The Hebrew word for "excellent things" in Prov. 22:20 is "shalosh" (#7991 in *Strong's Concordance*) and means "a triple (as a musical instrument), a triangle (or perhaps a three-stringed lute), a three-fold measure, a general of the third rank (upward, the highest)." It is translated in the King James Version as "captain, instrument of music, (great) lord, (great) measure, prince, three." It is taken from the word (#7969) meaning "three, third, thrice." Thus, these "excellent things" are three-fold things! Truths dealing with three dimensions. This is the manner in which the Father has written His counsels and knowledge that we might know the certainty of the words of truth (Ex. 23:14; II Sam. 23:9). It is interesting that the primary meanings of this word speak of the area of music. With each move of God from Luther to the present, the Lord has brought a new song to His Church. There was a song for the Outer Court, a song for the Holy Place, and the song of songs for the Holy of Holies. Each has its place, and when struck together by the hand of God, they provide a symphonic chord of truth, perfectly balanced and blended at every level.

All of us are hungry. Along the way, as with the prophet Elijah, we have been fed by ravens in the Outer Court. Then God led us to the woman of the Holy Place. But I pray that an angel (or messenger) will stop by and feed us with meat that is in season (Gal. 4:14; Rev. 1:20)! A many-membered angel with one mouth and one voice (I Cor. 1:10). I am thankful for what the ravens have brought. I praise Him for what the Woman, a Spirit-filled Church, can offer. But God wants us to eat of Himself, of His Word and of His Spirit beyond the rent veil. There is standing up a priest with Urim and Thummim so that we can eat the things of the Most Holy Place (Ezra 2:63). This is the "hidden manna" of Rev. 2:17. At one time, it was not lawful to consider these new creation realities (II Cor. 12:1-4), but now the Lamb has been killed and the table is spread. All things are now ready.

Only the living Word can help us now. I want my life to be changed. I am tired of going into meetings just for the sake of going into meetings. I am wearied to hear the voice of a man or a woman. Beloved, we must learn to listen for the Voice within the voice. I want to hear Him! There is a deep sense of hunger, a longing, and a reaching forth in many of your hearts. I pray that you will allow this living, creative Word to divide soul and spirit to transform your life (Heb. 4:12).

So then there were three feasts. The Feast of

Passover was in the first month (Ex. 12:1-2), and was a beginning of months unto Israel. God meets man in this first dimension as Jesus, the Saviour. We then seal that conversion or initial salvation with baptism in water in the Name of the Lord Jesus Christ for the remission of our sins and the circumcision of our hearts. Christ our Passover was sacrificed for us. The Lord Jesus, the Lamb of God, did more than atone for or cover our sins. Atonement is intrinsically an Old Testament concept. The blood of bulls and goats could but cover sin, and that annually. The blood of Jesus is better blood, nobler and stronger. He did more than cover my sin. He removed it as far as the east is from the west (Psa. 103:12)! He took it away. He removed it. I am a new creation that never existed before!

The second, the Feast of Pentecost, was in the third month. It was a separate feast pointing to a subsequent experience. This was a new experience, for it came with a new meal offering. I believe that speaking with other tongues as the initial evidence of receiving the Holy Ghost Baptism remains the Pentecostal distinctive (Acts 2:4; 8:18), but the real proof of a Pentecostal lifestyle is the law of God written on our hearts, for God gave the law at Sinai in the third month (Ex. 19:1). We have experienced Passover and Pentecost, but there is more. Something is stirring among God's people everywhere. There is a fresh Breath of heaven moving the curtains of the Tabernacle. Knowing that there is more in God for all of us, men are asking, "What's next?"

Don't let philosophy and vain deceit spoil you at this point. Just as surely as the first two feasts were fulfilled historically and experientially in Christ and His Church, so the Feast of Tabernacles will be the fullness of our portion. Hyper-dispensationalism has relegated this third feast to another time, the future, and to another people, the natural Jews. Thank God for men who are not afraid to kill this sacred cow. The Church is Abraham's Seed (Eph. 2:11-12). The Church is Spiritual Israel (Gal. 6:16; Rom. 2:28-29; 9:6-8). The Church is the Circumcision (Phil. 3:3). The Church is the Holy Nation (Matt. 21:42-43; I Pet. 2:9-10). The Church is the New Jerusalem, the City of the Living God (Matt. 5:14; Jn. 4:19-24; Gal. 4:21-31; Heb. 12:22-24; Rev. 21). My Christian friend, the Jew is you! The truths of the Feast of Tabernacles are breaking upon every nation. The Lord Himself is spreading a feast of fat things for His people that He might destroy the face of the covering cast over all people, and the veil that is spread over the nations (Isa. 25:6-9). We have been spoiled long enough (Col. 2:8; Mk. 7:13; Matt. 15:9).

The Seventh Month

The Feast of Passover was in the first month. The Feast of Pentecost was in the third month. Now we come to the principle of the seventh month. Peter gave us a key to understanding this.

II Pet. 3:8 KJV:

> *But, beloved, be not ignorant of this one thing, that one day is with the Lord as a thousand years, and a thousand years as one day.*

Reckoned from Adam, we are in a transition time between the sixth and seventh days. Reckoned from Jesus, we see the second day ending and the third day beginning. We now stand on the threshold of the seventh day from Adam or the third day from Jesus. A new day is dawning. The prophet declared that God would revive His people after two days, and in the third day He would raise them up (Hos. 6:1-3). Jesus confirmed that when He promised to raise up His body in three days (Jn. 2:18-22). The Lord has been casting out demons and doing cures for two days, but on the third day He will be perfected in a people (Lk. 13:31-32).

Search the Scriptures and discover what took place on the third day. That is very important. Then parallel what you find with what Jesus did on the Sabbath.

Next, keep in mind that the seventh day is a Sabbath. The principle of rest is seen throughout the scheme of the three major feasts of the Lord. The outline of the feasts given in Lev. 23 opens with the concept of the Sabbath (which is thoroughly treated in our notes on the book of Genesis). This is our situation now: Adam has labored for six days (Ex. 20:9-10). He has toiled all night and caught nothing. Now it is time for the Lord to work. Ministries everywhere are at their wit's end (Psa. 107:27). It will take more than a good idea to solve this one. Man has come to the end of his wisdom, intelligence, and skill. Only a vision that is born of God will stand today (I Jn. 5:4). We must learn to cease from our own efforts and let God work in us both to will and to do of His pleasure (Phil. 2:13). In Ezek. 44, there was no sweat on the linen garments of the Zadok priesthood.

Consider the lilies (Matt. 6:28-29). Without effort or struggle, they slowly became more glorious than Solomon. Consider the lilies, how they grow. They grow automatically, spontaneously, without trying, without fretting, without thinking, without work. So the Christ-life unfolds from the Divine germ planted in the new creation. The man who does not possess His indwelling life cannot be transformed, but the man who has it must be.

The Feast of Tabernacles, coming in the seventh month, is a feast of rest. The seventh month had three aspects:

1. First day — Blowing of Trumpets.
2. Tenth day — Day of Atonement.
3. Fifteenth day — Feast of Tabernacles.

An in-depth study of the feasts of the Lord is given in our notes on the book of Leviticus. We will not deal with the Feast of Passover or Pentecost here, and will only briefly touch on the Feast of Trumpets, as our primary concern is the Day of Atonement and its connection with the more excellent ministry.

The Feast of Trumpets is mentioned in Lev. 23:23-25 and Num. 10:1-10. It was on the first day of the seventh month. A trumpet blast awakened the nation to prepare for cleansing on the Day of Atonement and the harvest of the Feast of Tabernacles. The trumpet is a symbol of a clear Word from God at the mouth of His ordained minister (priest). Prophetic utterance is anointed utterance. The prophetic voice is the voice of the Lord, the voice of the Bridegroom (Jer. 33:11; Song 2:8; Rev. 19:10). This is the spoken Word of the Lord to His people through His servants the prophets (Isa. 58:1; Hos. 8:1; Ezek. 33:1-7). These ministries have been sounding since the 1940's and 1950's. Truths were proclaimed and sounded forth, such as the Church coming to maturity and perfection, the great preparation for the harvest ingathering, and the coming of the Lord again to His Church in glory. There was also a further call to cleansing, to holiness, and to separation unto the Lord; in other words, a call to the Day of Atonement!

I believe that the Church is presently experiencing that Day of Atonement. The Lord is cleansing us. This is the tenth day of the seventh month, the day of at-one-ment, a day when God is bringing the Church into a great balance. Isaiah saw this when he said,

Isa. 40:3-4 *Amplified Bible:*

*Prepare in the wilderness the way of the Lord —
clear away the obstacles — make straight and
smooth in the desert a highway for our God!
Every valley shall be lifted and filled up, and
every mountain and hill shall be made low; and
the crooked and uneven shall be made straight
and level, and the rough places plain.*

The highway is the high calling (Phil. 3:12-14), the upward calling to the top of Mt. Zion. It will lead us to the fifteenth day (the Bible number of rest) of the seventh month, the Feast of Booths or Ingathering, a world-wide harvest! An unprecedented move of the Holy Ghost in the midst of the Church!

But what is the Day of Atonement? To begin with, it was the most solemn of the feast days. It was the day when the nation and the sanctuary were cleansed. The Bible background for this feast is found in Lev. 16; 23:27-32; Num. 29:7-11; and Heb. 8-10. The Day of Atonement was fulfilled historically in the finished work of Jesus Christ and will be fulfilled experientially in His Body, the Church. There is no doubt that Jesus made a full and complete atonement, and there is no doubt that His Church has yet to fully appropriate and receive all that His atonement provided. This day of holy convocation was a day of fasting and prayer (Acts 27:9). It included the afflicting of the flesh and the subjugation of bodily appetites. It was a day for the affliction of the soul, which is our intellect, emotions, and will; our opinions, feelings, and desires. This Day of Atonement is a time of mourning, humiliation, repentance, purification, cleansing, and intercession. It is the final preparation for the harvest of Tabernacles and the coming of the Lord. It speaks to us of Gethsemane, the olive-press, the place of selling out to the will and purposes of the Father. The Day of Atonement is a time of reconcilation, perfection, and maturity. It is a time when sin is being judged.

Yet the emphasis here is not the sin question, but the "Son" question. Do you understand what Jesus has wrought for mankind? Have you considered the length and breadth of His finished work?

Gal. 3:13-14 KJV:

Christ hath redeemed us from the curse of the law, being made a curse for us: for it is written,

Cursed is every one that hangeth on a tree: That the blessing of Abraham might come on the Gentiles through Jesus Christ; that we might receive the promise of the Spirit through faith..

Jesus redeemed us from the curse of the law; that is, from sin, sickness, poverty, and death. There is a people who are shaking themselves from the dust that they might arise and walk in all that He died for! But it won't just happen. We must experience a preparation, a breaking, a humbling, a stripping, a making ourselves of no reputation (Phil. 2:1-11). The Day of Atonement is a day of fire, a day of cleansing, a day of purifying. But, most of all, this day is a day of forgiveness! God's dealings with us are not punitive, but therapeutic. He is correcting and adjusting His sons (Gal. 4:19; Heb. 12:5-11). He knows what it takes to make each of us squeal. God is dealing with sin in the camp, but this purging is being done on the basis of Jesus' finished work. Our focus is not on the sin, but the Saviour. He is revealing these things that He might remove them from our midst. God is pouring out a spirit of judgment and burning that His glory might be seen.

Isa. 4:1-6 KJV:

And in that day seven women shall take hold of one man, saying, We will eat our own bread, and wear our own apparel: only let us be called by thy name, to take away our reproach.

In that day shall the branch of the Lord be beautiful and glorious, and the fruit of the earth shall be excellent and comely for them that are escaped of Israel.

And it shall come to pass, that he that is left in Zion, and he that remaineth in Jerusalem, shall be called holy, even every one that is written among the living in Jerusalem:

When the Lord shall have washed away the

filth of the daughters of Zion, and shall have purged the blood of Jerusalem from the midst thereof by the spirit of judgment, and by the spirit of burning.

And the Lord will create upon every dwelling place of mount Zion, and upon her assemblies, a cloud and smoke by day, and the shining of a flaming fire by night: for upon all the glory shall be a defence.

And there shall be a tabernacle for a shadow in the daytime from the heat, and for a place of refuge, and for a covert from storm and from rain.

Forgiveness is the essence of the more excellent ministry. Forgiveness and healing go hand in hand throughout the Scriptures. God has preserved us and brought us to this day that we might be healed! This healing is not just in the physical realm. The marriage relationship is more than physical union. A husband and his wife must meet together in soul (mind) and spirit as well. God is dealing with the whole man. He wants to bring salvation and deliverance to our spirit, soul, and body (I Thess. 5:23; Heb. 4:12; II Cor. 1:10). This is exampled in the book of Nehemiah. Before I share that, let me show you a principle by which you can understand the context of any Old Testament book or setting. Everything that took place in the Old Covenant took place in one of three places:

1. The Land — Israel — Body.
2. The City — Jerusalem — Soul.
3. The Temple — Zion — Spirit.

In the days of Nehemiah, the Temple was restored. In other words, the spirit, or the center of worship in man, was rebuilt. At least one-third of us is all right! The name "Nehemiah" means "comforter." The Holy Ghost (Jn. 14:26; 15:26; 16:13) has come to make us whole. The walls of our city, or soul (mind) need to be repaired. He is rebuilding the human personality. Be transformed by the renewing of your mind (Rom. 12:1-2; II Cor. 3:18). Then the land, or the body, can be filled with the glory of the Lord! We must allow the healing flow of the river of God to wash over our spirits, our minds, and our bodies. We must let God deal with us. Let Him work. In this Day of Atonement, He wants to reveal our sin and bring it to the surface so that we might be cleansed, purified, and forgiven. He comes to convict, not to condemn. The Greek word for "confession" is "homologeo" and means "to speak the same thing." Let us agree with the Father about our need and let Him restore us.

It is so important how we respond to His fire. Are we groping along the wall trying to find the thermostat, or are we standing still while the bondages are consumed in the flame? The beast nature is subtle. Adam will do his best to preserve his lower life. He may even put on an apron to cover himself (Gen. 3:7). Many in the Church world have done just that. These are sporting a religious "front." Don't turn around, Adam! Someone may see you for what you really are. Let God be your garment. Let Him wrap Himself around His people and His ministers. Are you wearing an apron? Then hold on, because this message is going to turn you around a few times. The seventh day is dawning, the Day of the Lord, and the lid is coming off everything (I Cor. 3:1-15)!

Isa. 28:24-25 NIV:

When a farmer plows for planting, does he plow continually? Does he keep on breaking up and harrowing the soil?

When he has leveled the surface, does he not sow caraway and scatter cummin? Does he not plant wheat in its place, barley in its plot, and spelt in its field?

In this Day of Atonement, we are being plowed by the Lord. The plow is a sharp instrument and speaks of the Word of God. Are you willing for the sword of the Spirit to open you up that the Word might become flesh? The farmer doesn't continuously plow over and over again without ever coming to the end of that process. Plow it deep, harrow and disk it well, whatever processes are necessary to break up the ground and prepare it for planting. Then put the plow away. Some of us have been plowed. Others have resisted this sharp instrument. To plow literally means "to cut or engrave." The Word is a hammer and chisel that is fashioning His image in us. Zion shall be plowed like a field to bring forth a new creation in righteousness (Jer. 26:18; Mic. 3:12). But He will not always be threshing! There is a finality to His dealings (Job 14:14-15; Lk. 22:37). God will finish what He started.

Song 3:6 KJV:

Who is this that cometh out of the wilderness like pillars of smoke, perfumed with myrrh and frankincense, with all powders of the merchant?

This is His Church, coming out of the Day of Atonement into the fullness of the Feast of Tabernacles! Pillars suggest stability and uprightness. Smoke is a symbol of conquest and victory, as in a burnt offering when consumed or a city when subdued. We will have received all the odors of His graces as He conforms us to His glorious image. The anointing of the myrrh, and the sweet smell of frankincense, or worship. A people just like Jesus!

Isa. 41:13-16 NIV:

"For I am the Lord, your God, who takes hold of your right hand and says to you, Do not fear; I will help you.
Do not be afraid, O worm Jacob, O little Israel,

for I myself will help you," declares the Lord, your Redeemer, the Holy One of Israel.

"See, I will make you into a threshing sledge, new and sharp, with many teeth. You will thresh the mountains and crush them, and reduce the hills to chaff.

You will winnow them, the wind will pick them up, and a gale will blow them away. But you will rejoice in the Lord and glory in the Holy One of Israel."

The highest order of anything is to become it. We are being plowed that we might become His plow! He is going to thresh the nations in the Feast of Tabernacles. Only those who submit now to this baptism of fire (Jer. 23:29; Heb. 12:29) will become "a new sharp threshing instrument having teeth." Each tooth is one of the members of the Body of Christ, locally and universally. The scope and breadth of our influence will be to the extent that each of us allows the dealings of the Lord to work in our lives during the Day of Atonement. Let him open you and break the clods of your identity in Adam. Then He can plant the principal wheat, the Word of the Kingdom. Let Him level your surface (Isa. 40:1-3). You can pay Him now, or pay Him later. Receive the plow. Receive the Word.

Jas. 1:21 NIV:

Therefore, get rid of all moral filth and the evil that is so prevalent and humbly accept the word planted in you, which can save you.

Two Goats

I see two kinds of people in the Church today. So there were two goats for the Day of Atonement (Lev. 16:5-10).

1. There was the "Lord's goat." It was killed as a

sin offering and its blood or life poured out in the
Holiest of all for the sins of the nation.

　　2. There was also the "scapegoat." Hands were
laid on this animal and he was sent into the
wilderness.

Every Bible student knows that the Lord Jesus
Christ is typified by both goats. He is the Lord's Goat,
and our Sin Offering, for "God caused Christ, who
himself knew nothing of sin, actually to be sin for our
sakes, so that in Christ we might be made good with
the goodness of God" (II Cor. 5:21 *Phillips*).

Jesus is also revealed in the Scriptures as the
Scapegoat, for Isaiah said that "like sheep we had all
gone astray, we each had taken his own way, and on
Him the Eternal laid the guilt of all of us" (Isa. 53:6
Moffatt).

Truth is layered like an onion. I see another
application of the two goats. Regardless of the label on
the door or the doctrines men believe, people are the
same. Most folks want to get into this move of God
without paying the price. Everyone is looking for a
shallow place to cross the Jordan. The dilemma is
intensifying, for the longer the wait, the deeper and
wider the Jordan becomes in the day of harvest (Josh.
3:15)! The word "Jordan" means "descender," but
nobody wants to come down in this hour. God would
move mightily in any locale or city if each one could
lay down his toys. Since we haven't come down, He is
helping us now. He is bringing us down! Just as Jesus
cleansed the Temple at the beginning (Jn. 2) and the
end (Matt. 21) of His public ministry, so He cleansed
His Church at the beginning of this age (through the
ministry of Jesus and his apostles), and will cleanse
His Church at the end of this age. We were cleansed in
the Feast of Passover with water and blood, and we are
being cleansed in this Day of Atonement with fire
(Mal. 3-4). There is an outward washing with water,

and there is an inward purging by fire. The Day of Atonement is a baptism of fire.

Some will be like the Lord's goat and lay down their lives. The Lord's goat was chosen and killed. His blood was shed and poured out in the Presence of God for others. Learn this principle:

Lev. 17:11 KJV:

> *For the life of the flesh is in the blood: and I have given it to you upon the altar to make an atonement for your souls: for it is the blood that maketh an atonement for the soul.*

The Hebrew word for "life" here is "nephesh" and means "soul." Compare it with the Greek "psyche." This means that the soul life of the Lord's goat was poured out. This reveals the five senses of man, or man's intellect, emotions, will, desires, and attitudes. Man's frame of mind. The principle of the soul can be expressed in various ways:

1. The living soul (I Cor. 15:44-49).
2. The first man, Adam (I Cor. 15:44-49).
3. The Jacob nature (Gen. 32:24-32).
4. The Ishmael nature (Gen. 16:1-4).
5. The beast nature (Rev. 13:16-18).
6. The wild ass nature (Deut. 22:10).
7. The antichrist nature (I Jn. 2:18-22; 4:1-3).
8. The fleshly mind (Col. 2:18).
9. The natural mind (I Cor. 2:9-14).
10. The carnal mind (Rom. 8:1-6).

However it is said, we must be dealt with. There are no exceptions (Jn. 12:24). The way we think, the way we feel, what we want. All this must be poured out in the Day of Atonement. Now you understand, pastor, why a lot of your sheep have gotten "run" in their feet. The home and the local church are the places where you get dealt with. Every minister must face the testings of the lust of the flesh, and lust of the eyes, and the pride of life before he steps into the public arena of the more excellent ministry (Lk. 4:1-18). Because some never allowed the breaking to come in the private beginnings of their ministry, they are now being set aside and stripped publicly. You can get circumcised as a child or a man. It's up to you, but the longer you wait, the more it will hurt, and the more your blood or soul-life will flow.

Can't you hear that scapegoat as the sentence of death passed over his neighbor? "Whew! I'm glad that other fellow got the knife and not me. Why, everybody came up and laid their hands on me. I must be pretty important. Hey! Where are you taking me? We're leaving the camp ..."

The extremes of the faith message ignore the cross of Christ and the sovereignty of God. Jesus didn't just suffer for you in a substitutionary sense; He also suffered in your behalf that you might learn to suffer with Him. This kind of preaching and commitment hasn't been everybody's cup of tea, but we must be bold to declare the Gospel of the Kingdom before it is popular. As a takeoff to a certain song in the country music field, I and others could certainly say, "I was Kingdom when Kingdom wasn't cool!"

What happened to the scapegoat? He was led through the camp as everybody watched. He was taken and sent away by the "hand of a fit man into the wilderness" (Lev. 16:21). The word "fit" here means "time, or opportunity." In like manner, where did the woman of Rev. 12 go? She went into the wilderness! Compare this with the second chapter of Hosea. God is pleading with His people now. It's time to draw near (Isa. 55:1-3).

Which goat are you? The Lord's goat willingly lays down his life. He understands the plan of the Father and delights in the purposes of the One who sent Him.

His life is not his own. He is a love-slave. The scapegoat also dies, but the elements kill him! Which will it be for you and me? Are we going to empty ourselves in this Day of Atonement, or are we going to be dealt with in the wilderness? A lot of folks want to fly away and miss all this, but the flight has been cancelled due to inclement weather. We may as well unpack our bags. We can pay Him now, or pay Him later. Those who make this commitment know that the Kingdom of God is the will of God. A man who wants to save his own neck always has a "plan B" ready just in case. He has yet to learn that the Kingdom of God offers no alternatives, just "plan A" and the will of Him out of whose bosom we came. There never was a "plan B" in Gen. 1-3, for the Father slew the Lamb before He bruised the man. One thing is certain. The Mercy-seat covered the Ark, no more, no less. God's mercy does not extend beyond the law of His Word. Though His grace abounds, we are not going to get away with anything. There is a law of sowing and reaping (Gal. 6:7-8). Don't be stubborn. You might be dead right. God is looking for someone who will pour out his life for his brothers. I'm not a gloom-and-doom preacher, but some folks who have heard these truths preached for years are going to the wilderness with mama (the rest of the Church world who has played the harlot like Gomer of old) because they are refusing Him that speaks (Heb. 3:7-4:9; 12:25-29). There in the desolate place, the elements of circumstances will do what His mercy, grace, and blood offer them now. Let us fall on the Rock and be broken.

The Back Forty

Some may be thinking at this point, "Bro. Varner, when are we going to get to the meat of the more excellent ministry?" Beloved, these opening pages are the most important in this volume. Only those who pay a price will qualify for the king-priest ministry. Don't be in such a hurry. We've only begun.

We have seen the purpose of God in three dimensions. The third dimension involves the Feast of Tabernacles, particularly the Day of Atonement. In other words, we have been saved, we are being saved, and we shall be saved. I shared this at length in the second chapter of *Prevail: a Handbook for the Overcomer.* There I taught you that salvation is progressive in nature as well as being once-for-all. The word for "salvation" is "soteria" and means "a complete deliverance." So our spirit has been saved, our soul is being saved (our mind is being renewed), and our body shall be saved. The new birth is the beginning of our salvation.

II Cor. 1:10 KJV:

> *Who delivered us from so great a death, and doth deliver: in whom we trust that he will yet deliver us;*

I Thess. 5:23 KJV:

> *And the very God of peace sanctify you wholly; and I pray God your whole spirit and soul and body be preserved blameless unto the coming of our Lord Jesus Christ.*

Eph. 4:13 KJV:

> *Till we all come in the unity of the faith, and of the knowledge of the Son of God, unto a perfect man, unto the measure of the stature of the fulness of Christ:*

We are on the edges of the third dimension. The Church is coming to maturity. God is laying the foundation for a new feast. This is His day and He is doing it His way. He is so unpredictable these days. God isn't acting like He's supposed to. He has gotten too big to fit into our theological and eschatological box. As on that night on the storm-tossed lake, Jesus is showing up in a form that we did not expect. May we, like Peter, have enough sense to ask, "Lord, is that You?" Some think Him to be a devil. "This can't be God," some say. But men always cry that when their systems are at stake. One thing is certain. If this new thing is the Lord, then somebody is going to have to get out of the boat and walk on the Word. This thing is bigger than we think (Eph. 3:18-20).

When we first came into the Outer Court, the realm of being born again and baptized in water, we weren't a full thirty-fold (Matt. 13:23) ... we were one! The first dimension is from one to thirty. Please understand that I am not trying to stereotype the Body of Christ, or attempting to compartmentalize or segment God's people. I am simply using the words and principles of the Bible to convey truth to your spirit. In the earlier days of Kingdom/sonship teaching, there was a great emphasis on groups and companies. The result has been the hellish fruit of sectarianism and exclusivism. I am not excluding you or anyone else, but your level of commitment to the call and purpose of God may exclude yourself from His best. Every piece of Tabernacle furniture could fit into the Brazen Altar, showing the potential for all things in the heart of every born-again believer. You get what you pay for.

The Feast of Passover is from one to thirty. When we stepped into the Holy Place and the Feast of Pentecost, the Spirit-filled realm, we weren't sixty-fold all at once. We were thirty-one. Do you see what I am saying? Again, I am not trying to put you into a spiritual straitjacket. I am using words which the Holy Ghost teaches to communicate truth. There are three realms of Christian maturity, and the Most Holy Place is the realm in which Jesus is Lord and King of our lives. Matt. 13:23 is a good teaching tool.

Matt. 13:23 KJV:

But he that received seed into the good ground is he that heareth the word, and understandeth it; which also beareth fruit, and bringeth forth, some an hundredfold, some sixty, some thirty.

The Outer Court is from one to thirty. The Holy Place is from thirty-one to sixty. And the Most Holy Place is from sixty-one to one hundred. Can you see it? One hundred minus 60 equals 40! We are now entering the back forty. One preacher said, "We're west-bound with the hammer down." The back forty ... with all the stumps, and the snakes, and the sidewinders. The back forty ... those areas of our lives which have remained hidden until now. The back forty ... that part of our heart which no preacher or teacher has been allowed to approach. The back forty ... the strongholds and vain imaginations which must come down and be dealt with in the Day of Atonement!

The number forty is very prominent in the Bible, being a number denoting trial, discipline, learning, humbling, or testing. Sound familiar? "One of these days I'll let God deal with it," is the cry of the hour. Many Kingdom preachers have done with the adoption of Romans eight what others have done with the pre-tribulation rapture theory. We are no better, for the devil doesn't care what we believe, so long as it is in the future. Satan is a procrastinator. We are not ignorant of his devices or thoughts.

Hear me well. The Most Holy Place is a present reality. I am not saying that we have arrived, or that we are fully perfected, or that we have already put death under our feet. But I am saying that the blood of Jesus (Heb. 10:19-22) has opened the way for a people to step over the threshold of the seventh day. We can step through the rent veil. Like Esther, we stand in the throne-room but are not yet fully in the throne

(Esth. 4-5). We are by no means one hundred-fold, just sixty-one. When I was first converted, I was a baby in that dimension. I knew nothing. Like the man in John's Gospel, I was born blind. Two years later, when I was filled with the Holy Ghost and entered the Holy Place, I was a baby in that realm, knowing nothing of the gifts and graces of the Spirit. Now I'm just a baby in this third feast, and this writing is one of my first attempts to declare this new thing (Isa. 43:18-19). Don't dismiss truth if you don't understand it. Kill your pride. God may be saying something now that you have never heard or can't fully explain. My eyes have only begun to see the more excellent ministry. But I love God's servants and His people, and I will be bold to tell you what I know.

You and I are alike. All of us are facing the same thing now. We are on the back forty, and Jesus is becoming Lord in all areas of our lives. I'm not an "end-time" preacher. I'm a "new day" preacher. Don't take that and run with it or misrepresent this ministry. God hates labels, and so do I. The so-called "New Age Movement" is a satanic counterfeit to what I am declaring. That humanistic approach has nothing in common with the blood and the Lordship of Jesus. But let me show you something.

The prophet Simeon (Lk. 2:25-35) stood in one age and held another Age in his arms! I am not content to be part of a prophetic order that sees the Consolation of Israel and then dies in peace. I want to be part of that new thing, that tangible vision, the living, breathing Christ that is going to impact the nations. He is now but an infant, so fragile and vulnerable. He has yet to be circumcised, and to grow, and to be poured out. But He isn't going to come. He is here! The shadow of the old has given way to the sunlight of the new. "It" has become "He" (Hab. 2:1-4; Heb. 10:37). The message of the Old Covenant prophets was "He is coming." The reality of the New Covenant is that the Son is here and that He is speaking (Heb. 1). May we be patient to hear all that He is saying. Are you part of the voice that is about to leave the scene, or are you part of a new voice, a Light to lighten the nations?

One Measure Or Seven?

I want to provide another thought to introduce the more excellent ministry. Aside from the Tabernacle of Moses, I know of no better teaching to help you understand the scope of present truth than the book of Ruth. I have seen churches all over the East Coast changed by that teaching. I would encourage you to read and study the verse-by-verse notes that I have written on this wonderful book, and then link it with my verse-by-verse notes on the Song of Solomon.

The book of Ruth is applicable to our day, showing the development of the believer from conception to perfection. The first chapter is foundational. There we see the principle of the blood, the water, and the Spirit (I Jn. 5:8).

Ruth 1:16 KJV:

And Ruth said, Entreat me not to leave thee, or to return from following after thee: for whither thou goest, I will go; and where thou lodgest, I will lodge: thy people shall be my people, and thy God my God:

This verse reveals the principle of the blood, or of her conversion (Rom. 10:6-10). Confession was made unto salvation. She identified with the God of Abraham, Isaac, and Israel. She became a covenant woman. In type, she experienced Jesus as Saviour and was born from above.

Ruth 1:17 KJV:

Where thou diest, will I die, and there will I be

buried: the Lord do so to me, and more also, if
aught but death part thee and me.

Here is revealed the principle of the water, or the
truth of water baptism in the Name of Jesus Christ for
the remission of our sins and the circumcision of our
hearts (Acts 2:38; Col. 2:11-12). She thus sealed her
conversion. At this point, Ruth was born again and
baptized in water.

Ruth 1:22 KJV:

So Naomi returned, and Ruth the Moabitess,
her daughter in law, with her, which returned out
of the country of Moab: and they came to Beth-
lehem in the beginning of barley harvest.

This verse teaches the principle of the Spirit, or the
experience of the Holy Ghost Baptism with the initial
evidence of speaking with other tongues (Acts 2:4).
This was a time of firstfruits and is a type of the
Pentecostal experience, which is the firstfruits of the
Spirit (Rom. 8:23) and the earnest of our inheritance
(Eph. 1:13-14). Some feel that this is the fullness of the
Spirit, but we shall soon see that there is more than
Pentecost. Chapter one of Ruth can be summed up in a
familiar New Testament verse.

Acts 2:38 KJV:

Then Peter said unto them, Repent, and be
baptized every one of you in the name of Jesus
Christ for the remission of sins, and ye shall
receive the gift of the Holy Ghost.

In chapter two we see her development, and
chapters three and four her maturity. There is more in
God than we have ever dreamed. God is spreading a
feast in this day by the hand of His ministries. I grew
up in West Virginia, and "supper" was the main meal.
Beloved, the Feast of Tabernacles is the main meal! Do

you want to stay in chapter one of Ruth and sip, or do you want to sup? It's up to you (Rev. 3:20; Matt. 5:6; 6:33).

In the first two chapters, Ruth tasted of Passover and Pentecost, which constitute one measure. This speaks of an in-part realm. It is the realm of the law, which can bring nothing to conclusion.

Ruth 2:17 KJV:

So she gleaned in the field until even, and beat out that she had gleaned: and it was about an ephah of barley.

Are you content with one measure? Men go to the field and work all day for an ephah of barley. They go back the next day to work for another portion of the same measure. Every evening, Ruth came home with a tired back, and sore feet, and dirty hands, and one measure. That is Pentecost ... working for Jesus. Working all day ... day after day. And all we had to show for this labor was one measure.

Matt. 11:28-30 KJV:

Come unto me, all ye that labour and are heavy laden, and I will give you rest.

Take my yoke upon you, and learn of me; for I am meek and lowly in heart: and ye shall find rest unto your souls.

For my yoke is easy, and my burden is light.

There is a rest that is given and there is a rest that is found. The rest or peace that is given is bestowed in the Feast of Passover (Ruth 1). The rest or peace that is found is discovered in the Feast of Tabernacles (Ruth 3-4). In between is the covenantal yoke of learning and discipline which takes place in the part of the field belonging unto Boaz (Ruth 2:3), or the local church under the Lordship of Jesus. Now behold your King in the opening verses of chapter three. He is threshing the firstfruits of the harvest (Rev. 14:1-8)! This again reveals the Day of Atonement and provides a pattern for entering the Most Holy Place. Ruth going down to the threshingfloor and Esther going before the King of Persia teach us much about our pressing into the fullness of God. Ruth prepared herself according to Naomi's instructions.

Ruth 3:3 KJV:

> *Wash thyself therefore, and anoint thee, and put thy raiment upon thee, and get thee down to the floor: but make not thyself known unto the man, until he shall have done eating and drinking.*

While others slept, she put her life in jeopardy and marked the place where Boaz rested. So we have set our eyes upon Jesus and the throne of the Lamb. Let us go in and receive His mantle, His anointing, His more excellent ministry! Let us come softly and lie at His feet, not moving until He moves, not speaking until He speaks.

Ruth 3:15 KJV:

> *Also he said, Bring the veil that thou hast upon thee, and hold it. And when she held it, he measured six measures of barley, and laid it on her: and she went into the city.*

Here is the key. Bring the veil, which represents our limitations and that which binds us. We must take it. We must hold it and master it. Then Jesus, our Heavenly Boaz, will give us another six measures to add to our one measure. Six plus one is seven ... the fullness of Him that filleth all in all (Eph. 1:20-23)!

Which do you want? The leftovers on the edges of His promise, or the experience of a living union with Him who owns all the granaries? May God help us to stop polluting His sabbaths with our own wisdom and strength. Let our intellect and reasonings become dung that we may win Christ! I am fed up with my ministry. I must have His!

The Order Of Melchisedec

The priesthood of Melchisedec has been a mystery to most of the Church world. He is first mentioned in Gen. 14 in connection with Abraham. Some feel that this Melchisedec was Shem. Others teach that this was a Christophanie, or an appearance of Christ in the Old Testament. The time in which the father of the faithful met this priest is significant. Abraham had just defeated the heathen kings, bringing restoration and deliverance. This encounter was historic, a turning point for creation. Melchisedec gave bread and wine to Abraham, revealing the principle of flesh and blood. This rejuvenated Abraham, who, in turn, ministered this life to Sarah, who then bore Isaac. Hundreds of years later, God would visit another daughter of Abraham (Lk. 3:34). The virgin Mary was instructed by the angel Gabriel that God desired to take back that flesh and blood, and then wrap Him in swaddling clothes and lay Him in a manger (Lk. 2; Jn. 1:14; Heb. 2:14-18).

We must understand the truths of the Melchisedec priesthood if we are to understand the more excellent ministry. The Hebrew word for "Melchisedec" is "Malkiy-Tsedeq" (#4442, 4428, and 6664 in *Strong's Concordance*), which means:

1. (#4428, 4427) "king royal, to reign, to ascend the throne, to induct into royalty."

2. (#6664, 6663) "the right, equity, prosperity, justice, righteousness, cleanse, justify."

Psa. 110:1-4 NIV:

The Lord says to my Lord: "Sit at my right hand

until I make your enemies a footstool for your feet."

The Lord will extend your mighty scepter from Zion; you will rule in the midst of your enemies.

Your troops will be willing on your day of battle. Arrayed in holy majesty, from the womb of the dawn you will receive the dew of your youth.

The Lord has sworn and will not change his mind: "You are a priest forever, in the order of Melchizedek."

Other than Gen. 14:18, this name is found only in the above passage. In Hebrew, "Melchizedek" thus means "king of righteousness, king of justice, righteous rule, upright counselor, righteous judgment." Jesus is the King of Righteousness!

The Greek word for "Melchisedec" has the same meaning and is found in Heb. 5:6, 10; 6:20; 7:1, 10, 11, 15, 17, 21. Thus the word is found two times in the Old Testament and nine times in the New Testament for a total of eleven times. It is noteworthy that the epistle to the Hebrews provides the primary Scriptural basis for the study of Melchisedec, for that letter reveals the principles of the more excellent ministry. The word "Hebrews" means "descendants of Eber," and "Eber" means "passing over, come over, overcome, on the other side, region beyond, a shoot." There is a people who are passing over into a new order of ministry. They are moving beyond the Feast of Pentecost in the Holy Place and are passing over the threshold of the rent veil into the holiest of all. Like Joseph, their branch shall go over the wall (Gen. 49:22).

What is the more excellent ministry? Simply, it is the ministry of the Lord Jesus Christ from the Most Holy Place after the order (manner or similitude) of

Melchisedec. The Bible reveals the more excellent ministry to be the same as:

1. The High Priestly ministry (Heb. 4-10).
2. The King-Priest ministry (Rev. 1:6; 5:10).
3. The faithful priesthood (I Sam. 1-4).
4. The Zadok priesthood (Ezek. 44).
5. The royal priesthood (I Pet. 2).
6. The priesthood with Urim and Thummim (Ezra 2).
7. The priesthood of Melchisedec (Heb. 5-7).

Again, the realm or dimension out of which the more excellent ministry flows is the Most Holy Place. This is the realm of maturity and the Lordship of Jesus Christ, the Feast of Tabernacles, the third dimension "within the veil" into which our Forerunner has entered. The Most Holy Place is the realm of "perfection" which is the subject of the whole sixth chapter of Hebrews.

Heb. 6:1-3 KJV:

Therefore leaving the principles of the doctrine of Christ, let us go on unto perfection; not laying again the foundation of repentance from dead works, and of faith toward God,

Of the doctrine of baptisms, and of laying on of hands, and of resurrection of the dead, and of eternal judgment.

And this will we do, if God permit.

Heb. 6:19-20 KJV:

Which hope we have as an anchor of the soul, both sure and stedfast, and which entereth into that within the veil;

Whither the forerunner is for us entered, even Jesus, made an high priest for ever after the order of Melchisedec.

He has gone in and He hasn't come out. He won't

come out until His Body, the Church, goes in and stays in with Him. Then when He comes out, He will come out with His brethren in the more excellent ministry, and every eye shall see Him. Do you desire to be part of such a priesthood? Then ask the Lord to open your eyes to see the hope of His calling.

A brief analysis of the seventh chapter of Hebrews reveals nine major principles concerning the Melchisedec priesthood. A verse-by-verse exegesis is beyond the scope of this writing. However, I submit to you what has been revealed to me after having made such a study. The following are characteristics of the ministry of King Jesus and his brethren (Rom. 8:28-30; Heb. 2:6-13; Isa. 8:18):

1. This ministry is that of a prophet, priest, and king.
2. This ministry is unlimited.
3. This ministry is energized by the source of an endless life.
4. This ministry is eternal.
5. This ministry is immutable or unchangeable.
6. This ministry is universal, flowing unto all men.
7. This ministry springs from Judah, or praise.
8. This ministry brings perfection.
9. This ministry puts away the curse of the law, namely, sin, sickness, poverty, and death.

First of all, Jesus was a Prophet, Priest, and King. All three offices meet in Him. We shall discuss this truth at length later.

Second, the ministry of Jesus is unlimited. There is nothing in heaven, or in earth, or under the earth, which will not bow to Him. His is a ministry of the Spirit.

Third, the ministry of Jesus flows out of His own resurrection life. The same Spirit that raised Him from the dead quickens His people. This life ("zoe" in Greek) is uncreated and incorruptible.

Fourth, the ministry of Jesus is eternal. It will never end, for He will never end. Of the increase of His government and peace, there shall be no end.

Fifth, the ministry of Jesus is immutable. There won't be another priesthood. He is the last Word on the subject. There is no higher or better order.

Sixth, the ministry of Jesus is universal, ministering to all men without prejudice or partiality. To show the vast breadth and length of the more excellent ministry, we will confine our study about His better priesthood to this sixth principle. It will comprise this book and a future companion volume.

Next, we see that the ministry of Jesus springs out of Judah, which means "praise." Praise and worship are the key to the flow of the Spirit today. Minstrels are being raised up throughout the land. He is sending Judah first.

Also, we note that the ministry of Jesus brings perfection. The law could bring nothing to conclusion. Only the New Covenant in His blood can complete God's plan and bring to completion His design for the Church. He has begun a good work in us, and He will perfect that which concerns us.

Finally, the ministry of Jesus put away the curse of the law. He was our Redeemer, being made a curse for us, for cursed is every one that hangs on a tree. Sin, sickness, poverty, and death are under the feet of the Head of the Church.

As you can already see, we have an awesome path before us. To help us along the way, Sue Baird, teacher at Praise Tabernacle, did the following study concerning Melchisedec. She first noted that Abraham was "refreshed" after the first battle with the Mesopotamian kings, and then "readied" for the second battle of Gen. 14 (with the king of Sodom). He was encouraged in the meeting with Melchisedec, who gave him bread, beverage (wine), and blessing. These are the marks of

the more excellent ministry after the order of Melchisedec:

1. State of royalty — powerful (Heb. 7:1-2). He was
king of Salem, or peace (Jeru-salem), and a king and
priest who also prophesied to Abraham (Gen. 14:17-24).

2. Sacred — priestly (Heb. 7:1-2). He was first a king
and then a priest. This must be the order. Jesus cannot
be our Priest until He is our Lord. This produces the
state of Salem, or peace (Phil. 4:7).

3. Steadfastness — permanent (Heb. 7:3, 17, 21, 24,
28). The Bible gives Him no genealogy (no roots). He is
the Ancient of Days, the great I AM (Heb. 13:8 with
7:16).

4. Similitude of Jesus — perfect (Heb. 7:3, 26, 28; 5:9;
Psa. 110:4).

5. Springs from Judah — praise or praiseworthy
(Heb. 7:14; 13:15; Matt. 1:1; Lk. 3:23; Psa. 145; Rev.
5:10-13).

6. Superior order — preeminent (Heb. 7:9-14, 22;
Col. 1:18). This better Priesthood is greater than that of
Aaron, which was limited and in-part (Heb. 7:4-6).

7. Singleness of eye — not prejudiced (Heb. 7:3).
Abraham was not yet circumcised (Gen. 17:9-14; I Tim.
2:4-6; Lk. 11:34; Jn. 8:12).

8. Separated from sin, sickness, poverty, and death
— purged (Heb. 7:3, 16, 23-24; Jn. 8:51; 11:26; II Tim. 1:10;
II Cor. 6:14-7:1).

9. Servant to man — prayerful (Heb. 7:25; 9:24; I
Tim. 2:5; Ex. 20:19; Num. 16:48; Jas. 5:16; I Thess. 5:17;
Rom. 8:34).

These thoughts will help you toward a more detailed
study of Hebrews seven. Keep in mind also that the
Name of God that is related to the order of Melchisedec is "The Most High God" (Gen. 14:18). This Name
points to the highest realm and order of ministry, the
Most Holy Place. The Hebrew word for this Name is

"El-Elyon." The word for "burnt offering" or "ascending offering" is "olah" and is in the same word family. In the burnt offering, God received one hundred percent (Rom. 12:1-2). The Latin form of the latter is "holacausta." God is calling forth a ministry who will give all, and remain worshippers in every circumstance, especially as the smoke rises from the holocaust of personal pride and ambition. El-Elyon is the God who possesses heaven and earth, the God of fullness within the veil. Consider the following verses which speak of "The Most High God": Gen. 14:18-22; Num. 24:16; Deut. 32:8; II Sam. 22:14; Psa. 7:17; 9:2; 21:6-7; 45:3; 46:4; 47:2; 50:14; 56:2; 57:2; 73:11; 77:10; 78:17, 56; 83:18; 91:1, 8; 107:11; Isa. 14:14; Lam. 3:35, 38; Dan. 3:26; 4:17, 24, 25, 32, 34; 5:18, 21; 7:18, 22, 25, 27; Hos. 7:16; 11:7; Mk. 5:7. Lk. 8:28; Acts 7:48; 16:17; Heb. 7:1.

The prophet Daniel saw a day in which the "saints of the Most High" possessed the Kingdom. These most high saints will know the reality of the Most Holy Place and the more excellent ministry. We sing the chorus:

> The kingdom and dominion shall be given
> To the saints of the Most High;
> It is an everlasting one, I speak of life,
> For they shall never die.
> The covenant I made shall stand,
> Death disannulled by My own hand,
> And with mercy I will pass over
> These I've tried.
> This remnant seed that I've preserved
> Shall soon be seen upon the earth,
> And My glory rests
> On the saints of the Most High.

This Is The Sum

We continue our introduction of the more excellent ministry. As noted, chapter seven of Hebrews details the Melchisedec order. It describes and reveals the kind of ministry that flows out of Zion, the Throne of God.

Heb. 8:1-6 KJV:

Now of the things which we have spoken this is the sum: We have such an high priest, who is set on the right hand of the throne of the Majesty in the heavens;

A minister of the sanctuary, and of the true tabernacle, which the Lord pitched, and not man.

For every high priest is ordained to offer gifts and sacrifices: wherefore it is of necessity that this man have somewhat also to offer.

For if he were on earth, he should not be a priest, seeing that there are priests that offer gifts according to the law:

Who serve unto the example and shadow of heavenly things, as Moses was admonished of God when he was about to make the tabernacle: for, See, saith he, that thou make all things according to the pattern shewed to thee in the mount.

But now hath he obtained a more excellent ministry, by how much also he is the mediator of a better covenant, which was established upon better promises.

Verse one is variously rendered: "... the chief point is this ..." (ASV); "A crowning point ..." (*Rotherham*); "Now the main point of what we have been saying is this ..." (*Berkeley Version*); "He (Christ) has acquired a (priestly) ministry which is as much superior and more excellent (than the old) as the covenant of which He is the Mediator (the Arbiter, Agent)" (*Amplified Bible*)."

This is the sum. This is the bottom line. This is what it all adds up to. This is the eternal purpose of God, simplified and clarified. The whole Bible and the theme of this writing can be summed up in one statement: **There is a New Man in the Throne with a Ministry!**

First and foremost, this has been fulfilled in the Man Christ Jesus. The heart of the Father has ever cried for a new humanity in His image and likeness. Jesus is that Man, or, more specifically, the Head of that Man! God married Israel in the Old Testament and brought forth a Son, Jesus Christ. God divorced Israel on the grounds of adultery (see my notes on Jer. 3) and married again in the New Testament; He married the Church (spiritual Israel) and is producing a son, a corporate son, a many-membered son. Throughout the Scriptures, we see the pattern of a man, a maid, and a manchild. Don't misunderstand me, but God's ultimate intention is not a "spotless Bride." Rather, He longs for a son in His image to perpetuate His seed, His nature and His ministry, in the earth and universe. We will deal with the balance between brideship and sonship in the future volume on the more excellent ministry. A detailed study of that principle is now available in my notes on the book of Esther.

A New Man ... in the Throne ... with a Ministry. We have preached and taught concerning the "man" principle and the "throne" principle. God has restored present truth about the maturity of the saints and the authority of the believer. But I want to zero in on the "ministry" principle. We must know the "why" and the "how" of His priestly ministry. Let us discover that for which we were apprehended. What kind of ministry is it? How does it operate? How do I know that I have been chosen for such a ministry? As God helps us to answer these questions, He will enable us to discern between true ministries and those who are like "clouds without water" (II Pet. 2:13-17; Jude 12).

The secrets of this more excellent ministry are being revealed to a people who have been called to the top of the mountain of sacrifice (Gen. 22). Only the Father and the Son go to the top of the hill. Don't be afraid to step out and to rise up into this new thing. As Abraham and Isaac began their ascent up one side of the mountain, a lonely ram began his ascent up the other side, invisible to the offerer and the sacrifice. They met at the top in a manifestation of the Name of God. His biddings are His enablings. Those whom God calls, He equips. The proclamation of these principles in the earth is a priority of my Father. God's people must begin to grasp these truths. We must see the scope and the substance of the ministry of Jesus. Are you ready? Do you want to share His throne? Then come boldly, for His blood has made the Way!

God Lives In A Three-room House

I'll never forget the moment I first heard it. It rippled through my spirit. God whispered, "I live in a three-room House."

The Lord was about to transform my life and ministry. It was the spring of 1979 and Joann was soon to give birth to our first child. God said, "This year I am going to change you!" I have not been the same man, the same husband, the same father, the same pastor since I heard this Word. With the birth of April Dawn came the birthing of a new thing in my heart.

How many dimensions were in the Tabernacle of Moses? Of course, there were three: the Outer Court, the Holy Place, and the Most Holy Place. I was reminded of the words of Jesus, "Jesus saith unto him, I am the way, the truth, and the life: no man cometh unto the Father, but by me" (Jn. 14:6 KJV).

In the Outer Court, Jesus is the Way to God. In the Holy Place, Jesus is the Truth of God. But in the Most Holy Place, Jesus is the Life of God! God lives in a three-room house, and the third room is the living room! Add to that the words of Paul to the Corinthians,

"And now abideth faith, hope, charity, these three; but the greatest of these is charity" (I Cor. 13:13 KJV).

The Outer Court is the realm of faith. The Holy Place is the realm of hope. But the Most Holy Place is the realm of love. God lives in a three-room house. The third room is the living room, and the living room is the loving room! The Holy of Holies is the realm of His "agape" love.

I saw, too, that there was a fireplace in God's living room. In the Outer Court, we were baptized in water. In the second room, we were filled with the Holy Ghost, baptized in the Spirit. But the third dimension offers a baptism of fire (Jer. 23:29; Heb. 12:29). The Most Holy Place is the place of fire. Add to that Paul's discovery that there is a snake in the fireplace! The fire is the only thing that will reveal the snake, and the fire is the only thing that will consume the snake (Gen. 3:1; Lk. 9:5; Acts 28:5). Don't be frightened. Just shake off the beast. He can't hurt you.

God lives in a three-room house. The third room is the living room and the loving room. Over the place of fire in God's living room, there are no trophies on the mantle, for there is no competition in this realm, no fleshly strivings, no impressive performances. Look again and you will also see that there is no clock on the wall, because the Lofty One who is holy inhabits eternity (Isa. 57:15).

As babes, we were baptized in water. Our adolescence in God began with the baptism of the Spirit. On our way to becoming full-grown, we are now tasting of the baptism of fire. It's never been hotter. The pressures are unprecedented. He is choosing His own in the furnace of affliction (Isa. 48:10). Daniel felt the heat, and so will a Daniel ministry who stands ready to interpret the king's dream. God's sovereign hand within and the "hand" of His servants without (Eph. 4:11) have shaped the clay. The oven awaits. Irene

Lindsay's "Fires for Glory" (used by permission), expresses it so well:

> In the fires of our affliction,
> All predestined for our good,
> We can see the fourth man walking,
> Forming now a son of God.
> Lest our souls fall in that furnace,
> Be consumed by sorrow sore,
> He has sent the Holy Spirit,
> Our deliverance to insure.
> He knows what will purify us,
> Knows the way, has gone before,
> And He planned this fiery furnace,
> Not for an end, but as the door.
> For our body, soul, and spirit,
> As a substance to refine,
> From these fiery trials and sorrows,
> Shall emerge with glory shine.
> Not as a golden, evil image,
> As a heathen king did mold,
> But a precious holy image,
> A reflected son of God.
> So wait, my soul, wait on His workings,
> Wait, my spirit, patiently,
> Wait, my body, for the changing,
> Rising up triumphantly.
> In the ages yet unrolling,
> We shall still His glories share,
> For the plan of God is ceaseless,
> His salvation making bare.
> Mortal minds cannot receive it,
> This supernal plan so great,
> One that covers all the ages,
> Ending sin, and fear, and hate.
> So we give Him all the glory,
> Knowing fiery trials now
> Will present us in His likeness,
> All is well, that He allows.

The Mercy-Seat Is The Love-Seat

The third room, the Most Holy Place, is the living room. There is one piece of furniture in God's living room, the realm of singleness and simplicity (II Cor. 11:1-3; Matt. 6:22-23; Jas. 1:6-8). Our focus here is not upon two, but upon One. Not upon God and the devil, just God. Not upon the new man and the old man, just the new man. There is one piece of furniture in God's living room: the Ark of the Covenant and its golden lid, the Mercy-seat (Ex. 25:10-22; 37:1-9; 40:20-21).

The Ark of the Covenant typifies the person of the Lord Jesus Christ. All of the other pieces of furniture outside of this room speak of His work. The previous two arks, the one that preserved Noah and his family, and the one that spared Moses, also speak of Christ but are generally remembered more for what they did than for what they were. The Ark of the Covenant, made of wood and gold, reveals the person of Jesus Christ more than the purpose of Jesus Christ. The Father beholds who His Son is before viewing what His Son has done. It is the Ark (His Person) that supports the Mercy-seat (His work). From man's perspective, however, we will first view the work of Jesus before seeing His office, for until His ministry has performed changes in us, we are unable to draw near enough to God's holiness to behold the perfections of Jesus' person.

Here we see the Lord Jesus as the King of kings, and the Lord of lords, risen and exalted, seated at the right hand of the Father, resting in His victory over all enemies (Rev. 19:6). Here is revealed the principle of propitiation, which literally means "mercy-seat."

Rom. 3:25 KJV:

Whom God hath set forth to be a propit-
iation through faith in his blood, to declare his

righteousness for the remission of sins that are past, through the forbearance of God;

The Ark of the Covenant speaks of the Throne of God, wherein are seated the Glorious Church (Eph. 5:25-27) with Jesus as the Head of that Church (Eph. 1:22; 4:15; Col. 1:18). As noted, the Melchisedec Priesthood, the Feast of Tabernacles, and the Day of Atonement are all connected with the Ark. All of these truths are aspects of the more excellent ministry. The outworkings of this revelation knowledge will manifest the truths of the fullness of sonship, our full maturity, and our coming to the fullness of the stature of Christ. A Most Holy Place people will obtain their full inheritance, which includes the redemption of the body and immortality (Rom. 8; Eph. 4:13; I Cor. 13:8-13).

The Mercy-seat is the place where He sits! The Mercy-seat is a love-seat! It is the Throne of God, and, in particular, the throne of grace (Heb. 4:14-16). The throne of judgment has become the throne of grace. God's people have moved from Sinai to Zion. We are becoming the Ark of the Covenant in the Most Holy Place. We are becoming the propitiation and Mercy-seat of God in the earth ... mediators, reconcilers, medicine men, saviours, curers, peacemakers, healers of the breach, restorers of paths to dwell in! To balance this, remember that God's Mercy-seat totally covers His law, but no more. Any time man attempts to extend God's grace beyond the boundaries of His law, he is headed for disgrace. Our liberty in Christ can never become a license to sin.

I remember when I first heard the truth about the King and His Kingdom. There was something that brought an alarm to my spirit in 1969 when I began to see the third dimension, a realm beyond Pentecost. We were told in that small gathering behind closed doors, "Now don't tell anyone about these truths. This revelation knowledge is too deep for folks to understand." I know now why I wanted to jump up and shout, "But if these things are true, God wants His whole creation to hear the Good News!" There was then, and in many places now, no vision for evangelism. Just a heaping up of knowledge, which is power. If I know something that you don't know, I have an edge on you. But times have changed. Everybody is going to hear about it now.

Heb. 8:11 KJV:

> *And they shall not teach every man his neighbour, and every man his brother, saying, Know the Lord: for all shall know me, from the least to the greatest.*

There are other scribes like me who are not ashamed or afraid to speak the truth in love. I prophesy that the truths and concepts of the third dimension will begin to infiltrate the major streams of the Body of Christ this year. This thing is going down Main Street. His prophets are now praying for an open door of utterance into the Pentecostal, Charismatic, and Faith churches. It has rained. God has visited His people in giving them bread, and the news will reach even to Moab (Ruth 1:6). No longer will we focus on one emphasis or area of truth. We refuse to build on the sand, which is particles of rock. We must declare the whole counsel of God. This ministry is not limited to one stream of the Body of Christ. We want all men to know that Jesus is Lord! When Eve reached for knowledge, the heavens closed. That is happening now to every "hot dog" preacher who wants to come into the Holiest of all on his skateboard, cracking his bubble-gum. Many vehicles are going to be sent back to the factory due to faulty workmanship. Those who stick their heads in the water of His Word just to "pig out" on revelation will be disqualified from the army of the Lord. But those who will drink water from the hand (Eph. 4:11), as in the days of Gideon, with an eye of vigilance for their brethren, or the enemy who may be approaching, will constitute His overcoming people. Real revelation knowledge will purify you (Isa. 6). It will put you on your face.

I was dismayed almost twenty years ago when I first heard this message. How can a man or woman hear about the truths of the Most Holy Place and not change his lifestyle? Many today are bound with attitudes and motives which are sectarian, exclusive, and "holier-than-thou." Men use convention pulpits to wrangle over who is the "elect" and the "very elect." I remember a time in my own life and ministry when I knew about Sonship but had not the Spirit of the Son (Gal. 4:1-7). I was proud, and harsh, and critical. God has been working a real breaking in my spirit these last nine years. Little by little, and line upon line, He is changing me. He has revolutionized my thinking and is continually renewing my mind. When I began to preach, I was so full of legalism and exclusivism, and was especially hard on my brethren in the ministry. Having picked up that critical attitude from older ministries, I supposed it to be the norm until the Lord smote my heart. I have always been able to roar like a lion. But bold preaching and bold living must be tempered with the nature of the Slain Lamb. It is time for the lion and the lamb to lie down in one nature (Isa. 11). This is the spirit of the more excellent ministry.

Our King beckons us to come into His living room and sit with Him in His love-seat! He has extended the golden sceptre. Let us draw near by the blood of Jesus (the Brazen Altar of Moses' Tabernacle), with a true heart (the Laver), with full assurance of faith (the Golden Candlestick), having our hearts sprinkled (with the frankincense at the Table of Shewbread), and our bodies washed with pure water (the cleansing of the High Priest on the Day of Atonement). Let us come boldly (Heb. 10:19-22)! He now invites us.

Rev. 3:21 KJV:

To him that overcometh will I grant to sit with me in my throne, even as I also overcame, and am set down with my Father in his throne.

I will let every one who conquers sit beside Me on My throne (Living Bible).

Those who prove victorious I will allow to share My throne (Jerusalem Bible).

His blood has given us a direct access unto the Father (Eph. 2:18). The veil is rent and all that was hidden and concealed is now open and available. His glory now stands open before us, and there sits One who now summons a people to follow in His steps. Jesus is already seated, and is perfected. He has entered into His rest (Heb. 3-4). He is the Overcomer who sat down as the Forerunner after the order of Melchisedec. He lives forevermore, and His priesthood is eternal and unchangeable. He is the Firstborn among many brethren (Rom. 8:28-30). The Lord Jesus Christ is the Pattern of the more excellent ministry! Come with me now. Let us explore this new world. It's all right. Do not fear, for His is a ministry without condemnation.

Chapter Two

A Ministry
Without Condemnation

There are several key principles concerning the more excellent ministry that you must keep before you:

1. This ministry is the ministry of Jesus.
2. This ministry flows out of the Most Holy Place.
3. This ministry is beyond Pentecost.
4. This ministry is after the order of Melchisedec.
5. This ministry is to all men.
6. God lives in a three-room house.
7. The third room is His living room.
8. The third room is His loving room.
9. There is one piece of furniture in His living room.
10. The Mercy-seat is the love-seat, His throne.

Our basic text was Heb. 8:1-6. There are three other key Scriptures which form the basis of our study:

Heb. 4:14-16 KJV:

Seeing then that we have a great high priest,

that is passed into the heavens, Jesus the Son of God, let us hold fast our profession.

For we have not an high priest which cannot be touched with the feeling of our infirmities; but was in all points tempted like as we are, yet without sin.

Let us therefore come boldly unto the throne of grace, that we may obtain mercy, and find grace to help in time of need.

Heb. 5:1-2 KJV:

For every high priest taken from among men is ordained for men in things pertaining to God, that he may offer both gifts and sacrifices for sins:

Who can have compassion on the ignorant, and on them that are out of the way; for that he himself also is compassed with infirmity.

Heb. 7:26 KJV:

For such an high priest became us, who is holy, harmless, undefiled, separate from sinners, and made higher than the heavens;

Let us understand that what is said about the Lord Jesus Christ in the epistle to the Hebrews applies in principle to His Church.

I Jn. 4:17 KJV:

Herein is our love made perfect, that we may have boldness in the day of judgment: because as he is, so are we in this world.

... for we realize that our life in this world is actually His life lived in us (Phillips).

... we are living as He lives (Moffatt).

... we have become as He is (Jerusalem Bible).

We now present several major aspects of the more

excellent ministry, all of which together make up the word and ministry of reconciliation (II Cor. 5:17-21). The more excellent ministry is:

1. A ministry without condemnation.
2. A ministry without prejudice.
3. A ministry without walls.
4. A ministry without retaliation.
5. A ministry without profanity.
6. A ministry without idolatry.

We shall also discover that the more excellent ministry operates according to the power of the creative, spoken Word, and flows in two primary directions:

1. Forgiveness.
2. Blessing.

This, then, is the outline and the scope of our study in this present volume. These are the major principles which every saint must learn. We first behold Him who operates a ministry without condemnation.

Follow The Lamb

Somebody is going to follow Jesus all the way and sit down with Him in His throne, His love-seat (Rev. 3:21). These will identify with His ministry of mercy and compassion. Theirs is a ministry of purity, a ministry that knows only to give. The law of love is giving.

Jn. 3:16 KJV:

For God so loved the world, that he gave his only begotten Son, that whosoever believeth in him should not perish, but have everlasting life.

Jesus rent the veil and sat down at the right hand of the Father. There is a people who are following Him in fullness of faith and obedience. These will follow the Lamb at any cost. They love not their lives unto the death.

Rev. 14:1-5 NIV:

> *Then I looked, and there before me was the Lamb, standing on Mount Zion, and with him 144,000 who had his name and his Father's name written on their foreheads.*
>
> *And I heard a sound from heaven like the roar of rushing waters and like a loud peal of thunder. The sound I heard was like that of harpists playing their harps.*
>
> *And they sang a new song before the throne and before the four living creatures and the elders. No one could learn the song except the 144,000 who had been redeemed from the earth.*
>
> *These are those who did not defile themselves with women, for they kept themselves pure. They follow the Lamb wherever he goes. They were purchased from among men and offered as first-fruits to God and the Lamb.*
>
> *No lie was found in their mouths; they are blameless.*

There is no deceit in the hearts and mouths of the Church that John saw. They were literally "without stain" before the throne. These overcomers have His Father's name in their foreheads, having tapped into the kind and quality of relationship that Jesus had with the Father. These have the mind of Christ, which is the mind of the Father (Phil. 2:5). From that pure mind flows a pure river of life, the word and ministry of reconciliation.

We must follow the Lamb wherever He goes. So we ask, "Where did He go?" He has entered into that which is within the veil (Heb. 6:19-20), into the highest realm of life and ministry, into the highest call of all. Some have taken the revelation of "Christ in you" (Col. 1:27) to the extreme and have done away with a literal Jesus, but I tell you that there is a flesh-and-bones Man in the heavens! And He is coming again, literally (Lk. 24:36-43; Acts 1:9-11; 7:55-60; 9:1-7; Rev. 22:16-21; Zech. 13:6)! He is God, and can manifest Himself in any form He chooses.

Our Lord has ascended into the Most Holy Place realm of life and love. Now He beckons, "Come up hither." Let us partake of His divine nature. There is One seated in the throne, the Mercy-seat, the love-seat. We can be with Him where He is. Do you remember His words?

Jn. 14:2 KJV:

In my Father's house are many mansions: if it were not so, I would have told you. I go to prepare a place for you.

Jn. 14:12 KJV:

Verily, verily, I say unto you, He that believeth on me, the works that I do shall he do also; and greater works than these shall he do; because I go unto my Father.

Jn. 17:24 KJV:

Father, I will that they also, whom thou hast given me, be with me where I am; that they may behold my glory, which thou hast given me: for thou lovedst me before the foundation of the world.

God once told Moses that there was a place by Him. Abraham eventually came to the place that God had told Him of (Gen. 22:9). The prepared place of which our Lord spoke is the throne of God, the Mercy-seat in the living room! God's throne is not a big chair somewhere in outer space or in an earthly Jerusalem. The Greek word "thronos" means "the place and seat of authority," and refers to all executive authority that resides in the Name of Jesus (Matt. 28:18-20). Any takers? God is now inviting a ministry and a people into the holiest of all to share His ministry of life, love, and mercy. A people with a ministry just like Jesus, a ministry without condemnation.

The Untouchables

This new Man in the throne with a ministry is a many-membered Man, and His ministry is one of forgiveness and blessing. Let's look at Heb. 4:14-16 again.

Amplified Bible:

> *Inasmuch then as we have a great High Priest Who has (already) ascended and passed through the heavens, Jesus the Son of God, let us hold fast our confession (of faith in Him), for we do not have a High Priest Who is unable to understand and sympathize and have a fellow feeling with our weaknesses and infirmities and liability to the assaults of temptation, but One Who has been tempted in every respect as we are, yet without sinning. Let us then fearlessly and confidently and boldly draw near to the throne of grace — the throne of God's unmerited favor (to us sinners); that we may receive mercy (for our failures) and find grace to help in good time for every need — appropriate help and well-timed help, coming just when we need it.*

The Authorized Version uses the word "touched" in Heb. 4:15. This is the Greek word "sumpatheo" (#4834 in *Strong's*) and means "to feel sympathy with; to commiserate, have compassion." See also Heb. 10:34; I Pet. 5:8; Rom. 8:17; and I Cor. 12:26. This word is made up of two other Greek words:

1. "sun" (#4862) — "with."
2. "pasko" (#3958) — "to suffer" (used 42 times).

Compare it with the word "paska" — the word for

"passover." The Kingdom of God is not for half-hearted people. There is a passion and a price to be experienced. Many who teach sonship have not followed the Son! Their lifestyle declares to a world that is dying, "You cannot touch me. I am above you because I have revelation knowledge." We have been untouchable, cold, unfeeling, unloving, uncaring, calloused by our insatiable lust for more and greater revelation. We have loved our concepts more than the sinner. We have become Pharisees, compassing meeting after meeting, one convention after another. We have become hypocrites, and are more in need of God than are those we selfishly ignore (Matt. 23:15).

But whoever we are and whatever we believe, we love to go to Him, don't we? We love to cast our care, our anxieties and distractions, upon Him (I Pet. 5:7). What would you think if Jesus turned to you and said, "I don't have time for you today. I'm too busy being a Son! I'm the elect of the Father, and one of these days, perhaps you may attain the lofty heights of knowledge that I now enjoy." Aren't you glad that our Head is not like that? Neither are His ministers.

It has become ironic that those who have preached so hotly and heavily against Babylon and the harlot mother have become like her. The word "Jezebel" means "chaste, not dwelling, intact, untouchable, untouched, unproductive, noncohabitating, without husband, virgin, adulterous, base, unexalted, licentious." The great harlot systems (Jer. 50-52; Rev. 17-18) have never received seed (the Greek word is "sperma") and the Word of the Kingdom from the husband ministries of Eph. 4:11. But Babylon is a spirit, and this Jezebel spirit is still working and operating in some who have "come out of her." Those nondenominational denominations. The ungodly attitude of sectarianism and exclusivism is the spirit of Jezebel!

In the old order, we feared lest someone or something would contaminate our "holiness," which was nothing more than the filthy rags of external legalism. We dressed the baby before it was born. But now we are in the "new order." Sadly enough, we are still afraid lest someone or something contaminate our "revelation." If our holiness or our revelation is that fragile, perhaps we had better take inventory. Better yet, let us receive a fresh revelation of Him who is holy, for He walked in the midst of death and hell, and remained the spotless Son of God. He is life, and He swallowed up death. He is light, and He dispels all darkness. There is no fear in Him!

We can go to Jesus and find help and mercy. Can others come to us and find the same? Are we a throne of judgment or a throne of grace? Are we belching out smoke and thunder from Mt. Sinai, killing men with the law of sin and death (Heb. 12:18-21)? The attitude and mentality of that Old Covenant mountain is, "Keep away! I'm a great big angry God, and if you don't believe Me, I'll come and consume you in a moment!" Little wonder that God's people, then and now, ask and intreat that the Word should not be spoken to them any more, for they could not endure that which was commanded (Heb. 12:19). Preacher, there are two ways that you can suffer: as a Christian, or as a fool. If you are harsh and obnoxious in the pulpit and accustomed to beating the Woman (the Church) with the Word, be man enough to see that your problems are self-inflicted. The devil didn't have a thing to do with it, unless it was the devil in you!

We are a New Testament people. We have left the realm of the tangible and the natural. We are in the spirit and have come unto Mt. Zion, the mountain of grace and truth (Jn. 1:17). You won't find any prejudice there. You won't find the Jezebel spirit of sectarianism. But I'll tell you what is there: ministries just like Him and a people with His nature. These flow out of the love-seat in the living room with a quickening Word that says to all, "Come unto me ..."

Compassion On The Ignorant

The more excellent ministry is a ministry without condemnation. Consider God's kind of forgiveness:

Heb. 5:1-2 — *The Living Bible:*

The Jewish High Priest is merely a man like anyone else, but he is chosen to speak for all other men in their dealings with God. He presents their gifts to God and offers to Him the blood of animals that are sacrificed to cover the sins of the people and his own sins too. And because he is a man he can deal gently with other men, though they are foolish and ignorant, for he, too, is surrounded with the same temptations and understands their problems very well.

... the ignorant and erring ... (ASV).

... the ignorant and deluded ... (The Twentieth Century New Testament).

... the ignorant and wayward ... (Berkeley).

... for those who have no knowledge and for those who are wandering from the true way ... (New Testament in Basic English).

The more excellent ministry has compassion on the "ignorant." This is the Greek word "agnoeo" (#50) and means "not to know (through lack of information or intelligence); to ignore (through disinclination); not understand; unknown." Compare the English word "agnostic." This principle is found in Luke's Gospel: "Then said Jesus, Father, forgive them; for they know not what they do. And they parted his raiment, and cast lots" (Lk. 23:34 KJV).

We must show mercy to those who do not know about the more excellent ministry. The ignorant are those who have yet to hear this message and the present truth (II Pet. 1:12) of what the Spirit is saying to the Church. There are spiritual agnostics everywhere who have never heard of the third dimension. Some have never heard of Pentecost (Acts 19:1-6)! I learned today that here in Onslow County of eastern North Carolina only 27% of the population go to church. We've got to reach these folks. We must love them. But what about all the different churches? Don't get me wrong. I hate religious systems and the traditions of men that enslave God's people. But we must love every tribe!

If we could stop and listen for a moment, we would hear a groan from the throne, the intercession of Him who has already entered in. From the top of Zion He disturbs and torments me with the haunting sobs of a broken heart. I'm a praiser. I love the song and the dance. I love to play instruments of music unto the Lord and shout His praises, but I am hearing a still, small voice. O God, give us a ministry like Yours! A ministry of forgiveness and blessing. A ministry without condemnation and prejudice that looks down its religious nose at those who don't know what we know. Brethren, I can't speak for you, but something is happening in our local area, and all over the East Coast. It is a sovereign work of God. Ministries are opening up and receiving the heart of a servant. His love is changing us! We are reaching out in His name, and many lives are being set free. God is drawing and apprehending people from every quarter. This truth of the Feast of Tabernacles is being proclaimed and received by many. Friend, if you will lift up your eyes to new horizons, you will see an unlimited, progressive vision begin to unfold. Be balanced. Be sensible. But above all, be open to receive all men!

I'm not trying to bring everyone under one big umbrella. Babylon is going to fall. The Psalmist described our ministry in that regard when he said, "O daughter of Babylon, who art to be destroyed; happy shall he be, that rewardeth thee as thou hast served us. Happy shall he be, that taketh and dasheth thy little ones against the stones" (Psa. 137:8-9 KJV).

The Living Bible:

> *Blessed is the man who destroys you as you have destroyed us.*

I love to take what Babylon has produced and dash it against the Rock, the Word of God (Rev. 18:6). Every idol and every teaching that has brought confusion to the people of God must be addressed. Bro. C. L. Moore, a prophet of the Lord, once told me that I would "kick the bricks out of men's foundations." God has some battering rams in the earth. Bricks are man-made. I am called to pull down strongholds, but I love people. I hate the systems, but I care about the people who are bound by them.

God is shaking everything. One ministry after another, even on a national scale, is being dealt with. The stars are falling from heaven. Some lead dominoes are already down. They weren't the first, and they won't be the last. Get ready, pastors. The saints are going to turn back to the local church. Get your motives cleaned up, brethren. You're going to be handling the finance that once was wasted on Ishmael. There is a people that God is gathering from every direction. As they reach out to us, we must receive them. We cannot cut them off. Do not look and judge with the natural eye. Do what Jesus does from the mercy-seat of grace and see the end from the beginning. Then you can begin to judge after the Spirit. To receive this fresh vision, go to your local area, and let your assembly and your ministry be the glory of God that will cover your surroundings. The hand of God is placing people in strategic places all across this nation. We are not to be a garden enclosed and a fountain sealed, but we are to release the fragrance of the King. Let His wind blow upon us that the spices of His ministry might flow out. God wants to break out of your belly, the Temple of the Holy Ghost. He wants to roar out of Zion with a ministry of life.

Christ In You The Hope Of Glory

There is a mystery Christ. As we unfold this sacred secret, you will begin to understand the greatness of Him who indwells you.

Col. 1:25-29 KJV:

> *Whereof I am made a minister, according to the dispensation of God which is given to me for you, to fulfil the word of God;*
> *Even the mystery which hath been hid from ages and from generations, but now is made manifest to his saints:*
> *To whom God would make known what is the riches of the glory of this mystery among the Gentiles; which is Christ in you, the hope of glory:*
> *Whom we preach, warning every man, and teaching every man in all wisdom; that we may present every man perfect in Christ Jesus:*
> *Whereunto I also labour, striving according to his working, which worketh in me mightily.*

"Christ" is a transliteration of the Greek "Christos," which means "the anointed one." There is an Anointed One who lives within you (Gal. 4:6). We have been filled with the Holy Ghost. To better see this, let us remember that there were three kinds of people who were anointed in the Bible:

1. The prophet (I Kg. 19; II Kg. 2).

2. The priest (Ex. 40).
3. The king (I Sam. 16).

There is a "prophet" in every Spirit-filled Christian. Please understand that I am not making all of you prophets in the ministry-gift sense of the word (Eph. 4:11), but I want you to realize that there is a prophetic anointing in the hearts of God's people. A prophet is God's mouthpiece, one who speaks for another. There is an anointing, an ability within you to declare God unto men.

There is a "priest" in every Spirit-filled Christian. A priest is one who brings men unto God. There is a priestly anointing, an ability within you to release the mercy and compassion of the Lord, to love people and bring them to Jesus.

There is a "king" in every Spirit-filled Christian. A king is one who rules in the Name of the Lord. Where the word of a king is, there is power. There is a kingly anointing, an ability within you to rise up and take authority over your circumstances in the Name of Jesus!

The Christ within is a prophet, priest, and king. Add to that the truth that Jesus gave us in Luke's Gospel.

Lk. 17:20-21 KJV:

And when he was demanded of the Pharisees, when the kingdom of God should come, he answered them and said, The kingdom of God cometh not with observation:
Neither shall they say, Lo here! or, lo there! for, behold, the kingdom of God is within you.

The Christ nature, the new nature, is within you, and the Kingdom is within you. In other words, the Christ is to produce the Kingdom. Then consider Rom. 14:17 and begin to see the release of the more excellent ministry.

1. The prophet speaks, producing righteousness.
2. The priest speaks, producing peace.
3. The king speaks, producing joy.

All this is within you. Christ is the image of God (II Cor. 4:4). The image is in the seed (I Pet. 1:23). All that the King is, and all that the King does, is in you. The dispensation of the grace of God is seen and understood in Col. 1:25-29. He has poured the Spirit of His Son into our hearts that we might become containers and then dispensers of the life of God (II Cor. 3:6). When the Holy Ghost came in, He brought a prophet, priest, and king! But the killer called "condemnation" has stifled the flow of God. It has kept this anointing in check. Stop putting yourself down. Do you remember what Jesus said?

Jn. 7:38 KJV:

He that believeth on me, as the scripture hath said, out of his belly shall flow rivers of living water.

The Greek word for "flow" here is "rheo," from which we derive the English word "rhetoric." Out of a man's belly would flow divine rhetoric, faith-filled words! What are the "rivers" that Jesus mentioned?

1. The prophet — out of the belly (Jn. 7:38).
2. The priest — out of the sanctuary (Ezek. 47:1-12).
3. The king — out of the throne (Rev. 22:1-2).

You may be asking, "But, Brother Varner, where is the manifestation of all this? Why don't we see the release of God's Kingdom in our midst?" The answer is simple. We have believed the lie of our accuser. Satan comes and whispers, "You can't have the promise." If we know better, He tries again, "You can have the promise, but you can't have it now." If that won't discourage us, he adds, "You may have the promise, you may have it now, but it won't last." How sad that men have agreed with the adversary instead of the Father (Amos 3:3). Why are we bound?

Song 4:12-16 KJV:

A garden enclosed is my sister, my spouse; a spring shut up, a fountain sealed.

Thy plants are an orchard of pomegranates, with pleasant fruits; camphire, with spikenard,

Spikenard and saffron; calamus and cinnamon, with all trees of frankincense; myrrh and aloes, with all the chief spices:

A fountain of gardens, a well of living waters, and streams from Lebanon.

Awake, O north wind; and come, thou south; blow upon my garden, that the spices thereof may flow out. Let my beloved come into his garden, and eat his pleasant fruits.

The Church is a garden, a spring, and a fountain. But we have remained inclosed, shut up, and sealed. We are closed in to our own little world. As in the days of the prophet Haggai, we have each run to his own house while the House of the Lord lies waste. Let us consider our ways. All of us have been hurt. We have retreated to our castle and pulled up the drawbridge. Having filled the moat with alligators, we have said to others, "Just keep away. Leave me alone." Nobody told us that when Jesus comes in, He brings His friends, and His friends will hurt you.

Song 5:1 KJV:

I am come into my garden, my sister, my spouse: I have gathered my myrrh with my spice; I have eaten my honeycomb with my honey; I have drunk my wine with my milk: eat, O friends; drink, yea, drink abundantly, O beloved.

We must get beyond our personal feelings and loose

the Christ. The above passage in chapter four reveals nine kinds of fruit. With the exception of the pomegranate, these were imported, having been brought in from another country. So the fruit of the Spirit (Gal. 5:22-23) has been imputed and imparted from another nature, the divine nature! The fruit of the Spirit is the nature of Jesus. We must forgive ourselves so that the spices of His life and love can flow out to the creation. We must ask the Lord to forgive us for the times in which we have condemned ourselves and others. A blow brings a flow (Jn. 7:38) as the north wind (the Holy Spirit in convicting power) kills everything but the evergreens of His life (Jn. 16:8-11), dealing with our stubbornness and unbelief. May the Breath of God come and show us the insanity of our continually condemning ourselves.

The Jubilee Ministry On The Other Side Of The Wilderness

The more excellent ministry after the order of Melchisedec brings correction, adjustment, restoration, and deliverance in this age and the ages to come. This order is coming into being now. The Greek verb for "made" in Heb. 7:16 is "ginomai," which shows that this ministry is "becoming." This is true concerning the ministry of Jesus and His Church.

Heb. 7:16 KJV:

Who is made, not after the law of a carnal commandment, but after the power of an endless life.

Heb. 5:7-10 KJV:

Who in the days of his flesh, when he had offered up prayers and supplications with strong crying and tears unto him that was able to save him from death, and was heard in that he feared;

*Though he were a Son, yet learned he obedience
by the things which he suffered;
And being made perfect, he became the author
of eternal salvation unto all them that obey him;
Called of God an high priest after the order of
Melchisedec.*

Jesus is our Mercy-seat. He is the lid to Jacob's well. The familiar story in the fourth chapter of John shows a Well on the well. He will no longer allow us to draw from the Jacob nature. We will have to move Him aside to get to the bitter water. Like the woman of Samaria, we have been married to five husbands, our five natural senses. We have walked after the flesh, and not the Spirit. Not being satisfied, we have gone on to flirt with number six, representing all that appeals to man. Now we are meeting the Seventh Man, the Perfect Man, the Lord from heaven. He is showing us how to show mercy. Drop your waterpot and become a waterpot. Lower yourself into Him and then run into the city with the good news.

The ministry of Jesus Christ is to all men. He is the Pattern for all who share His administration of forgiveness and blessing. He who was the Prince of Peace, the Recipient of peace, has now become the King of Peace, the Administrator of peace. In like manner, the Christ who indwells us is a prince, a king's son. The Christ within will become the Lord within. The Residing One will become the Presiding One.

Isa. 9:6 KJV:

For unto us a child is born, unto us a son is given: and the government shall be upon his shoulder: and his name shall be called Wonderful, Counsellor, The mighty God, The everlasting Father, The Prince of Peace.

Heb. 7:1-2 KJV:

For this Melchisedec, king of Salem, priest of the most high God, who met Abraham returning from the slaughter of the kings, and blessed him;

To whom also Abraham gave a tenth part of all; first being by interpretation King of righteousness, and after that also King of Salem, which is, King of peace;

The first four chapters of Luke's Gospel provide a tremendous revelation of Jesus' ministry without condemnation. It is covered in more detail on pages 129-139 of *Prevail*.

In Luke 1:35 we see that Jesus was born of the Spirit. In Luke 3:21-22 He was baptized in water and filled with the Holy Ghost. Although the uniquely begotten Son of God received more that day at the Jordan than the in-part measure of Pentecost, the principle remains. The Pattern Son was born of the Spirit, baptized in water, and filled with the Spirit.

Jn. 3:34 KJV:

For he whom God hath sent speaketh the words of God: for God giveth not the Spirit by measure unto him.

Acts 10:38 KJV:

How God anointed Jesus of Nazareth with the Holy Ghost and with power: who went about doing good, and healing all that were oppressed of the devil; for God was with him.

Jesus was then led (Rom. 8:14) by that same Spirit into the wilderness to be tested by the adversary in the areas of the lust of the flesh, the lust of the eyes, and the pride of life. The same holds true for all His followers. The servant is not above his Lord. There can be no real anointing upon our lives and ministries until we have been dealt with in these three dimensions.

Lk. 4:1, 2 KJV:

And Jesus being full of the Holy Ghost returned from Jordan, and was led by the Spirit into the wilderness,

Being forty days tempted of the devil. And in those days he did eat nothing: and when they were ended, he afterward hungered.

I Jn. 2:15-17 KJV:

Love not the world, neither the things that are in the world. If any man love the world, the love of the Father is not in him.

For all that is in the world, the lust of the flesh, and the lust of the eyes, and the pride of life, is not of the Father, but is of the world.

And the world passeth away, and the lust thereof: but he that doeth the will of God abideth for ever.

The Pattern was tested in the area of the lust of the flesh (Lk. 4:1-4). This deals with the realm of self-satisfaction. Some use the anointing for their selfish gain. The devil said, "If thou be the son of God, command this stone that it be made bread." But Jesus wouldn't do it. He quoted Deut. 8:3 and overcame in this realm.

Second, Jesus was tested in the area of the lust of the eyes (Lk. 4:5-8). This speaks of materialism and the love of money (I Tim. 6:10). Some use the anointing to make money and merchandise off God's people (II Pet. 2:3). Jesus refused the glitter of the world systems, quoted Deut. 6:13; 10:20, and won the second round. A true son cannot be bought.

Third, the Lord was tested in the area of the pride of life (Lk. 4:9-13). Some use the anointing to be seen of men and to receive man-worship. They want to be popular or somebody's favorite preacher. Jesus quoted Psa. 91:11 and Deut. 6:16, overcoming the evil one by the Word of God.

Our Lord returned after that testing (Acts 1:8) in the power and ability of the Spirit. He went immediately to His home town and His home church. The Pattern Son stood up in the synagogue in Nazareth to read from Isa. 61, declaring the Year of Jubilee, the Year of Liberty: "The Spirit of the Lord is upon me, because he hath anointed me to preach the gospel to the poor; he hath sent me to heal the brokenhearted, to preach deliverance to the captives, and recovering of sight to the blind, to set at liberty them that are bruised, To preach the acceptable year of the Lord" (Lk. 4:18-19 KJV).

> *He hath sent me forth to proclaim to captives a release ... (Rotherham).*

> *To announce to prisoners, "You are free!" (Beck).*

> *To publish a release to the captives ... to dispense freedom to the oppressed* (Emphatic Diaglott).

> *To send away in release those who are broken by calamity, to herald forth that epochal period of time ... (Wuest's Expanded Translation).*

The Jubilee ministry of the Son of God is a ministry without condemnation. He has come to release all the:

1. Beggars ("the poor").
2. Brokenhearted.
3. Bound ("the captives").
4. Blind.
5. Bruised.

This is the call. This is the invitation. There is enough of the nature of God to swallow up all that death! And all without fear of contamination. O Lord, give us grace. The Master ate with publicans and sinners (Matt. 9:10-11; 11:19; 21:31-32). When God first showed me that He was going to deliver His creation by forgiving it, I was not aware of the real meaning of Lk. 4:18-19.

One of the keys is found in verse 18. The English Bible mentions the word "deliverance" and the phrase "set at liberty." The Greek reveals that the same word is used for both. This word is "aphesis" (#859 in *Strong's*) and means "freedom; pardon." It is rendered in the King James as "deliverance, forgiveness, liberty, remission." It is from the verb "aphiemi" (#863) which means "to send forth" or "to send away from."

Concerning "aphesis," *Thayer's Lexicon* adds that it means "to depart or send forth, yield, emit, let go, let alone, let be, disregard, to leave, not to discuss now, give up a debt by not demanding it, keep no longer, permit, allow, not to hinder." Bullinger added, "dismiss, set free, or to express the discharge or acquittal of a defendant; to remit the punishment, where the guilty person is dealt with as if he were innocent." *Vine's Dictionary* notes two roots:

1. "apo" — "from."
2. "hiemi" — "to send."

The word "aphesis" is used in the Septuagint (LXX), the Greek Old Testament, in Isa. 58:6; 61:1 ("release"); in Esth. 2:18 ("exemption" from taxation); and Lev. 16:26 ("forgiveness"). Of the fifty or so instances of "aphesis" in the LXX, 22 are found in Lev. 25 and 27 for the Hebrew "yobel" (or Year of Jubilee), and five in Deut. 15:1-9 for the Hebrew "samat" (the release of debts in the Year of Jubilee). In general, it is more often used to denote the release of captives and slaves (Isa. 61:1; Jer. 34:8, 15, 17; Ezek. 46:17). In Judaism, "aphiemi" and "aphesis" are found as terms for forgiveness in Josephus and Philo.

It is abundantly evident that "aphesis" is a Jubilee word, for it conveys the principles of liberty and release out of the prison house! This wonderful word is found seventeen times in the New Testament. Prayerfully consider these verses and then rejoice that One has come to teach us how to forgive and not to condemn.

Matt. 26:28 KJV:

For this is my blood of the new testament, which is shed for many for the remission of sins.

Mk. 1:4 KJV:

John did baptize in the wilderness, and preach the baptism of repentance for the remission of sins.

Mk. 3:29 KJV:

But he that shall blaspheme against the Holy Ghost hath never forgiveness, but is in danger of eternal damnation:

Lk. 1:77 KJV:

To give knowledge of salvation unto his people by the remission of their sins,

Lk. 3:3 KJV:

And he came into all the country about Jordan, preaching the baptism of repentance for the remission of sins;

Lk. 4:18 KJV:

The Spirit of the Lord is upon me, because he hath anointed me to preach the gospel to the poor; he hath sent me to heal the brokenhearted, to preach deliverance to the captives, and recovering of sight to the blind, to set at liberty them that are bruised,

Lk. 24:47 KJV:

And that repentance and remission of sins should be preached in his name among all nations, beginning at Jerusalem.

Acts 2:38 KJV:

Then Peter said unto them, Repent, and be baptized every one of you in the name of Jesus Christ for the remission of sins, and ye shall receive the gift of the Holy Ghost.

Acts 5:31 KJV:

Him hath God exalted with his right hand to be a Prince and a Saviour, for to give repentance to Israel, and forgiveness of sins.

Acts 10:43 KJV:

To him give all the prophets witness, that through his name whosoever believeth in him shall receive remission of sins.

Acts 13:38 KJV:

Be it known unto you therefore, men and brethren, that through this man is preached unto you the forgiveness of sins:

Acts 26:18 KJV:

To open their eyes, and to turn them from darkness to light, and from the power of Satan unto God, that they may receive forgiveness of sins, and inheritance among them which are sanctified by faith that is in me.

Eph. 1:7 KJV:

In whom we have redemption through his blood, the forgiveness of sins, according to the riches of his grace;

Col. 1:14 KJV:

In whom we have redemption through his blood, even the forgiveness of sins:

Heb. 9:22 KJV:

And almost all things are by the law purged with blood; and without shedding of blood is no remission.

Heb. 10:18 KJV:

Now where remission of these is, there is no more offering for sin.

The "deliverance" of His more excellent ministry in Lk. 4:18 is revealed nine times as "remission" and six times as "forgiveness." This word describes a release from bondage and imprisonment. In the Jubilee, all the doors were opened and all the captives went free! The land reverted back to the original owners. So the earth will once again be given to man as we experience the paradise Jesus has reclaimed. Jesus confirmed or secured the promises made unto the fathers (Rom. 15:8; Acts 3:13). He is the Son (seed) of Abraham and David (Matt. 1:1). He has the land and the throne. He has inherited the earth and the right to rule it. The Abrahamic Covenant gave Him the promise and the Davidic Covenant the legal right to appropriate the promise.

Gen. 1:26 KJV:

And God said, Let us make man in our image, after our likeness: and let them have dominion over the fish of the sea, and over the fowl of the air, and over the cattle, and over all the earth, and over every creeping thing that creepeth upon the earth.

Heb. 2:6-9 KJV:

But one in a certain place testified, saying, What is man, that thou art mindful of him? or the son of man, that thou visitest him?

Thou madest him a little lower than the angels; thou crownedst him with glory and honour, and didst set him over the works of thy hands:

Thou hast put all things in subjection under his feet. For in that he put all in subjection under him, he left nothing that is not put under him. But now we see not yet all things put under him.

But we see Jesus, who was made a little lower than the angels for the suffering of death, crowned with glory and honour; that he by the grace of God should taste death for every man.

God is going to deliver His creation by forgiving it. He has come to preach or proclaim "forgiveness" to the captives, to "forgive" them that are bruised.

Forgiveness And Blessing

There's a Man in the throne with a ministry. He has been ordained to deliver and set at liberty the creation. The purpose of this ministry is to forgive the creation. This word and ministry of reconcilation is a creative word, spoken forth to forgive and to bless in the Name of the Lord. The word out of the love-seat in the Most Holy Place flows forth in five practical areas, as we forgive and bless:

1. God.
2. Ourselves.
3. Everyone in our home and family.
4. Everyone in our local assembly.
5. Everyone in the ministry.

The principle is simple: the Lord forgave us, and then He blessed us. The proof or fruit of forgiveness is the blessing of the Lord resting upon our lives. This shows that He has forgiven us and released us from our sins. Praise His Name!

First of all, have you forgiven God? That may sound strange, so let us clarify this first question. God hasn't done anything wrong, nor can He. He is God. As our Father, He is always right, and always knows what we need when we need it. But because of His dealings with us as sons, we sometimes react instead of respond to His ways. Some men are shaking their fist at Him. "Why, Lord?" is the secret cry of many who have kicked against the pricks (Acts 9:5). Are you upset and angry with Him? Has He brought you in paths not to your liking? Has He ever ignored you as you quoted your favorite faith Scriptures? Did you name it and claim it and see nothing happen? Can you praise Him and worship Him in honesty? Do you want to praise Him? To bless the Lord is to give Him praise and worship. Some who have no desire to bless the Lord are mad at God. Many of these have become critical and condemning of themselves and others because they are that way with the Lord! Such are ignorant of the love-seat ministry. Every problem in personal relationships in the home and local church can be traced back to a need in one's own personal relationship with Jesus. We must forgive and bless God. We must release Him out of the self-inflicted bondage of our own impatience. Stay sweet, Joseph. You are coming out of prison to reign.

Once we have made things right with the Lord, we must forgive and bless ourselves. Have you agreed with His word of release to your life, or are you walking with the evil one, who is ever accusing you? Can you bless yourself? Do you know how to receive? The grace of receiving is as important as the grace of giving. God gave us the best when He gave Jesus. In Him, as new creatures, we are the best. Others deserve the best, His life, through us. We are not sinners saved by grace. We are the sons of God saved by grace (I Jn. 3:1-3). The Lord says to us, "I have forgotten your past. I have forgotten what you were, and now I deal with you as you are, and I see your end from the beginning." Let us follow His example. We must forgive ourselves to create a channel for His blessing. We must bless as the Lord blesses. We must look at ourselves and others through His eye of faith. Bury the past. Rejoice that you have been forgiven. You have become His instrument of blessing in the earth.

The hardest place to be spiritual is in the home. Have you ministered His forgiveness and blessing to everyone in your family? Brothers, can you say to your wife, "Honey, forgive me. If I didn't live in such a briar patch, I wouldn't call you a thorn in my flesh." We must have enough of His life and love to forgive and bless all our relatives. Somebody said, "That's rough. I don't think that I can do that." Then brace yourself for His reponse, "I don't think that you are ready for My more excellent ministry." Nobody knows us like our mate or children. The spirit of grace must be poured out among us. When God got ready to bring a nation out of bondage, He put a Lamb in every house (Ex. 12:3)!

Once I have released God, myself, and all those in my home, I am ready to go to church. Just as the Tabernacle of Moses was pitched in the center of the camp, so the local church, the house of the Lord, is central to our lifestyle. Everything we are and do revolves around God and His people. We must forgive and bless everyone in our local assembly. This principle must first work among the leadership. As elders, we are to lead by example. Authority flows out of relationship. If you don't know me or trust me, I won't be allowed to speak into your life. Pastors cannot be kings and overlords with an attitude that says, "This is my

church and these are my people. The service can begin
now that I have arrived." Are we intimidating the
saints? Have we become as Mt. Sinai that keeps folks at
a distance? Can the sheep get close to us? Can they find
grace to help in time of need? May God give us
understanding in these things. We are sheep as well as
shepherds. When we turned to Jesus, He freely forgave
us, without prejudice or hesitation. Now He expects us
to speak the same kind of word to all the people and our
fellow ministers. Once the leaders get right, the saints
will follow, having learned to forgive and bless in the
local church.

Have you forgiven God? Yourself? Your family?
Your brothers and sisters in Christ? Then pass the
final test. Forgive and bless everyone in the ministry
who has touched your life. Somebody says, "But,
Brother Varner, you don't understand. There are
some ministries who have really hurt me!" Yes, I
know that. But I also know that men receive the kind
and quality of ministry that they deserve (I Sam. 8-12).
You will have to forgive the ones who hurt you, and
have compassion on the ignorant and those who are
out of the way. Everybody has walked through hard
places. Some have experienced deep wounds. But God
has brought us into this day to heal us and bind us up
(Hos. 6:1-3). In my twenty years of ministry, I have
been wounded in my spirit by more than one preacher.
As I look back to those days, I know why God allowed
some pretty rough men to grace my life. In my
youthful zeal, I needed that restraint. To make a very
long story short, I have come to a place in God where I
am thankful for every ministry that has ever spoken
into my life. Each was uniquely gifted to teach me
something, either by a positive or negative example.
The Holy Ghost has blended and woven a marvelous
tapestry of covering for my steps (Prov. 31:22). These

men and women have brought me to this day and to the threshold of the Most Holy Place.

Remember, these last four areas flow from our personal relationship with the Lord. Forgive and bless Him, and then begin to minister His life to others. Abide in the Vine, and His life will live through you.

Not Imputing Their Trespasses Unto Them

The king-priest ministry of the Lord will not impute the sins and trespasses of men to them. It preaches a great big Jesus and a wee little devil. Our eyes are focused on Him who is the Author and the Finisher of our faith.

But we must maintain a balance as we understand that this teaching is not a license to sin. God couldn't forgive you and me until we repented. All men have been reconciled, but not all men have been saved. The veil has been rent from the top to the bottom. The way has been made and the forgiveness of sins is available, but we must appropriate the finished work of Jesus through the experience of repentance and faith, the two elements of conversion. I am not holding out a blanket of unconditional forgiveness and blessing, but when broken humanity or our brothers and sisters begin to cry out for grace to help in time of need, we must not refuse them. In that moment, we will be as Sinai or Zion. In that moment, we will be a throne of judgment, condemning, criticizing, railing, and cursing; or we will be a throne of grace, forgiving, blessing, and speaking words of life and comfort.

Paul talked about this principle in his letter to the Corinthians. It must be understood, but with balance: "Therefore if any man be in Christ, he is a new creature: old things are passed away; behold, all things are become new. And all things are of God, who hath reconciled us to himself by Jesus Christ, and hath given to us the ministry of reconciliation; To wit, that God was in Christ, reconciling the world unto himself, not imputing their trespasses unto them; and hath committed unto us the word of reconciliation. Now then we are ambassadors for Christ, as though God did beseech you by us: we pray you in Christ's stead, be ye reconciled to God. For he hath made him to be sin for us, who knew no sin; that we might be made the righteousness of God in him" (II Cor. 5:17-21 KJV).

... and has given us the work of making peace ... (N.T. in Basic English).

... not counting their sins against them ... (Phillips).

... not reckoning unto them their offences ... (Rotherham).

It was God (personally present) in Christ, reconciling and restoring the world to favor with Himself, not counting up and holding against (men) their trespasses (but cancelling them); and committing to us the message of reconciliation (Amplified Bible).

... gave us the work of handing on this reconciliation ... and He has entrusted to us the news that they are reconciled ... (Jerusalem Bible).

... not putting down on the liability side of the ledger their trespasses, and lodged in us the story of the reconciliation (Wuest's Expanded Translation).

Beloved, God was in Christ doing this, and now the Christ is in you! We will not keep a "log" or an inventory once we sit down with Jesus in the Mercy-seat. The word for "imputing" in verse 19 is "logizomai" (#3049 in *Strong's*) and means "to take an inventory, estimate." It is rendered in the King James as "conclude, account, count, esteem, impute, lay to charge, number, reason, reckon, suppose, think." This word is found forty-one times in the New Testament, including eleven times in the fourth chapter of Romans.

The word "logic" is an English derivative. Faith is contrary to reason. We walk by faith and not by sight. Men cannot follow their logic and be part of the more excellent ministry. The reason why we cannot see our brothers clearly is because of the beam or the "log" in our eye. Others are judged after the flesh and not by the Spirit. We like to keep score. Good records are needed to play the game of religious blackmail. We won't let men forget. Perhaps we are smarter than God. We remember what He has forgotten. Some feel that Jesus told us not to judge. To the contrary (Jn. 7:24). In the following passage, the Judge shows us how.

Matt. 7:1-5 NIV:

Do not judge, or you too will be judged.

For in the same way you judge others, you will be judged, and with the measure you use, it will be measured to you.

Why do you look at the speck of sawdust in your brother's eye and pay no attention to the plank in your own eye?

How can you say to your brother, "Let me take the speck out of your eye," when all the time there is a plank in your own eye?

You hypocrite, first take the plank out of your own eye, and then you will see clearly to remove the speck from your brother's eye.

Jesus came to minister. He came to serve others. He has delegated this responsibility and "ministry" of reconciliation to His Church. The word "diakonia" is used in II Cor. 5:18 (compare it with the English "deacon"). The king-priest ministry is a servant ministry. It is also a mature ministry, for we are "ambassadors" of His peace. This is the word "presbuteros," or "elder." Jesus said it this way, "Blessed are the peacemakers: for they shall be called the children of God" (Matt. 5:9 KJV).

The "children" of God are the "huioi" or the "sons" of God. This is the plural form of "huios," the word used in the New Testament to describe a full-grown son. Paul used a form of "huios" (#5207) in Rom. 8 to speak about our "adoption" ("huiothesia") or placement as the sons of God. We are called to be peacemakers and reconcilers, to stand between two warring spirits and swallow up the death and hell in both of them without being contaminated. This high calling is also described in James and I Corinthians.

Jas. 3:14-18 KJV:

> *But if ye have bitter envying and strife in your hearts, glory not, and lie not against the truth.*
>
> *This wisdom descendeth not from above, but is earthly, sensual, devilish.*
>
> *For where envying and strife is, there is confusion and every evil work.*
>
> *But the wisdom that is from above is first pure, then peaceable, gentle, and easy to be intreated, full of mercy and good fruits, without partiality, and without hypocrisy.*
>
> *And the fruit of righteousness is sown in peace of them that make peace.*

I Cor. 1:30 KJV:

> *But of him are ye in Christ Jesus, who of God is made unto us wisdom, and righteousness, and sanctification, and redemption:*

Jesus is the Wisdom of God. He is the Gift from above (Jn. 3:16; II Cor. 9:15; James 1:17). His Lamb-like nature is reproduced in the brethren of whom He is not ashamed. These ambassadors of peace, these peacemakers, are:

1. Pure ("clear, chaste, holy").

2. Peaceable (no fighter, no retaliation).
3. Gentle ("moderate, patient").
4. Easy to be intreated (can be approached).
5. Full of mercy and good fruits (fullness).
6. Without partiality ("not seeing through").
7. Without hypocrisy ("unfeigned, genuine").

Can you see the kind of ministry that is made in the image of Jesus? Men can hear this message with their reason and miss altogether what I am saying, or they can hear these truths by the Spirit and be transformed by the renewing of their minds.

The Abomination Of Condemnation

The more excellent ministry is a ministry without condemnation. There is an attitude among many of God's people that alarms me. It is a mentality that says, "I cannot have anything. I cannot do anything. I cannot be anything. And if I can, it won't last!" The God in me despises that kind of stinkin' thinkin'. What does the Bible say about this unhealthy frame of mind?

Prov. 17:15 KJV:

He that justifieth the wicked, and he that condemneth the just, even they both are abomination to the Lord.

The Hebrew word for "abomination" here (#8441 in *Strong's*) means "something disgusting (morally); an abhorrence, especially idolatry or idol." It comes from a root (#8581) which means "to loathe, detest." This verse teaches us that it is a disgusting thing to justify one's own sinfulness and wickedness, and it is equally disgusting when we commit the abomination of condemnation! Compare this with some other verses in Proverbs that use the same word.

Prov. 11:1 KJV:

A false balance is abomination to the Lord: but a just weight is his delight.

Prov. 12:22 KJV:

Lying lips are abomination to the Lord: but they that deal truly are his delight.

Prov. 20:10 KJV:

Divers weights, and divers measures, both of them are alike abomination to the Lord.

There is a prophet, priest, and king in you. The Anointed One longs for release. But His life has been locked in the garden, held down by the undergrowth of old-order concepts and sin-conscious preaching. The spring is shut up and the fountain sealed.

Stop condemning the just! Stop condemning the redeemed! Stop condemning yourself and others that He has washed in His blood. Don't justify the lawlessness of the beast nature, but don't rail on the righteousness of God. Jesus never condemned the just. Jesus never condemned anybody (Jn. 8:11-12).

Jn. 3:16-17 KJV:

For God so loved the world, that he gave his only begotten Son, that whosoever believeth in him should not perish, but have everlasting life.

For God sent not his Son into the world to condemn the world; but that the world through him might be saved.

Jn. 5:24 KJV:

Verily, verily, I say unto you, He that heareth my word, and believeth on him that sent me, hath everlasting life, and shall not come into condemnation; but is passed from death unto life.

Jn. 8:11-12 KJV:

She said, No man, Lord. And Jesus said unto her, Neither do I condemn thee: go, and sin no more.

Then spake Jesus again unto them, saying, I am the light of the world: he that followeth me shall not walk in darkness, but shall have the light of life.

Jn. 20:21 KJV:

Then said Jesus to them again, Peace be unto you: as my Father hath sent me, even so send I you.

It is an abomination to condemn the just. The "just" are those who have been justified by His grace, those who have been made righteous by His blood. Jesus Himself declared and announced this good news.

Acts 13:38-39 KJV:

Be it known unto you therefore, men and brethren, that through this man is preached unto you the forgiveness of sins:

And by him all that believe are justified from all things, from which ye could not be justified by the law of Moses.

The Amplified Bible in these verses speaks of the "removal of sin" and that we have been set free and "absolved (cleared and freed) from every charge!" Jesus has justified you and me from all things. The Greek word for "justified" is from the root word "dikaios" (#1342) and means "equitable (in character or act); by implication, innocent, holy." It is translated as "just, meet, right, righteous."

Justification by faith was the cry of the Protestant Reformation. It is sad that most Christians do not understand this glorious truth. Most have been taught that justification means that God looks upon the believer "just as if he had never sinned." No! That cannot be. That would be God saying, "I know that you sinned, but I'll act like you didn't." That is how man forgives. He forgives, but he won't forget. This humanistic view of justification says, "You sinned. I'll act like you didn't. But you did." Learn this, child of God, and learn it now. Real Bible justification says, "You never sinned!" The blood of bulls and goats could not take away sin (Heb. 9:13; 10:4). That Old Testament blood could only "cover" the sin, which is the basic meaning of the word "atonement." But the better blood of Jesus Christ, the blood of the New Covenant, did more than cover our sin; His blood, the blood of the Lamb of God, took away sin! He removed it!

Jn. 1:29 KJV:

The next day John seeth Jesus coming unto him, and saith, Behold the Lamb of God, which taketh away the sin of the world.

Psa. 103:12 KJV:

As far as the east is from the west, so far hath he removed our transgressions from us.

Isa. 43:25 KJV:

I, even I, am he that blotteth out thy transgressions for mine own sake, and will not remember thy sins.

Heb. 8:12 KJV:

For I will be merciful to their unrighteousness, and their sins and their iniquities will I remember no more.

Justification is a legal term. The word "justify" is a judicial term meaning "to acquit, to declare righteous, to pronounce sentence of acceptance." The guilty one (man) stands before God the Righteous Judge, but instead of a sentence of condemnation, he receives a sentence of acquittal. Justification is a state of acceptance into which one enters by faith. This acceptance is a free gift of God made available through faith in Jesus Christ (Rom. 1:17; 3:21-22). By nature, unregenerated man is not only a child of the evil one, but also a transgressor and a criminal (Rom. 3:23; 5:6-10; Col. 1:21; Tit. 3:3). In regeneration (the new birth) man receives a new heart and a new nature; in justification man receives a new standing that includes:

1. The remission of the penalty of death.
2. The restoration to favor.
3. The imputation of righteousness.

The source of justification is the grace of God (Rom. 3:24; Tit. 3:7). It originates in the heart of God. Realizing not only our lack of righteousness, but also our inability to attain to it, He in His kindness decided to provide His righteousness for us. It was His grace that led Him to provide it. He was under no obligation whatever to do it. In His grace He had regard to our guilt, and in His mercy, to our misery.

The ground of justification is the blood of Jesus Christ. He paid for this righteousness given to us (Rom. 3:24; 5:9; Heb. 9:22). God remitted the penalty and restored man to favor. In justification our sins were not excused, but punished and then removed through the Person and work of the Lord Jesus Christ. His resurrection validated the purchase (Rom. 4:25), and the sending forth of the Holy Spirit to make that truth known to us revealed our acceptance in the Beloved (Acts 2:1-38; Eph. 1:6-7).

The means of justification is faith (Rom. 3:26-30; 5:1; 10:10). Faith is the condition or the instrument which appropriates the righteousness of Jesus Christ.

Rom. 5:1-2 KJV:

Therefore being justified by faith, we have peace with God through our Lord Jesus Christ:

By whom also we have access by faith into this grace wherein we stand, and rejoice in hope of the glory of God.

We commit the abomination of condemnation whenever we speak against those whom Jesus has saved by His blood. Our words must become constructive, not destructive. This is not a day to tear down, but to build up. To further illustrate this, consider these four verses from the eighth chapter of Romans.

Rom. 8:1 KJV:

There is therefore now no condemnation to them which are in Christ Jesus, who walk not after the flesh, but after the Spirit.

Rom. 8:15 KJV:

For ye have not received the spirit of bondage again to fear; but ye have received the Spirit of adoption, whereby we cry, Abba, Father.

Rom. 8:18 KJV:

For I reckon that the sufferings of this present time are not worthy to be compared with the glory which shall be revealed in us.

Rom. 8:39 KJV:

Nor height, nor depth, nor any other creature, shall be able to separate us from the love of God, which is in Christ Jesus our Lord.

For the child of God who has been justified by the blood of Jesus, we see that there is:

1. No condemnation.
2. No bondage or fear.

3. No comparison.
4. No separation.

What is our response to these truths? What shall we say to these things? Will we agree with the Father, or will we practice the idolatry of the abomination of condemnation?

Rom. 8:30-35 KJV:

> *Moreover whom he did predestinate, them he also called: and whom he called, them he also justified: and whom he justified, them he also glorified.*
>
> *What shall we then say to these things? If God be for us, who can be against us?*
>
> *He that spared not his own Son, but delivered him up for us all, how shall he not with him also freely give us all things?*
>
> *Who shall lay any thing to the charge of God's elect? It is God that justifieth.*
>
> *Who is he that condemneth? It is Christ that died, yea rather, that is risen again, who is even at the right hand of God, who also maketh intercession for us.*
>
> *Who shall separate us from the love of Christ?*

I'll tell you who. I will, and you will, when we condemn the just. I can almost picture God standing with His hands on His hips saying, "How dare you? Who do you think you are? Are you smarter than I am? I have justified you by my grace. I command you to repent and change your mind about yourself and your brethren!"

The Accuser Of Our Brethren Is Cast Down

The Christ is in you: prophet, priest, and king. He is there to produce the Kingdom of God: righteousness, peace, and joy in the Holy Ghost. You are God's garden, and spring, and fountain. What will release it all?

Rev. 12:9-11 KJV:

And the great dragon was cast out, that old serpent, called the devil, and satan, which deceiveth the whole world: he was cast out into the earth, and his angels were cast out with him.

And I heard a loud voice saying in heaven, Now is come salvation, and strength, and the kingdom of our God, and the power of his Christ: for the accuser of our brethren is cast down, which accused them before our God day and night.

And they overcame him by the blood of the Lamb, and by the word of their testimony; and they loved not their lives unto the death.

Satan is our adversary. He has deceived the whole world through fear. He is the "accuser" of the brethren. This word is "diabolos" and means "to throw or hurl through, to slander, to speak against." *The Amplified Bible* says here, "He who keeps bringing charges ..." The enemy is throwing everything at us now. There has gone forth a flood out of his unholy mouth. But we can quench every one of his fiery darts and accusing thoughts by the blood of Jesus (Eph. 6:16).

Let us arise in faith (Rom. 10:17). Let us take the Word of God and cast him down! This scene in Rev. 12 has and will happen corporately, but it must happen individually. Then will be released the flow of the more excellent ministry. Then will come the Kingdom and the rule of God as righteousness, peace, and joy fill the land. Then will the power of the Christ within come forth, and we will hear the voice of the prophet, priest, and king. We're not seeing much now because we have exchanged the truth for the lie (Rom. 1:23-25). With the help of Satan and his ministers, we have formed certain images of ourselves and others in our minds until these reasonings have become strongholds which must be torn down.

II Cor. 10:3-6 KJV:

> *For though we walk in the flesh, we do not war after the flesh:*
> *(For the weapons of our warfare are not carnal, but mighty through God to the pulling down of strong holds;)*
> *Casting down imaginations, and every high thing that exalteth itself against the knowledge of God, and bringing into captivity every thought to the obedience of Christ;*
> *And having in a readiness to revenge all disobedience, when your obedience is fulfilled.*

II Thess. 2:3-4 KJV:

> *Let no man deceive you by any means: for that day shall not come, except there come a falling away first, and that man of sin be revealed, the son of perdition;*
> *Who opposeth and exalteth himself above all that is called God, or that is worshipped; so that he as God sitteth in the temple of God, shewing himself that he is God.*

The word for "pulling down" and "casting down" in II Cor. 10:4-5 is the same word. It is the word "kathaireo" (#2507), which means "to lower; (with violence) demolish; make extinct." It is found nine times in the New Testament, including the following verses.

Lk. 12:18 KJV:

> *And he said, This will I do: I will pull down my barns, and build greater; and there will I bestow all my fruits and my goods.*

Acts 19:27 KJV:

> *So that not only this our craft is in danger to be set at nought; but also that the temple of the great goddess Diana should be despised, and her magnificence should be destroyed, whom all Asia and the world worshippeth.*

This reveals the principle of the "fenced cities" in the Old Testament. Our minds and the way that we think can become a walled city. Those walls are coming down. These strongholds, or the thoughts and concepts that have such a strong hold on our minds, come in two forms:

1. Satan's reasonings — His purpose is to make us distrust and discredit the Christ, the Word of God. "Hath God said?" has ever been his favorite ploy.

2. Our own reasonings — These bear the fruit of fear, guilt, and shame.

The Greek word for "imaginations" in II Cor. 10:5 is "logismous" and means "reasonings." All human logic must be demolished! As the Israelites of old were to destroy all the heathen images in the days of Ezra and Nehemiah, so let us deal with spiritual idolatry and adultery in these days when Jesus is building His Church.

The truth of the woman bringing forth the manchild in Rev. 12 has varied applications. Are you aware that the spirit ("pneuma") of man is in the masculine principle, and the soul ("psyche" — some have called her "Sue Kay") of man is in the feminine gender or principle? The soul or mind is feminine, constituting the womb wherein are conceived the words that we speak (Matt. 12:34-36). Every word that goes out of our mouths is an ambassador of life or death (Prov. 18:21). Will we give birth to Christ or to Adam, to the new nature or the old, to the manchild or the monster?

There are two generations in every generation, sons and snakes. Let us bring forth life!

Isa. 53:8 KJV:

He was taken from prison and from judgment: and who shall declare his generation? for he was cut off out of the land of the living: for the transgression of my people was he stricken.

Matt. 3:7 KJV:

But when he saw many of the Pharisees and Sadducees come to his baptism, he said unto them, O generation of vipers, who hath warned you to flee from the wrath to come?

The King is showing us how to release the nature of the Son from within by speaking words of life. We must lay aside the sin of condemning ourselves. Put your feet on what the five natural senses are telling you (Josh. 10:24-25), and begin to believe what God has said about you. Everything else, all that is outside of the Christ nature, is a lying vanity and is idolatrous. Believe it. Walk it. Talk it, "until every thought acknowledges the authority of Christ" (II Cor. 10:5 *Phillips*).

We Are Fighting A Memory

The Head of the more excellent ministry never condemns. When Jesus forgives, He forgets. Most folks are struggling with the mistakes of the past. The war is over. The civil war within has ceased (Isa. 40:1-2; Rom. 7:24-25). Jesus has crossed the finish line and won the victory! The good fight of faith is to believe and receive His finished work. We are fighting a memory.

Isa. 26:13-14 NIV:

O Lord, our God, other lords besides you have ruled over us, but your name alone do we honor.

> *They are now dead, they live no more; those departed spirits do not rise. You punished them and brought them to ruin; you wiped out all memory of them.*

Eph. 2:1-6 NIV:

> *As for you, you were dead in your transgressions and sins,*
>
> *In which you used to live when you followed the ways of this world and of the ruler of the kingdom of the air, the spirit who is now at work in those who are disobedient.*
>
> *All of us also lived among them at one time, gratifying the cravings of our sinful nature and following its desires and thoughts. Like the rest, we were by nature objects of wrath.*
>
> *But because of his great love for us, God, who is rich in mercy,*
>
> *Made us alive with Christ even when we were dead in transgressions — it is by grace you have been saved.*
>
> *And God raised us up with Christ and seated us with him in the heavenly realms in Christ Jesus,*

We are new creatures in Christ. His blood has washed away our sin. We are free in Him. The old man has been crucified with the affections and lusts. Tradition teaches that the old man is still alive. The fruit of believing this is that the Christ lies dormant, entombed within the darkness of our soul. We are fighting a memory. The old man is dead, but his socks are in the drawer and his picture is on the dresser. He's dead and gone, but his influence is still around. The memory of him still lingers. It's simple. Just get rid of his things. Burn them if you have to.

Rom. 7:1-4 KJV:

> *Know ye not, brethren, (for I speak to them*

that know the law,) how that the law hath dominion over a man as long as he liveth?

For the woman which hath an husband is bound by the law to her husband so long as he liveth; but if the husband be dead, she is loosed from the law of her husband.

So then if, while her husband liveth, she be married to another man, she shall be called an adulteress: but if her husband be dead, she is free from that law; so that she is no adulteress, though she be married to another man.

Wherefore, my brethren, ye also are become dead to the law by the body of Christ; that ye should be married to another, even to him who is raised from the dead, that we should bring forth fruit unto God.

Our first husband has died, and now we are married to Christ. Our first husband was energized by the law of sin and death. Our Heavenly Boaz is the gentle Saviour, the Husband of the Church. Settle it, friend. The old man is dead. The sixth chapter of Romans teaches us to know that, to reckon that (as an absolute), and to yield our members (especially the tongue) accordingly (Rom. 6:1-14).

Rom. 6:6 KJV:

Knowing this, that our old man is crucified with him, that the body of sin might be destroyed, that henceforth we should not serve sin.

Gal. 2:20-21 KJV:

I am crucified with Christ: nevertheless I live; yet not I, but Christ liveth in me: and the life which I now live in the flesh I live by the faith of the Son of God, who loved me, and gave himself for me.

> *I do not frustrate the grace of God: for if*
> *righteousness come by the law, then Christ is*
> *dead in vain.*

The verbs "is crucified" and "am crucified" are the same word. It is the verb "sunestauromai" and is literally, "I have been crucified with Christ." It is perfect passive indicative, showing action that has been completed in the past with ongoing results in the present. The other verbs in Romans six are in the aorist or "snapshot" tense, showing action that took place at a definite point of time in the past. *Phillip's* rendering of Gal. 2:20 says, "I died on the cross with Christ."

In the book of Esther, Haman the Agagite, the descendant of Esau, speaks of the old man. I declare to you that Haman is dead! He was hanged on the gallows of Calvary. The Hebrew word for "gallows" means "to suspend, hang up, hang upon a cross, or to crucify" and is found eight times in the book of Esther, the number of a new day or a new beginning. We have been born again.

Jesus Christ has dealt with satan and the carnal mind. We are not to give place to either (Eph. 4:24-27). In Luke 23:27-43, we see three men on crosses. The One in the middle was God in the flesh, Immanuel. The one on the right was Adam in the flesh. The one on the left was satan in the flesh. The one who earlier said, "If you are the Son of God, command these stones to be made bread," returned that day to be hanged (Matt. 4:3; Jn. 12:31; 14:30; 16:11; 19:28). He said, "If you are the Christ, save yourself and us." This is the spirit of him who tries to to save his own neck. Contrast him with the Lamb who laid down His life without opening His mouth. What a scene! God was in the middle. Adam was on the right, and satan on the left. Adam was reinstated and reunited to the paradise of His Kingdom, but the son of perdition found no repentance. Satan has been convicted and bound, and now the Church must enforce his defeat. We must enforce the law (Rom. 8:1-4). Haman is no longer in the Kingdom, but His influence and his decree must be dealt with (see my notes on the eighth chapter of Esther). The decree of death must be reversed. A new law must be instituted. And with the new law comes a new priesthood (Heb. 7:12). Later in the story, we see the necessity of the destruction of the sons of Haman as well (Gal. 5:19-21). Stop talking, preaching, singing, and thinking about Haman. Haman is dead. The house of Haman has perished. Start talking, preaching, singing, and thinking about the Lord Jesus Christ and his eternal victory over all enemies. Let your praises be the celebration of His glorious triumph!

Adam has died. He was hanged on the tree. The Last Adam came to bring a lasting end to the first Adam. This is rough, but stop munching on dead men's bones. Jesus has forgiven you. He has forgotten what you were. His love covered the multitude of your sins. In like manner, our father Abraham disobeyed God from the beginning. He left Ur of the Chaldees with his father Terah and his nephew Lot. He went down to Egypt in the time of famine. He lied about Sarai. God interceded for a liar. Abraham later joined himself to Hagar the Egyptian, and produced the wild man Ishmael. God didn't speak to him for thirteen years! Hear the words of the apostle concerning this patriarch: "He staggered not at the promise of God through unbelief; but was strong in faith, giving glory to God; And being fully persuaded that, what he had promised, he was able also to perform" (Rom. 4:20, 21 KJV).

That's not a contradiction. That's the result of the grace of God! What about Paul himself? He was a murderer who persecuted the early Church. Can you see him pounding down the road to Damascus with a pocketful of warrants? He went into Christian homes and dragged men and women, boys and girls, out into the streets to be beaten and killed. Listen to his personal testimony of knowing God's forgiveness: "Make room for us in your hearts. We have wronged no one, we have corrupted no one, we have exploited no one" (II Cor. 7:2 NIV).

Thank God for His grace! Like many of you, I have been hurt by other Christians, and even by other preachers. I'm not saying that I won't remember. I'm saying that I can't remember! Hallelujah! Believe it, my friend. We have been shadow-boxing, beating the air, fighting a memory ...

I'm not excusing sin. I'm not watering down sin. But the king-priest ministry after the order of Melchisedec has been sent to deliver, not to condemn the world. We have been invited to participate in this more excellent ministry. Jesus longs for an overcoming Church to sit with Him in the love-seat, there to be the channel of His light and life.

Some brothers haven't made half the mistakes that I have made, but they are ever condemning themselves. Cast down the accuser! Let salvation, and strength, and the Kingdom of our God, and the power of His Christ come forth. Let righteousness, peace, and joy fill the land as we hear the voice of the prophet, priest, and king. Beloved, for most of my ministry, I was a "professional fighter." On occasion, I have been harsh, and arrogant, and legalistic. The law of sin and death is a spiritual "wife-beater." There have been times when I have whipped the saints with the Word of God. I have handled the Word of God deceitfully in those moments, using His Hammer to make my point rather than to let that same Hammer help my hardness of heart. Thank God for His deliverance. I still struggle in some of those areas whenever I cease to reckon myself dead to sin and alive unto God. A man's character is what he is under pressure. Tribulation is pressure. In the times when I get my eyes off the Lord Jesus and His all-inclusive victory, I drift off into the never-never land of Adam's dream. God put Adam to sleep (Gen. 2:21), and he didn't wake up until four days later (Jn. 11:39; II Pet. 3:8). Adam is asleep, but Christ is awake. Adam is dead, but Christ is alive forever more! I have lived Adam's nightmare, for I used to be like David, the man of war.

I Kg. 5:1-5 KJV:

> And Hiram king of Tyre sent his servants unto Solomon; for he had heard that they had anointed him king in the room of his father: for Hiram was ever a lover of David.
> And Solomon sent to Hiram, saying,
> Thou knowest how that David my father could not build an house unto the name of the Lord his God for the wars which were about him on every side, until the Lord put them under the soles of his feet.
> But now the Lord my God hath given me rest on every side, so that there is neither adversary nor evil occurrent.
> And, behold, I purpose to build an house unto the name of the Lord my God, as the Lord spake unto David my father, saying, Thy son, whom I will set upon thy throne in thy room, he shall build an house unto my name.

Rom. 16:20 KJV:

> And the God of peace shall bruise Satan under your feet shortly. The grace of our Lord Jesus Christ be with you. Amen.

It's the God of peace who wins the victory. The man of war, the old man, must perish so that the lover, the man of peace, the new man, can come forth to build God a house of devotion. Are you a fighter, or are you a lover, seated with Jesus in the love-seat in the living room? There is a Man in the throne with a ministry, a ministry without condemnation. He bids us come. Let us arise and sit down with Him in the heavenlies (Isa. 52:1-3; Eph. 2:1-6).

I challenge you. Open your heart. If you still have on your apron, your religious mask, take it off. I know it hurts. It's been there a long time. But there is One who knows all about it. There is so much that only you and He know about. Let Him heal you. Let Him deliver you from the abomination of condemnation. Let Jesus begin to pour in the oil and wine, and bind you up.

The Lord stands ready to forgive you and bless you. You can come now to the throne of grace and find help. Only then can you begin to feel the need of those who are still in the Outer Court and the Holy Place. Only then will you be able to hear the distant cries of those who are without the camp. Only as you allow Him to comfort you, can you effectively minister the reality of His life and love to others.

He is drawing us together. This is not a day to shrink back in fear. Now is the time to draw near ... near to God and His people. He is linking us together. We are becoming an interlocking chain of a new humanity (Rev. 20:1-3) that will appropriate the finished work of Jesus and bind Satan, enforcing his defeat. Only God can make us one. Only God can make us whole. Only God can tear down the walls between us and bring us into the joint-participation of His ministry, a ministry without condemnation and prejudice.

Chapter Three

A Ministry Without Prejudice

We have already learned that the more excellent ministry, the king-priest ministry of Jesus Christ, is the ministry of forgiveness and blessing through the living, creative Word. It flows out of the Most Holy Place from the Mercy-seat of God. It is a ministry without condemnation. It is also a ministry without prejudice.

Gal. 4:6-7 NIV:

Because you are sons, God sent the Spirit of his Son into our hearts, the Spirit who calls out, "Abba, Father."
So you are no longer a slave, but a son; and since you are a son, God has made you also an heir.

The spirit of Moses was imparted to the seventy elders. The spirit of Elijah came upon Elisha. The Spirit of Jesus has been sent into our hearts! His Spirit is holy, free of all condemnation, bitterness, revenge, and self-pity, which is the devil's baby-sitter free of charge. We must have His nature. Somebody says, "I want the power." Well, the Greek word "dunamis" means "power, ability, might, or strength." It is power that is inherent within a nature, according to *Thayer's Lexicon*. God is love (I Jn. 4:7-8). If the love of God is there, the power of God will be there. The opposite of love is hate, and hate is prejudice.

Gal. 5:5-6 NIV:

> *But by faith we eagerly await through the Spirit the righteousness for which we hope.*
>
> *For in Christ Jesus neither circumcision nor uncircumcision has any value. The only thing that counts is faith expressing itself through love.*

Faith is in Christ, and Christ is in you. There is a new dimension of faith which is being energized by a new dimension of love. The new dimension of faith is His faith, an unprecedented display of the might and power of God. It's coming. The new dimension of love is His love which flows from the Mercy-seat. *The Amplified Bible* here says that this faith is "activated, and energized, and expressed, and works" through the love of God (I Jn. 3:1-18).

Rom. 1:17 KJV:

> *For therein is the righteousness of God revealed from faith to faith: as it is written, The just shall live by faith.*

The phrase "from faith to faith" is literally "out of faith into faith." Faith in the abstract gives way to faith in substance. Out of shadow and into reality. Out of Old Testament faith and into New Testament faith. Our faith is not found in the eleventh chapter of Hebrews. I love this "faith" chapter of the Bible, and there is much we can learn from it. But did you ever notice that all the people mentioned there are Old Testament saints? Heb. 11 faith is Old Covenant faith.

Heb. 11:13 KJV:

These all died in faith, not having received the promises, but having seen them afar off, and were persuaded of them, and embraced them, and confessed that they were strangers and pilgrims on the earth.

Heb. 11:39-40 KJV:

And these all, having obtained a good report through faith, received not the promise:

God having provided some better thing for us, that they without us should not be made perfect.

You can do two things with the Heb. 11 kind of faith:

1. You can die.
2. You can die without the promise.

Our faith is not in Heb. 11. One Person is conspicuously missing. The greatest Name of all is not to be found in the "faith" chapter. But read on.

Heb. 12:1-2 KJV:

Wherefore seeing we also are compassed about with so great a cloud of witnesses, let us lay aside every weight, and the sin which doth so easily beset us, and let us run with patience the race that is set before us,

Looking unto Jesus the author and finisher of our faith; who for the joy that was set before him endured the cross, despising the shame, and is set down at the right hand of the throne of God.

Our faith is in Heb. 12! Our faith is His faith (Gal. 2:20). The Bible tells us in Mk. 11:22 to have the faith of God. Jesus Christ is the Author and the Finisher of our faith. He conquered death and obtained the promise, and that same kind and quality of faith has been planted in every child of God (I Pet. 1:23)! Now learn something else about Old Covenant faith.

Heb. 11:2 KJV:

For by it the elders obtained a good report.

Heb. 11 faith is "good report" faith. How many were saved, or filled, or healed? How big is your building, or choir, or budget? All the important things. To men, that is. God isn't impressed. I know you've heard this testimony: "Pray for me that I'll make it through. All I want is to hear Him say, 'Well done!' All I want is a good report card." I want more than a good report card. I want to conquer death and obtain the promise, and He has promised that we can live!

If Heb. 11 faith is "good report" faith, then Heb. 12 faith, His faith, is "no reputation" faith (Phil. 2:1-11). It's the kind of faith that heals the sick, and then says, "Shhh! Don't tell anybody." Are you still interested? There's a price to pay to share the more excellent ministry. Some are waiting for that price to be right. Some opportunists are anxious for the right moment when they can step from behind the curtain and say, "I brought in the Kingdom." Wake up, brethren. We're not going to bring in the Kingdom ... the Kingdom is going to bring us in!

The power of God is released by the love of God. The love of God is the absence of hate, and hate is prejudice.

Mother's Love And Father's Love

A man and a woman rightly related reveal the image of God.

Gen. 1:26 KJV:

And God said, Let us make man in our image, after our likeness: and let them have dominion over the fish of the sea, and over the fowl of the air, and over the cattle, and over all the earth, and over every creeping thing that creepeth upon the earth.

Gen 5:1-2 KJV:

This is the book of the generations of Adam. In the day that God created man, in the likeness of God made he him;

Male and female created he them; and blessed them, and called their name Adam, in the day when they were created.

God is neither male nor female (Jn. 4:23-24), yet He is characterized by both. We must have a fresh restoration of the love of God in our homes and churches.

It is necessary to have "mother's love" in our midst. This side of the love of God is always accepting, though acceptance does not necessarily mean approval. "Mother's love" is unconditional, free from requirements. We don't have to meet a certain standard of dress or doctrine with this love. If little Johnny breaks the neighbor's window with his baseball, Mother won't disown little Johnny. Mother will always love you. What safety! What security!

Eph. 4:1-3 NIV:

As a prisoner for the Lord, then, I urge you to live a life worthy of the calling you have received.

Be completely humble and gentle; be patient, bearing with one another in love.

Make every effort to keep the unity of the Spirit through the bond of peace.

Can you imagine the kind of home or local church where "mother's love" is flowing? It doesn't matter what a person has said or done, he is accepted. Unfortunately, most folks only want this side of God's love. It must be balanced with "father's love." What a difference when there is a real daddy in the house! His love is firm, an earned respect that will not let us have our way. He loves little Johnny, too. But Johnny is going to pay for the neighbor's window. Strong government and order in the home and local church is part of the love of God. Whenever a real daddy speaks, the kids may say, "You don't love me!" The interpretation to those tongues is, "You won't let me have my way!"

Heb. 12:5-11 NIV:

And you have forgotten that word of encouragement that addresses you as sons: "My son, do not make light of the Lord's discipline, and do not lose heart when he rebukes you,

Because the Lord disciplines those he loves, and he punishes everyone he accepts as a son."

Endure hardship as discipline; God is treating you as sons. For what son is not disciplined by his father?

If you are not disciplined (and everyone undergoes discipline), then you are illegitimate children and not true sons.

Moreover, we have all had human fathers who disciplined us and we respected them for it. How much more should we submit to the Father of our spirits and live!

Our fathers disciplined us for a little while as they thought best; but God disciplines us for our good, that we may share in his holiness.

No discipline seems pleasant at the time, but painful. Later on, however, it produces a harvest of righteousness and peace for those who have been trained by it.

God has ordained two institutions: the home and the local church. There is a pattern and order to note here. Jesus is the Head of both. Then comes the man, the woman, and the children. Many truths can be learned as we parallel the natural family and the spiritual family.

THE HOME	THE LOCAL CHURCH
Jesus Christ	Jesus Christ
The man	The senior pastor
The woman	The other elders and deacons
The children	The saints

The man is a husband and a father. The woman is a wife and a mother. The pastor is a husband ministry to the other leadership and a father to the saints. The elders and deacons are a wife ministry to the pastor and a mother to the saints. Mother will always love you. Father won't let you do your thing. Together, we see the image of God, the love of God. This is the Day of Atonement, a day of purification, a day of purging, a day of preparation, fitting us for the final thrust into the Feast of Tabernacles.

II Pet. 1:19 KJV:

We have also a more sure word of prophecy; whereunto ye do well that ye take heed, as unto a light that shineth in a dark place, until the day dawn, and the day star arise in your hearts:

The Son is also the Sun (Mal. 4:2). The Christ within is the Daystar which rises to dispel the darkness. We have been brought out of darkness into His marvelous light. Darkness is ignorance. Light is understanding (Eph. 1:18). He brought us out of darkness, superstition, fear, and tradition. Every kind of prejudice is a form of ignorance. The more excellent ministry is a ministry without prejudice. The light of God has dawned and is leading us on.

Prov. 4:18 KJV:

But the path of the just is as the shining light, that shineth more and more unto the perfect day.

Rev. 21:21 KJV:

And the twelve gates were twelve pearls; every several gate was of one pearl: and the street of the city was pure gold, as it were transparent glass.

The word "transparent" is "diaphaino," which means "to shine through." It is the same word as "dawn" in II Pet. 1:19 — "until the day shine through." God is looking for a resting place, a people through whom He can shine with His nature of light. All of humanity is saying, "We would see Jesus." That's the cry of the Spirit today. There is something within me that is desiring the dawning of His nature. The breaking forth of the Christ within is destroying the darkness and bringing the light of revelation and understanding upon my spirit. There is but one "street" in the city. What do you do on a street? You walk on it. The city is a people (Matt. 5:14) with a golden walk, letting His divine nature govern their steps. Gold perishes. Gold is corruptible. What have golden streets to do with an incorruptible inheritance? Gold and what it can buy mean nothing to the spiritual man.

I Pet. 1:4 KJV:

To an inheritance incorruptible, and undefiled, and that fadeth not away, reserved in heaven for you,

I Pet 1:7 KJV:

That the trial of your faith, being much more precious than of gold that perisheth, though it be tried with fire, might be found unto praise and honour and glory at the appearing of Jesus Christ:

I Pet. 1:18-19 KJV:

Forasmuch as ye know that ye were not redeemed with corruptible things, as silver and gold, from your vain conversation received by tradition from your fathers;

But with the precious blood of Christ, as of a lamb without blemish and without spot:

The Daystar is rising. The light is shining. A new day is dawning. A new priesthood is on the horizon. A ministry without darkness, a ministry without prejudice.

His Judgment Was Taken Away

Phil. 3:1 NIV:

Finally, my brothers, rejoice in the Lord! It is no trouble for me to write the same things to you again, and it is a safeguard for you.

We have already talked about the purpose of God being revealed in three dimensions. The Tabernacle of Moses consisted of the Outer Court, the Holy Place, and the Most Holy Place. God lives in a three-room house. The third room is the living room (Jn. 14:6). The third room is the loving room (I Cor. 13:13). There is one piece of furniture in God's living room: the Ark of the Covenant with its golden lid, the Mercy-seat. This is the love-seat, the throne of grace. There is a Man in the throne with a ministry (Heb. 8:1-6). This is the king-priest ministry after the order of Melchisedec, a forgiving and blessing order. This more excellent ministry is a ministry without condemnation, a ministry without prejudice. We saw that the Pattern Son proclaimed the ministry of Jubilee (Luke 4:18). He came to preach deliverance, or "forgiveness" — He came to set at liberty or to "forgive" them that are bruised.

Matt. 12:20 KJV:

A bruised reed shall he not break, and smoking flax shall he not quench, till he send forth judgment unto victory.

A smoking flax is a dimly burning wick. Jesus was gentle. The fruit of the Spirit is gentleness. We need to be bold as a lion (Prov. 28:1), but we need the nature of the Lamb as well. We must identify with the hurts, the needs, the cries of people. Forgive yourself first. If you have had to suffer, then know that the Father allowed it as He apprehended you for this ministry. There's not a son of God ever called to the top of Mt. Zion that won't have to follow the Pattern.

I Pet. 3:18 KJV:

For Christ also hath once suffered for sins, the just for the unjust, that he might bring us to God, being put to death in the flesh, but quickened by the Spirit:

Somebody will have to fellowship His sufferings if the creation is to be brought to God. Philip the evangelist went down to the desert and met the Ethiopian eunuch who was reading Isa. 53:7-8. "Do you understand what you are reading?" asked Philip. He then got into the chariot, and, beginning at those verses, preached Jesus.

Acts 8:32-33 KJV:

The place of the scripture which he read was this, He was led as a sheep to the slaughter; and like a lamb dumb before his shearer, so opened he not his mouth:
In his humiliation his judgment was taken away: and who shall declare his generation? for his life is taken from the earth.

His judgment, or justice, was taken away. The natural mind says, "That's not fair. That's not logical." The Latin word for "meat" is "karne" —the carnal mind is a meathead. Adam is ignorant. He's smart enough to be dumb. He avoids responsibility that way. But responsibility is our response to His ability, and only in His strength can we become like the Slain Lamb. Jesus was led by the Spirit (Rom. 8:14). The ox Christ Jesus could carry the load and keep His mouth shut. Who was His shearer? Certain tribes will have a problem with this, but His shearer was His Father!

Isa. 53:10 NIV:

> Yet it was the Lord's will to crush him and cause him to suffer, and though the Lord makes his life a guilt offering, he will see his offspring and prolong his days, and the will of the Lord will prosper in his hand.

Men in any generation who speak out against the strongholds of prejudice are going to get bruised. Jesus was a corn of wheat who fell into the ground and died (Jn. 12:24). He was the Seed and the Living Word (Jn. 1:1-4). He was planted in the earth in death and burial and came forth in the harvest of His resurrection as the Firstfruits of them that slept. Jesus suffered, not only during the passion of Gethsemane and Calvary, but all the while he tasted of the realm of death, the realm to which He subjected Himself for thirty-three years. He suffered, and bled, and died. Not fair, you say? From Adam's perspective, His whole life wasn't fair. He was tempted in all points like as we are, yet without the sin of complaining. Some of you have been called to the top of the mountain. The thrones of the kings are in Zion. And the tombs of the kings are in Zion. There's one with your name on it, a custom-designed death to self and all that self wants.

Gen. 50:20 NIV:

*You intended to harm me, but God intended it
for good to accomplish what is now being done,
the saving of many lives.*

The patriarch Joseph is one of the most outstanding
types of Jesus Christ in the Old Testament. He was
"petted" by his father Jacob, "pitted" by his jealous
half-brothers, "potted" in the house of Potiphar when
he refused the harlot, and "putted" on the throne as
the lord of the harvest. What was Joseph's secret? He
stayed sweet in the prison house. He continued to pray
and to stay sensitive to the Holy Ghost so that his
words meant life for some and death for others. Joseph
paid a price, but no one has ever suffered like the
Lamb of God. Are you aware of the origin of all
suffering?

Rev. 13:8 KJV:

*And all that dwell upon the earth shall worship
him, whose names are not written in the book of
life of the Lamb slain from the foundation of the
world.*

All suffering began and ended with the Slain Lamb.
Behold your God. Behold His head, His wisdom. He's
too wise to make a mistake. He made you, and you're
not a mistake. Behold His hands, His power. He's too
powerful to fail. Behold His heart, His love. He loves
you too much to hurt you. I'm not looking for a demon
under every bush and around every corner. The
deliverance ministry is valid and part of the manifestation of the authority of the Kingdom, but it has been
heavily abused, sometimes ignorant of the ways in
which the Father deals with His sons.

Hos. 6:1-2 NIV:

Come, let us return to the Lord. He has torn us

to pieces but he will heal us; he has injured us but he will bind up our wounds.

After two days he will revive us; on the third day he will restore us, that we may live in his presence.

I Cor. 4:11-13 NIV:

To this very hour we go hungry and thirsty, we are in rags, we are brutally treated, we are homeless.

We work hard with our own hands. When we are cursed, we bless; when we are persecuted, we endure it;

When we are slandered, we answer kindly. Up to this moment we have become the scum of the earth, the refuse of the world.

Do you believe that? God tears, then He heals. That's a principle for training children. The one who spanks them is the one who reassures them and prays with them. God has allowed some of you to be puzzled, misrepresented, ostracized, and cast out as the scum of the earth. At this point, some may be saying, "Varner, you are out of your mind!" No, friend, I may be out of your mind. The carnal mind says, "It's not fair." The mind of Christ doesn't say a word except, "Father, into your hands I commit my spirit." If the sons of God are to minister His vengeance, then we must be free of all vengeance. And how can I be free from retaliation if I haven't had occasion for revenge? I have had to walk through some hellholes where I was 150% right, and still got blamed for it. The minute I complain, I disqualify myself for this ministry. It's all right to complain, just make sure that He is the only One who hears it. His yoke is easy and His burden is light. We can walk through these places and come out without the smell of smoke on us. The Lord gives us strength to walk through those broken-hearted experiences without gritting our teeth. One thing's for sure. I'm going to stay in the woodshed or go around the same mountain again and again until I learn to keep my mouth shut. Then when I do speak (Isa. 50:4), I can say, "My beloved enemies, in the Name of my Lord who is my Pattern and Example, I forgive and bless you out of Zion."

Isa. 48:10 KJV:

Behold, I have refined thee, but not with silver; I have chosen thee in the furnace of affliction.

Matt. 20:16 KJV:

So the last shall be first, and the first last: for many be called, but few chosen.

Now we know why few are chosen. They don't want the heat. Can we say with the three Hebrew children, if God delivers us or if He doesn't, we refuse to bow? We will not worship the image of self-pity and resentment. Again, this won't sit well with certain theologies, but there were some in the faith Hall of Fame who did not accept deliverance that they might obtain a better resurrection (Heb. 11:35). Settle it now. To share His throne is going to cost you everything.

II Kg. 18:4 KJV:

He removed the high places, and brake the images, and cut down the groves, and brake in pieces the brasen serpent that Moses had made: for unto those days the children of Israel did burn incense to it: and he called it Nehushtan.

Some are worshipping at the altar of their sufferings. They flaunt their spiritual pedigree in the face of younger Christians. "Nehushtan" means "a piece of brass." It took fire to mold that brazen serpent. Don't be proud of your sufferings. Don't worship the furnace that God wants you to forget. It served its purpose. Don't let fiery trials and ordeals become idols in your mind. Some say, "You don't know what I've been through for God." The Outer Court deals with the external, the Holy Place with the internal, and the Most Holy Place with nature or being. Don't get so wrapped up in what God is doing in you that you lose sight of Him who is doing it. We've suffered, but it's nothing compared to His suffering. If we can't keep pace with the footmen (Jer. 12:5), what will we do when the horses get here (Rev. 6)?

What has all this to do with the more excellent ministry? First of all, I must count the cost. Second, I must learn to forgive and bless. If so, I'm a son. If not, I'm a bastard. The wheat and the tares have matured. It's harvest time. We are learning to forgive and bless ourselves and others. We are to love our neighbor as ourselves. You must be willing to learn to worship in every circumstance. All the accuser can do is whisper and intimidate. Cast him down with the Word of the Lord. The monkey on your back will fall off. "But, Brother Varner, what about the folks who won't forgive me?" Pray for them. Release them to the hand of the Father. The important thing is that you are free. Then it's easier to deal with our mate and everybody else. If patience is a fruit of the spirit, then impatience is a work of the flesh. All those who are apprehended for the more excellent ministry have to experience the fellowship of His sufferings.

Would You Die For A Creep?

Heb. 5:2 — *The Amplified Bible:*

> *He is able to exercise gentleness and forbearance toward the ignorant and erring, since he himself also is liable to moral weakness and physical infirmity.*

What is prejudice? It is hate, and hate is learned

behavior. Put two little five-year-old boys on a swing set and they will play with each other. No matter that one is white and the other black. Somebody will have to teach them the difference. You don't get prejudiced overnight. It's not important how we learned it or from whom we learned it. The point is, we learned it!

The "ignorant" are folks who aren't aware, folks who don't understand, or perceive, or consider — it's never crossed their mind because the Holy Ghost has never enlightened that dimension of their thinking. When folks who don't know want to know, we have a responsibility to show them a better way. It's a sin when they reach out to us and we don't reach back. A lot of us are like Peter. He had all his preconceived ideas and his formula down pat. But God shook him up real good!

Acts 10:9-16 KJV:

On the morrow, as they went on their journey, and drew nigh unto the city, Peter went up upon the housetop to pray about the sixth hour:

And he became very hungry, and would have eaten: but while they made ready, he fell into a trance,

And saw heaven opened, and a certain vessel descending unto him, as it had been a great sheet knit at the four corners, and let down to the earth:

Wherein were all manner of fourfooted beasts of the earth, and wild beasts, and creeping things, and fowls of the air.

And there came a voice to him, Rise, Peter; kill, and eat.

But Peter said, Not so, Lord; for I have never eaten any thing that is common or unclean.

And the voice spake unto him again the second time, What God hath cleansed, that call not thou common.

This was done thrice: and the vessel was received up again into heaven.

"Rise, Peter. Kill your prejudice and take unto yourself the creeping things!" Peter saw the Body of Christ. There are all kinds of people in every church. One preacher said, "Sure, I pastor a spirit-filled church ... it's filled with all kinds of spirits!" The Dove of the Holy Spirit has flown the Pentecostal coop and lighted upon every denomination, and we can begin to see the book of Acts in a new light. If you will liken the Jews to the classical Pentecostals and the Gentiles to the Charismatics, it makes for interesting study. I can hear Peter now. "But, Lord, they didn't get it one, two, three." If they get it three, two, one, praise the Lord! Let's rejoice that God is moving. Joel was a true prophet who spoke of these days.

Joel 2:28 KJV:

And it shall come to pass afterward, that I will pour out my spirit upon all flesh; and your sons and your daughters shall prophesy, your old men shall dream dreams, your young men shall see visions:

The Good Shepherd is also the Good Samaritan (Lk. 10:29-36). Man went down from Jerusalem, the place of God's presence, to Jericho, the place of the curse (Josh. 6:18, 26). Adam fell, and was left in a stricken condition. Religion came down the road twice, to forever witness to us that it cannot help broken humanity. The priest and the Levite came by chance, but Jesus came by choice. He poured in the oil of His Spirit and the wine of His blood. He then carried the man to an inn, the local church, and placed him under the care of the pastor, the innkeeper. The Good Samaritan provided two pennies, or enough to take care of the man for two days (II Pet. 3:8). Don't worry. After that, He'll be back to take care of the balance!

This is a hard question, but would you lay down your life for a creeping thing (Acts 10:12)? Would you die for a creep? Jesus did. He died for me.

Ten Kinds Of Prejudice

Jesus loves everybody. I'm not saying, "God loves you just as you are." Rather, He sees what you can become and what you are going to be. He's not prejudiced, but neither will He tolerate sin. This isn't greasy grace and "sloppy agape." This isn't the sweet "Hallelujah, thank you, Jesus" kind of plastic, candy-coated religious hype. The God that I'm preaching is a consuming fire (Heb. 12:29). In the Outer Court, we met the Son, our Saviour. In the Holy Place, we met the Holy Spirit, the indwelling Christ. In the Most Holy Place, we are meeting the Father and the way in which He deals with every son whom He receives.

The Old Testament Levitical order of priesthood was limited. It only ministered to one nation. Some ministries only cater to one doctrine or emphasis. But the New Testament order of priesthood after the similitude of Melchisedec is unlimited, ministering to all men of all nations. It is important to know that there are three kinds of nations:

1. Nations.
2. Denominations.
3. Imaginations.

We will never evangelize the nations of the earth until we send this Gospel of the Kingdom into the world between our ears. The word for "world" is "kosmos" and means "a system, order, or arrangement of things." It can speak of the way that we think, our frame of mind. The dark continents of the soul need to be converted. There are concepts that are ungodly and idolatrous. That world, or cosmos ... that world, or arrangement of our thought patterns, must be reached for the Lord. We must send the Word of the Lord to evangelize the prejudice that still exists in our imaginations. Those "nations" must come to the Lord. The more excellent ministry is a ministry without prejudice. It does not choose whom it loves.

There are ten kinds of prejudice. The list could be longer, but these are the major principles:

1. Racial.
2. Sexual.
2 Chronological.
4. Geographical.
5. Educational.
6. Financial.
7. Physical.
8. Denominational.
9. Ministerial.
10. Doctrinal.

The first kind of prejudice is racial. I'm grateful for all the ministries in the land who see this particular area of need. But I humbly submit a word of caution: don't ride the horse into the ground. It's only one of ten kinds of prejudice, and some of those other areas are just as bad as racial bigotry.

God has done a beautiful work in our local area. Some of my closest colleagues in eastern North Carolina are black. Let me give honor to these pastors: L. O. Sanders and Milton Sullivan from Jacksonville, Willie Murray and Ezekiel Murriel from Beaufort, S. E. Saunders and Walter Barbour from Goldsboro, Walter Jones and Daniel Williams from Havelock, Paul Thomas and Dexter Wingfield from Greenville, Elbert Kilpatrick from Kinston, Donald Wright from Rocky Mount, Julius Petteway and Darryl Thomas from New Bern, Robert Bratcher from Rose Hill, and L. J. Tillery from Clinton, among others. Pastor Steve Everett from Cape Coral, Florida, who was an elder under L. O. Sanders of Jacksonville, and with whom I have traveled extensively throughout the East Coast, the Caribbean, and South America, is one of the finest teachers in the nation.

North Carolina is full of bigotry. I have been in Richlands for ten years. When I first moved here, some of the saints in the black community called and asked if it was all right for them to attend our services. I was shocked and angered at the mentality of our locale. I've learned one thing in twenty years of ministry: people are crazy! Blacks want to be white, and white folks lay out in the sun trying to get black. I don't have a struggle with racial prejudice in my own heart. That's not to say that I don't need help in some other area. The prejudices I wrestle with may not bother you at all. Let's be merciful to one another.

Because race is such a sensitive issue, I have mentioned it first. Something must also be said about a teaching called the "Identity" message, or British Israelism, which says that only the white, Anglo-saxon races constitute the Israel of God. This teaching appeals to the soul or intellect of men under the guise of revelation knowledge. It requires a view of the seed of God as being natural, whereas the Israel of God has always been a spiritual people. This middle-of-the-road position bears the fruit of elitism and exclusivism. It is a feeble attempt to sew up the veil that Jesus rent. If I were God, I'd bring a great revival through the blacks of this country and the Third World nations of the earth. To these ministries I say, "Rise up, brethren! Let nothing spoil you through philosophy and vain deceit!"

How do you overcome racial prejudice? Just put a "g" in front of "race" and you get "grace"! Grace is bigger than race! How dare we feel otherwise? The king-priest ministry of Jesus ministers to all men, and all races. Jesus is color-blind. There is no racial prejudice in the more excellent ministry. I've met a lot of preachers who know somewhat about the Kingdom, but are biased and opinionated when it comes to race. I've heard them crack their jokes. God is going to crack them! Without that breaking, they will never sit in His throne. The Melchisedec priesthood is a universal ministry. It is a ministry to the whole world, to all nations. If we are truly born of the Spirit (and His wind blows all over the world), we will have a world-wide vision.

Acts 10:34-35 KJV:

> *Then Peter opened his mouth, and said, Of a truth I perceive that God is no respecter of persons:*
> *But in every nation he that feareth him, and worketh righteousness, is accepted with him.*

The second kind of prejudice is sexual. This is the battle of the sexes, the walls and fears that exist between men and women. The scope of this writing will not permit me to address the issue of women preachers. I have dealt with that in an eight-tape series called "The Ministry of Women." It is sad that the ignorance and the arrogance of some brethren have hindered such a great ministry. Ladies, I'm in your corner. Somebody said, "The virgin Mary was the first one to carry the Gospel!"

I remember the early 1970's when it seemed like all we preached was church government and divine order. A fresh wave of that is in the land under different brands and handles. I'm glad for that, but I want to beseech you in this area. The "discipleship controversy" evolved because men, husbands in the home and shepherds in the church, went too far. The extremes of authority and submission have gone beyond the limits to play God with people's lives. The whole principle of authority and submission is not to be an end in and of itself. It is, rather, to be a glorious means to an even more glorious end. This is a shocker, but did you know this truth?

All authority and submission is under the curse ...

What? Yes, you heard me right. It wasn't until after the fall of man that the husband was to rule over the wife (Gen. 3:16). Prior to the fall, they were one. There was no need for authority and submission; it was swallowed up in simplicity and union. In order for authority and submission to operate, there must be two wills. One will must come under and submit to the other will. For that reason, we see that obedience is not the ultimate goal. There is something greater than me submitting to His will. The highest order of anything is to become it! We are to come into union with His will ... one will. Jesus was the Pattern for this. He who was rich became poor. The Word was made flesh. He condescended from the realm of perfect order and worship to this lower realm of death and chaos. He identified with broken humanity, and, as such, lowered Himself into a relationship of authority and submission to the Father. Prior to that, He and the Father were one. He lowered Himself even further and submitted to Joseph and Mary, and to the law.

Now lest you think that I am belittling the truth of authority and submission, let me state that this was the only principle by which Jesus Christ walked out from under the curse, bringing us up and out with Him! We were in His loins. So I preach and practice government. I always have. I have been labeled "Babylon" and "old order" because I still pastor a local church. I've seen both sides of the coin. On the one hand, men teach that authority and submission is all-important; others are teaching that authority and submission are not important at all. Guess where the truth is? The first crowd is killing folks with legalism;

the other is killing folks quicker with license. Paul dealt with both issues in His letter to the Galatians, showing us that law and lust will abort the seed of God.

Submission does not denote inferiority. The man is not better or smarter than the woman. There are wonderful differences. For example, men are head-liners and women are fine printers. If the woman is the weaker vessel, then the man is the weak vessel (I Pet. 3:1-7). I have already taught you that a man and a woman rightly related reveal the image of God. It takes both. Two become one. There is a realm of perfect union where that which is in-part shall be done away. I know that the local church is a shadow of that reality. I am aware of what the "deeper life" teachers are saying; I should ... I've helped to teach some of them. I also know that we haven't arrived. The experience of Eph. 4:13 is still ahead of us. Some may read this and self-destruct. "Praise God, I'm free! I submit to no man," is the banner of a wild man. But we still need husbands in the home and pastors in the church. Let us follow the Leader. Jesus arrived at full stature by tasting fully of submission to the will of the Father. Brethren, face it. God is raising up some women to speak His Word. Like Deborah of old (Judg. 4-5), there are women in the land who are forerunners of the Kingdom.

Acts 2:17-18 NIV:

> *In the last days, God says, I will pour out my Spirit on all people. Your sons and daughters will prophesy, your young men will see visions, your old men will dream dreams.*
>
> *Even on my servants, both men and women, I will pour out my Spirit in those days, and they will prophesy.*

Gal. 3:28 NIV:

> *There is neither Jew nor Greek, slave nor free,*

male nor female, for you are all one in Christ Jesus.

Eph. 4:13 NIV:

Until we all reach unity in the faith and in the knowledge of the Son of God and become mature, attaining to the whole measure of the fullness of Christ.

The third kind of prejudice is chronological. Somebody says, "I don't like young people." Don't worry. They don't like you, either. Jesus ministers to all men, regardless of race, sex, or age. Two of the most neglected areas in the local church are ministries to the youngest saints and the eldest saints. The Lord took time to pick up babies and bless them in spite of some apostles who felt that there were more important things to do. Think of the great ministries in the Body of Christ for a moment, and then consider that somebody at one time had to change their stinky diapers. My David is seven months old. Just this week, he got his first tooth. My Jonathan is seven years old. Just this week, he got his first little league uniform. Who knows what a child may become? Moses in the bulrushes, Samuel at Shiloh, the baby Jesus in the manger ... these little boys became mighty prophets, men who could shake a nation. Thank God for the Jochebeds, and Hannahs, and Marys of this generation. Keep praying, mother. Your little man will become great in the Kingdom of God. Then what about the senior citizens of the Bible? What of these super saints? Moses started his ministry at the age of 80. Life began at 55 for King Jehoiachin following his release from a Babylonian prison. Time won't permit us to tell of Simeon the prophet and Anna the prophetess. Suffice to say that old age is not a problem with God. Just ask Abraham and Sarah.

Matt. 21:16 KJV:

And said unto him, Hearest thou what these say? And Jesus saith unto them, Yea; have ye never read, Out of the mouth of babes and sucklings thou hast perfected praise?

Psa. 92:12-15 KJV:

The righteous shall flourish like the palm tree: he shall grow like a cedar in Lebanon.
Those that be planted in the house of the Lord shall flourish in the courts of our God.
They shall still bring forth fruit in old age; they shall be fat and flourishing;
To shew that the Lord is upright: he is my rock, and there is no unrighteousness in him.

Acts 2:17 KJV:

And it shall come to pass in the last days, saith God, I will pour out of my Spirit upon all flesh: and your sons and your daughters shall prophesy, and your young men shall see visions, and your old men shall dream dreams:

The fourth kind of prejudice is geographical. All kinds of stereotypes are turned loose here. When I moved from Maryland to North Carolina in 1977, folks affectionately referred to the new kid on the block as the "Yankee preacher." I was a northerner in those days, and ignorant of the finer things in life. Seriously, when asked if I liked collards, I innocently replied, "I like everybody!" Anyway, we have attached our prejudices to certain regions in the nation. Here are some of the lies we have perpetrated: New England saints are the frozen few; if you are from California, you're strange; all of God's people south of the Mason-Dixon line (do you have one of those in your spirit?)

have hound dogs and drive pickups; the list could go on and on. "Where are you from, boy?" Who cares?

It doesn't help when geographical prejudice is a major issue of dispensationalism. I am speaking about the traditional focus upon the natural Jews as the chosen people of God. Something must be said here about the "Holy Land." The heathen Naaman thought there was something special about dirt from Palestine (II Kg. 5:17-18). American Christians have trafficked enough wood from Israel to rebuild Noah's Ark and enough water from the Jordan to float it. I covered this truth in the first chapter of the *Prevail* book, but I say again, "The Jew is you!" I'm not anti-Semitic. I'm pro-Jesus. He and His Church are the Seed of Abraham (Gal. 3:7, 16, 29).

Jn. 4:19-24 NIV:

> *"Sir," the woman said, "I can see that you are a prophet.*
>
> *Our fathers worshiped on this mountain, but you Jews claim that the place where we must worship is in Jerusalem."*
>
> *Jesus declared, "Believe me, woman, a time is coming when you will worship the Father neither on this mountain nor in Jerusalem.*
>
> *You Samaritans worship what you do not know; we worship what we do know, for salvation is from the Jews.*
>
> *Yet a time is coming and has now come when the true worshipers will worship the Father in spirit and truth, for they are the kind of worshipers the Father seeks.*
>
> *God is spirit, and his worshipers must worship in spirit and in truth."*

The fifth kind of prejudice concerns education, and whether you have it or not. Who cares? Somebody says, "Varner, you must be an educated man. You've written almost forty books, including studies on one-third of the books of the Bible. How many degrees do you have?" Well, that depends. I have three or I have 98.6... which ones do you want to talk about? Paul was a smart man. He knew that education was good fertilizer. If you use it right, it will help things grow; if not, you can keep piling it up or hang it on the wall and let it stink. Better yourself any way that you can. Don't forget that it takes the anointing to break the yoke. The two greatest Apostles of the early Church were complete opposites. Paul was educated; Peter was not. God cut each of them out of a predetermined mold. Some preachers have told me that my writings will cause God's people to become intellectuals. What these guys really mean is that once the Church knows what they know, they'll have to get with it and feed God's people. Other preachers have been intimidated by my knowledge of the Scriptures. What they need to know is that I learned much of it while sitting at the feet of men who didn't finish high school. There is no educational prejudice in the more excellent ministry. Jesus died for all men, regardless of their I.Q.

Phil. 3:4-8 KJV:

Though I might also have confidence in the flesh. If any other man thinketh that he hath whereof he might trust in the flesh, I more:

Circumcised the eighth day, of the stock of Israel, of the tribe of Benjamin, an Hebrew of the Hebrews; as touching the law, a Pharisee;

Concerning zeal, persecuting the church; touching the righteousness which is in the law, blameless.

But what things were gain to me, those I counted loss for Christ.

Yea doubtless, and I count all things but loss for the excellency of the knowledge of Christ Jesus

my Lord: for whom I have suffered the loss of all
things, and do count them but dung, that I may
win Christ,

The sixth kind of prejudice concerns money, and
whether you have it or not. Again, who cares? The
material riches of this world are only valuable to the
natural man. A spiritually minded man wants something more precious: the more excellent ministry, and
to be conformed to the image of Christ. Somebody said,
"Every man has his price." I don't believe that. The
city of Rev. 21 is a people. The twelve gates of the city
are twelve experiences which progressively unfold
from the nature of Christ within. When you walk
through the gate of Issachar, which means "reward,"
you come into a place with God where you can't be
bought. The root of all evil is the love of money, and
you don't have to have any to love it. Again, there are
two extremes in the land. Some tell us that financial
prosperity is all-important, and others teach that it
doesn't matter at all. Poverty was part of the curse
(Deut. 28). The wealth of the sinner is laid up for the
just, and the wealth of the nations is going to come into
the Church (Isa. 60; Rev. 22). But God's wealth is
wealth to be given away. Prosperity means that you
always have enough. In this Day of the Lord, some are
being abased in this area, while others are abounding.
If you have made mammon your god, get ready for the
stripping. If you have walked around in your beggar's
garment and second-hand shoes, get ready for the
stripping of your pride as you learn how to receive.
Jesus and his brethren love all men, regardless of the
size of their pocketbook.

I Tim. 6:6-11 KJV:

But godliness with contentment is great gain.
For we brought nothing into this world, and it is
certain we can carry nothing out.

And having food and raiment let us be therewith content.

But they that will be rich fall into temptation and a snare, and into many foolish and hurtful lusts, which drown men in destruction and perdition.

For the love of money is the root of all evil: which while some coveted after, they have erred from the faith, and pierced themselves through with many sorrows.

But thou, O man of God, flee these things; and follow after righteousness, godliness, faith, love, patience, meekness.

Phil. 4:11-12 KJV:

Not that I speak in respect of want: for I have learned, in whatsoever state I am, therewith to be content.

I know both how to be abased, and I know how to abound: every where and in all things I am instructed both to be full and to be hungry, both to abound and to suffer need.

The seventh kind of prejudice is physical, and how we look or don't look, whether or not we think ourselves attractive. Fat people want to be skinny and skinny people want to be fat. Tall folks walk around all slumped over and short folks walk around in platform shoes. Good looks are a must to perform in Babylon's circles. Fashion and finesse are big business. I guess that the Baptist's garb wouldn't have made the cover of the latest Roman magazine. I don't know if camel's hair was in vogue then. Jesus doesn't look into your closet when He comes to call. He looks into your heart. Again, look good. Be clean. Project the wholesomeness of Christ. You can fluff and buff the outer man all you want, but it's the beauty of the inward man that will last. Times haven't changed much. This kind of prejudice existed in the early Church.

Jas. 2:1-5 NIV:

My brothers, as believers in our glorious Lord Jesus Christ, don't show favoritism.

Suppose a man comes into your meeting wearing a gold ring and fine clothes, and a poor man in shabby clothes also comes in.

If you show special attention to the man wearing fine clothes and say, "Here's a good seat for you," but say to the poor man, "You stand there" or "Sit on the floor by my feet," have you not discriminated among yourselves and become judges with evil thoughts?

Listen, my dear brothers: Has not God chosen those who are poor in the eyes of the world to be rich in faith and to inherit the kingdom he promised those who love him?

The Worst Kind Of Prejudice

The more excellent ministry is a ministry without prejudice. Jesus Christ loves all races, both sexes, all ages, all local areas, and pours out His life to all men, regardless of education, finance, or appearance. But the worst kind of prejudice is religious prejudice. These strongholds are the toughest to bring down. I am speaking about denominational, ministerial, and doctrinal prejudice.

The eighth kind of prejudice is denominational. This is a sectarian spirit of exclusivism. This includes the nondenominational denominations. From Luther to the present, men have been building their kingdoms. The land is filled with these walled cities, houses that men have built. But Jesus taught us to build the house upon the rock and not upon the sand. Sand is particles of rock. It can prove dangerous to build our doctrine or ministry on one emphasis. We must declare the whole counsel of God. The wind has already started to blow. Babylon is coming down. But you have to remember that Babylon is a spirit. This warfare is not against flesh and blood, but against principalities and power in the heavenlies (Eph. 6:12). In Gen. 11, we see a people who want to make a name for themselves. Anyone can do that, regardless of the label on the door. The sad thing is to see the people who are locked behind these ecclesiastical walls. Sadder yet are the preachers who have chosen to be bound to the breast of the great whore rather than to draw from the life of El-Shaddai. God is raising up men now who will bridge the gap between the various streams. He is getting ready to send Daniel into Babylon. The Levitical order of priesthood only ministers to one nation or denomination. The more excellent ministry after the order of Melchisedec speaks the Word of the Lord to all nations or denominations.

Matt. 28:18-20 NIV:

> Then Jesus came to them and said, "All authority in heaven and on earth has been given to me.
> Therefore go and make disciples of all nations, baptizing them in the name of the Father and of the Son and of the Holy Spirit,
> And teaching them to obey everything I have commanded you. And surely I am with you always, to the very end of the age."

The ninth kind of prejudice is ministerial. This has to do with your favorite preacher. Paul warned the Corinthians about that, pointing out their immaturity and carnality. Do you like a certain kind of ministry? Maybe you are drawn to the preacher who rants and raves, whose neck bulges out, and who spits on the first three rows. Somebody else says, "I can't stand all that emotion and noise. I like somebody who just stands and teaches the Word." The covering for the Church (the virtuous woman) is made of tapestry with different textures, colors, and hues, yet woven together into a fabric that cannot be broken, a seamless robe to cover His body. God has gotten so big these days that there is no man, message, method, or movement on this planet that has a corner on Him. We need all the ministries. Each has his place. He who is the Bread of life ascended and divided Himself into five loaves. There are differences of ministries and anointings. Don't make an idol out of your favorite preacher. God may have to smash that image (Rom. 1:23-25).

I Cor. 3:1-7 KJV:

And I, brethren, could not speak unto you as unto spiritual, but as unto carnal, even as unto babes in Christ.

I have fed you with milk, and not with meat: for hitherto ye were not able to bear it, neither yet now are ye able.

For ye are yet carnal: for whereas there is among you envying, and strife, and divisions, are ye not carnal, and walk as men?

For while one saith, I am of Paul; and another, I am of Apollos; are ye not carnal?

Who then is Paul, and who is Apollos, but ministers by whom ye believed, even as the Lord gave to every man?

I have planted, Apollos watered; but God gave the increase.

So then neither is he that planteth any thing, neither he that watereth; but God that giveth the increase.

Prov. 31:22 KJV:

She maketh herself coverings of tapestry; her clothing is silk and purple.

Eph. 4:11 KJV:

And he gave some, apostles; and some, prophets; and some, evangelists; and some, pastors and teachers;

The tenth kind of prejudice is doctrinal prejudice, perhaps the stickiest of all. You may ask, "Brother Varner, isn't it important to know what we believe?" Sure it is, but these days it may be more important to know in Whom you believe! The first principles aside (Heb. 6:1-2), your doctrine is going to change. Don't nail your theology or eschatology down too tight. You may be embarrassed later when you have to pull it up and do it over. We must preach a sound, sane, sensible word. The centrality and preeminence of the Lord Jesus Christ must be our primary concern. The more excellent ministry can reach into every denomination, touch any preacher, and be effective in the midst of any doctrine. Above all, it won't cut a brother off because of what he believes. I get calls and letters all the time begging me to write a book on certain controversial issues. I'm not a coward or a politician. I want to be like the Lord in the fifth chapter of Joshua. He didn't take sides. I want to be for Him, and He is for Himself! I could spend more time in this section musing about the "hot" topics of 1988, but five years from now the fads will change again. A man could get himself killed for preaching justification by faith in Luther's day. We've come a long way, dear ones. You don't have to defend the truth. The truth will defend you. Preach the Word. Come to the Feast of Tabernacles. God will take care of your toys back at home.

Ex. 34:23-24 NIV:

Three times a year all your men are to appear before the Sovereign Lord, the God of Israel.
I will drive out nations before you and enlarge your territory, and no one will covet your land when you go up three times each year to appear before the Lord your God.

Acts 5:20 NIV:

"Go, stand in the temple courts," he said, "and tell the people the full message of this new life."

Acts 20:27 NIV:

For I have not hesitated to proclaim to you the whole will of God.

Jesus Has Invaded The Land

Jesus is not prejudiced in any of these ten areas. He has called us to have the same attitude (Phil. 2:5). We'll pay the price to walk in His ministry. When I began to pastor, the Lord whispered a secret in my ear: "Whatever you do and however you do it, you will be criticized." I have been praised and I have been cursed. Don't believe it when preachers tell you that it doesn't matter what people say. We care, because we need encouragement like everybody else. We have hurts and discouragements like everybody else. It does matter to me what people say and think, but it doesn't move me (Acts 20:24). I will obey God and not man. I can't be a manpleaser and the servant of Christ. Please don't misrepresent this ministry as I have shared it with you. I am not trying to create unity and bring everybody together under one banner. Unity cannot be created. It can only be kept. Thank God for every effort to get God's people together, but unity is based on seven absolutes.

Eph. 4:4-6 KJV:

*There is one body, and one Spirit, even as ye are
called in one hope of your calling;*
One Lord, one faith, one baptism,
*One God and Father of all, who is above all, and
through all, and in you all.*

We are not to have religious prejudice. We are to be
open to minister to anybody. But only the Holy Ghost
can network the Body of Christ. It has to be by the
Spirit.

Jesus has invaded the land. He has declared war on
the walled cities of our thinking. The inhabitants of the
land, the heathen concepts that have kept us in
darkness, are terrified. The sinners in Zion are afraid.
Fearfulness has surprised the hypocrites (Isa. 33:10-17).

I have loved the book of Joshua for many years. The
Lord opened it to me in 1981, and I have since written a
volume of notes on it. The name "Joshua" in the Old
Testament is the same as "Jesus" in the New. It means
"God is my salvation." Jesus Christ is our Heavenly
Joshua, the Captain of our salvation. He has invaded
the land that He might drive out the heathen and
possess the inheritance. It is interesting to note the
varied responses and reactions of the inhabitants of
the land to this Heavenly Intruder. This separate
study is available on nine tapes. Here is the outline of
that teaching:

1. Joshua himself — humble adoration.
2. The city of Jericho — fearful isolation.
3. Rahab the harlot — household salvation.
4. The Gibeonites — arrogant deception.
5. The five kings — fierce confederation.
6. Achan — secret rebellion.
7. The children of Joseph — haughty exaltation.
8. The two-and-a-half tribes — wrong motivation.

All of this is happening in the Church today. The Lord is drawing near in the Day of Atonement to cleanse us so that He can take His rightful place as the Head of the Church. Note especially the reaction of the Gibeonites:

Josh. 9:22-24 KJV:

And Joshua called for them, and he spake unto them, saying, Wherefore have ye beguiled us, saying, We are very far from you; when ye dwell among us?

Now therefore ye are cursed, and there shall none of you be freed from being bondmen, and hewers of wood and drawers of water for the house of my God.

And they answered Joshua, and said, Because it was certainly told thy servants, how that the Lord thy God commanded his servant Moses to give you all the land, and to destroy all the inhabitants of the land from before you, therefore we were sore afraid of our lives because of you, and have done this thing.

Jesus has invaded the land. We are that land. Thy Kingdom come, Thy will be done in earth as it is in heaven. He has come to cleanse the Temple and to tear down every wall. The Gibeonites tried to beguile or deceive Joshua. The beast is subtil. They ended up as bondmen, slaves to the law of sin and death. They were allowed to minister to the house but not to the Lord (Ezek. 44). Verse 24 explains the purpose of their scheming. They were sore and they were afraid ... they were sore afraid. I've encountered some Gibeonites along the way who are ever nursing their hurts, a running sore. Their resentment has become bitterness. The Gibeonites were afraid for their "lives" — this is the Hebrew word "nephesh" and means "soul." The Greek equivalent is "psyche." Note that "lives" is plural, pointing to the soul comprising the intellect, emotions, and will; in other words, our opinions, feelings, and desires — our way. My greatest struggles in this walk have come when I wanted to do God's will my way. We must not draw back unto perdition, but must believe to the saving of the soul. God has come to deal with our prejudice, whether its source is a family spirit or our parroting someone else's bias. God is going to deal with this Jacob nature.

Gen. 32:24-32 KJV:

> And Jacob was left alone; and there wrestled a man with him until the breaking of the day.
>
> And when he saw that he prevailed not against him, he touched the hollow of his thigh; and the hollow of Jacob's thigh was out of joint, as he wrestled with him.
>
> And he said, Let me go, for the day breaketh. And he said, I will not let thee go, except thou bless me.
>
> And he said unto him, What is thy name? And he said, Jacob.
>
> And he said, Thy name shall be called no more Jacob, but Israel: for as a prince hast thou power with God and with men, and hast prevailed.
>
> And Jacob asked him, and said, Tell me, I pray thee, thy name. And he said, Wherefore is it that thou dost ask after my name? And he blessed him there.
>
> And Jacob called the name of the place Peniel: for I have seen God face to face, and my life is preserved.
>
> And as he passed over Penuel the sun rose upon him, and he halted upon his thigh.
>
> Therefore the children of Israel eat not of the sinew which shrank, which is upon the hollow of the thigh, unto this day: because he touched the hollow of Jacob's thigh in the sinew that shrank.

Jacob was created but Israel was formed (Isa. 43:1). I shared concerning this time of Jacob's trouble on pages 112-114 of the *Prevail* book. The supplanter had his rendezvous. The trickster met his match. God was the aggressor. He has singled us out. We have been left alone for a face-to-face encounter, a heart-to-heart talk. Our name, or nature, must be changed. We have manipulated and maneuvered to get our way. That day is over. So we wrestle until the breaking ... the breaking of the day and the rising of the daystar. The *Amplified Bible* says of verse 27, "(The Man) asked him, 'What is you name?' And (in shock of realization, whispering) he said, 'Jacob (supplanter, schemer, trickster, swindler)!'" He touched me. This was more than a love-tap, for this word for "touched" is used elsewhere in the Old Testament to describe the smiting of Job; it was also used in Isa. 53 by the prophet to tell of the smitten and stricken Messiah. God knocked the fire out of Jacob, and He is knocking the fire out of our prejudices. The deceiver's thigh was hollow, speaking of the vanity and futility of what man can produce. A hollow thigh is like a husk of corn ... there's no real life in it. Men who preach sonship without the Spirit of the Son are a sounding brass and tinkling cymbal ... a gong that is big and loud on the outside but empty on the inside. You can spot a phony, and you can tell if a man is real, if He's been with Jesus. The world is groaning and crying for somebody who's got the goods. Jacob's thigh shrank (Jn. 3:30). He went forth with a different kind of walk, walking in the sunlight of a new day. Jacob became Israel, a prince with God, a man who had power with God and men, and who had prevailed. This is the man in the throne with a ministry, a ministry without prejudice, a ministry without walls.

Chapter Four

A Ministry Without Walls

The king-priest ministry of Jesus is a ministry without condemnation or prejudice. We have learned that there are ten kinds of prejudice. Each of these areas is a wall that must be destroyed in the name of the Lord. He is delivering us from being so narrow and proud. The pond is bigger than the lily pad we live on. No one experience in God does it all for you. He is opening us up and broadening us out.

There are two kinds of vines: those that creep and those that climb. We have already seen that the old man is a creepy crawler. Adam is prejudiced. Jesus died for the creep. The new nature, the Christ nature, is a climber. An example of this is a Joseph ministry in the earth, a ministry who will reach out and feed his brethren.

Gen. 49:22 KJV:

Joseph is a fruitful bough, even a fruitful bough by a well; whose branches run over the wall:

Joseph is a climbing vine. You can take a vine that is a creep and say, "Climb!" Then prop it up, nail it up, or hold it up. Come back in a few days. Because of an inward nature, the creeping vine will be right back on the ground. That's a real lesson for pastors who are wearing themselves out trying to get a creep to climb. The ministry without prejudice lets the Christ nature climb all over its own wall instead of climbing all over his brother. You can't hold down the new man. He has to ascend by the inner impulse of an eagle nature.

Everything outside of the Christ nature is a lying vanity. The walls aren't even real. They only exist in the carnal mind of men. In the mind of Christ, which was the mind of the Father, there are no walls. Jesus Christ destroyed them all in the rending of the veil of His own flesh.

Eph. 2:14-18 KJV:

For he is our peace, who hath made both one, and hath broken down the middle wall of partition between us;

Having abolished in his flesh the enmity, even the law of commandments contained in ordinances; for to make in himself of twain one new man, so making peace;

And that he might reconcile both unto God in one body by the cross, having slain the enmity thereby:

And came and preached peace to you which were afar off, and to them that were nigh.

For through him we both have access by one Spirit unto the Father.

... the wall which kept us apart ..." (Williams).

... and broke down the barrier of the dividing wall ... (New American Standard).

... and has broken down (destroyed, abolished) the hostile dividing wall between us ... (Amplified).

The word for "wall" here is "phragmos" (#5418 in *Strong's*) which means "a fence, or inclosing barrier." It goes back to "phrasso," which means "to block up, to silence, to stop." What has silenced the prophet, priest, and king? What has kept the garden inclosed and the fountain sealed? The walls that we think are between us. The same word is used in Luke's Gospel where Jesus compelled us to go to the hedges of our own thinking and ask them to repent.

Lk. 14:23 KJV:

And the lord said unto the servant, Go out into the highways and hedges, and compel them to come in, that my house may be filled.

The word used to show that Jesus has "broken down" these walls is "luo" (#3089), which means "to loosen, to reduce to the constituent particles." It is also used in I Jn. 3:8 where Jesus "destroyed" the works of the devil. Our King took the devil apart. From God's perspective, there are no more walls. From the viewpoint of the Mercy-seat, the throne of grace, the veil is rent. Our citizenship is in the heavens. From that vantage point, we can look at ourselves and our brethren. From man's perspective, the walls are still there, looming insurmountable from the vantage point of the dust. If you will change the spelling of w-a-l-l to w-i-l-l, you will know why men are still fighting each other. They will not bend. They will not change their minds. They will not let go of their prejudices, though these walls are vanities ... nothings ... idols (I Sam. 15:22-23). Note that Jesus broke down the "middle" wall of partition; that's where the wall is, in the middle of man, in the soul which contains the will.

Every wall is the pride and conceit of the carnal mind. It is a fence and hedge that must be torn down. In Num. 13:28, the Israelites refused to enter the land because of unbelief. Their excuse: the giants and the walled cities. A walled city is a blinded mind (II Cor. 4:1-4). The stubbornness of man's prejudices is thicker than the Iron Curtain. You can't get close to some folks because of the citadel, the fortress between their ears. The devil is not our problem ... what we think about the devil is our problem.

Prov. 18:11 KJV:

The rich man's wealth is his strong city, and as an high wall in his own conceit.

And like a high wall in his imagination ... (Rotherham).

... like a bulwark — so he thinks ...(Moffatt).

... a high protecting wall ... (Amplified).

The Day of the Lord is going to bring down "every high tower" and "every fenced wall" (Isa. 2:10-18; 30:8-14). False prophets in the pulpit and false prophets in the form of the words we speak have built the wall. Whether in the form of the systematic deception of man-made contemporary eschatology, or certain habits of unscriptural thought and speech, these walls cannot stand in His Kingdom. Saul is mad. The anointing has left him. David has already been anointed and is now being groomed to take his place. No wonder that the madman tries to pin folks to his wall (I Sam. 18:11; 19:10; 20:25). The "overflowing shower" and "great hailstones" of Ezek. 13 are descriptive of a remnant Church energized by the Holy Ghost (the "stormy wind"). This is the Lord roaring out of Zion to declare that Jesus has broken down every wall.

To be carnally minded is death. To be spiritually minded is life and peace (Rom. 8:1-6). There is a priesthood exampled in Acts 23:1-3 which judges after the law of sin and death. The ministry which smites in anger is indeed a "whited wall." This is the Greek word "koniao" (#2867), which means "dust, lime, whitewash." These are the "whited sepulchres" of Matt. 23:27 which sin against the brethren and wound the anointing in the midst of the people (I Cor. 8:12).

We are experiencing days of unprecedented spiritual warfare, but we need not fear the giants and their walled cities (Deut. 1:28; 3:5). The walls of Babylon are coming down (Jer. 50:14-16; 51:12, 58). Read II Cor. 10:3-6 in the *Amplified Bible*, and then rejoice in the victory of Jesus!

Who Is The Man Of Sin?

We will deal with the spirit of antichrist and the mark of the beast in the chapter about a ministry without idolatry. For now, let us understand that the mind is the battleground. King Saul sat on a "seat" by his wall. Jesus warned against the Pharisees who loved to sit in Moses' "seat." John even mentioned "the seat of satan" in Rev. 2:13 to be in Pergamos, which means "strongly united, closely knit or married, tough texture, elevated, height, citadel." Satan's throne is in the carnal mind. He is perched in the lofty heights of man's imagination.

II Thess. 2:1-4 NIV:

Concerning the coming of our Lord Jesus Christ and our being gathered to him, we ask you, brothers,

Not to become easily unsettled or alarmed by some prophecy, report or letter supposed to have come from us, saying that the day of the Lord has already come.

Don't let anyone deceive you in any way, for that day will not come until the rebellion occurs and the man of lawlessness is revealed, the man doomed to destruction.

He will oppose and will exalt himself over

everything that is called God or is worshiped, so that he sets himself up in God's temple, proclaiming himself to be God.

Paul wrote this epistle to correct the "any-minute" teaching about the coming of the Lord. The key word in this passage is "temple" — the place where the man of sin sits. There are two Greek words for "temple":

1. (#2411) "hieron": "a sacred place; the entire precincts of the Temple (at Jerusalem, or elsewhere)."

2. (#3485) "naos": "to dwell; fane, shrine, temple."

The word "hieron" is used throughout the Gospels and the book of Acts to describe the Temple at Jerusalem, a literal building made with hands, and which passed away in A.D. 70. Its only other mention is I Cor. 9:13. The word "naos" is used in the Gospels and the book of Acts to speak of the "inner sanctuary" itself. Note also Jn. 2:19 and Acts 7:48; 17:24. All the other references in the Pauline epistles (including II Thess. 2:4) and the thirteen references in the book of Revelation use "naos," the real Temple, a spiritual building not made with hands, eternal in the heavens.

I Cor. 3:16-17 KJV:

Know ye not that ye are the temple of God, and that the Spirit of God dwelleth in you?
If any man defile the temple of God, him shall God destroy; for the temple of God is holy, which temple ye are.

I Cor. 6:19 KJV:

What? know ye not that your body is the temple of the Holy Ghost which is in you, which ye have of God, and ye are not your own?

Eph. 2:21 KJV:

In whom all the building fitly framed together

groweth unto an holy temple in the Lord:

II Thess. 2:4 KJV:

Who opposeth and exalteth himself above all that is called God, or that is worshipped; so that he as God sitteth in the temple of God, shewing himself that he is God.

Concerning the rebuilding of a temple in Jerusalem, see my notes on Ezekiel 40-48. The man of sin sits in the real Temple, which we are. This is the spirit of antichrist, or that which is "instead of" the anointing; in other words, humanism. The man of sin is sinful man and the way he thinks. The man of sin is the carnal mind, enthroned behind the walls of his own making. This is the attitude that says, "Move over, Jesus. I'm going to rule today." The old man is a beast. He is so insecure ... he has to "shew" or convince himself that he is God.

II Thess. 2:5-12 KJV:

Remember ye not, that, when I was yet with you, I told you these things?

And now ye know what withholdeth that he might be revealed in his time.

For the mystery of iniquity doth already work: only he who now letteth will let, until he be taken out of the way.

And then shall that wicked be revealed, whom the Lord shall consume with the spirit of his mouth, and shall destroy with the brightness of his coming:

Even him, whose coming is after the working of satan with all power and signs and lying wonders,

And with all deceivableness of unrighteousness in them that perish; because they received not the love of the truth, that they might be saved.

> *And for this cause God shall send them strong delusion, that they should believe a lie:*
> *That they all might be damned who believed not the truth, but had pleasure in unrighteousness.*

Who is the hinderer and the restrainer in this passage? If it's the Holy Ghost that goes out with the Church in a pre-tribulation rapture, then how are folks going to get saved in the tribulation? Maybe it will be through 144,000 Jewish evangelists raised up overnight to do without the Holy Ghost what the Church has not been able to do with the Holy Ghost in 2,000 years. You need a vivid imagination to believe that (II Cor. 10:3-6).

I dealt with this whole chapter of II Thess. in an eight-tape series called "God's Two Greatest Mysteries" — the mystery of godliness (I Tim. 3:16) and the mystery of iniquity. In Luke 13:10-17, we see a bound woman, a blind ruler in the synagogue (the man of sin in the temple), and a blessed Redeemer. That woman, which could represent either the Church or the soul, had been bound by satan for eighteen years — that's six plus six plus six, the Bible number for bondage. The number 666 reveals man, man, man — man in fullness, the tares in full maturity. There are only two men on the planet — Adam and Christ; and both of them are many-membered. We have already learned that the only thing the serpent can eat is dust (Gen. 3:14-18; Isa. 65:25). The first man Adam is a man of dust. The only place that satan can live, and move, and have his being is in the carnal mind. Now you can better understand the emphasis on the renewing of the mind, or the transformation of the soul (the whole second chapter of the *Prevail* book). As you are conformed to the image of Jesus, you starve the devil!

He who now letteth will let, until he be taken out of the way. He who now restrains and withholds will continue to hinder until he literally "becomes in the midst." The Greek word here is "ginomai," which is always used to show something that is "becoming." The man of sin is the carnal mind that sits in the temple. His discovery is his undoing. Then shall that wicked one be revealed, whom the Lord will destroy with the brightness or manifestation of His coming or "presence." The Daystar is arising. The Son of man will swallow up the man of sin. Don't complain about how dark it is. Just turn the light on. This antichrist attitude is after the effectual working of satan, whose sole purpose is to blind your mind (II Cor. 4:1-7) and keep you in the dark, lest you understand the more excellent ministry. If you listen to his whisperings, you will reject the love of this truth; then will come the strong delusion of believing "the lie" — the lie that says that the old man is still alive and that satan is alive and well on planet earth. He's roaring, all right, and he will tear us apart until we see the finished work of Christ and believe it by appropriating the benefits of the New Covenant, until the Church arises in the earth to be a witness unto principalities and powers that Jesus Christ is Lord (Eph. 3:8-11)!

The simplicity of what I am saying is this: satan loves to divide people. God adds and multiplies; the devil subtracts and divides. Can you imagine what would happen in a home or local church where everyone believed the truth? We would put the devil out of business. He wouldn't be able to condemn us, and we wouldn't allow any prejudices or walls to keep us apart. Well, get ready, Church! Now you know the plan of God and the intent of the prayer of Jn. 17. He will judge the earth by that Man whom He has ordained, a Man in the throne with a ministry, a ministry without walls.

Ten Kinds Of Walls

We have looked at ten kinds of prejudice. Now understand that there are ten kinds of walls. In other words, any of these areas of prejudice can be at work in any of the following relationships. As you can see, this subject is getting bigger! What are the various areas in which we can be divided?

1. Walls between an individual and Jesus.
2. Walls between a local church and Jesus.
3. Walls between a husband and wife.
4. Walls between a parent and child.
5. Walls between an employer and employee.
6. Walls between sheep, or between shepherd and sheep.
7. Walls between shepherds.
8. Walls between local churches.
9. Walls between local areas.
10. Walls between nations.

Rom. 8:16-17 KJV:

The Spirit itself beareth witness with our spirit, that we are the children of God:

And if children, then heirs; heirs of God, and joint-heirs with Christ; if so be that we suffer with him, that we may be also glorified together.

Eph. 5:31-32 KJV:

For this cause shall a man leave his father and mother, and shall be joined unto his wife, and they two shall be one flesh.

This is a great mystery: but I speak concerning Christ and the church.

I Pet. 3:7 KJV:

Likewise, ye husbands, dwell with them according to knowledge, giving honour unto the wife, as unto the weaker vessel, and as being heirs together of the grace of life; that your prayers be not hindered.

Christ and His Church are heirs together of the grace of life. Again, there is a needed balance between brideship and sonship. I preach both. There are a lot of brothers hung up in the bride realm who can't see sonship. Others have bogged down in sonship who need to experience the truths of being His Bride. This is beautifully illustrated for us at the cross.

Jn. 19:26-27 KJV:

> *When Jesus therefore saw his mother, and the disciple standing by, whom he loved, he saith unto his mother, Woman, behold thy son!*
> *Then saith he to the disciple, Behold thy mother! And from that hour that disciple took her unto his own home.*

You that are preaching brideship, behold sonship. The essence of sonship is our being conformed to the image of the Lord Jesus Christ that we might be given dominion in His Name. The restoration of Sarah was great, but why was she restored? To bring forth Isaac, the manchild, the son of promise. You that emphasize sonship, behold your mother (Gal. 4:26). Don't despise her when she is old. Brideship precedes sonship. Until I can relate to Jesus as my Husband, my Lord, my Lover, I will not be able to relate to Jesus as the Elder Brother into whose image I am being changed. Until we can submit to His authority and become worshippers, there will be no impartation of His dominion. Don't let semantics throw you. We get overboard with stereotypes and terminologies and box ourselves in. We are heirs together of the grace of God. Let's move on with Him so we can tear down these ten kinds of walls.

Heirs Together Of The Grace Of Life

The Song of Solomon has been a closed book. It shouldn't be, for there are seven different ways of teaching it: literally, dispensationally, devotionally, allegorically, psychologically, governmentally, and prophetically. I have written a volume of verse-by-verse notes on this song of songs for the Holy of Holies.

There are different applications for Rev. 12. There we see a woman clothed with the sun, His light and life. The moon, which could represent the law, or the powers of darkness, are under her feet. On her head is a crown with twelve stars, speaking of divine government. The first seven chapters of the Song of Solomon take the Shulamite from conception to perfection and bring us to Rev. 12:1. In the final chapter of the Song we see the birth of a son. The woman bears a manchild in chapter eight. A man, a maid, and a manchild.

To quickly highlight this, note that the King brings the maiden into His chambers in chapter one. From that beginning point of conception, she moves into chapter two and the Feast of Pentecost at the banquet of wine. Song 2:4 beautifully parallels Acts 2:4. Follow her through chapters three, four, five, six ... by the time she gets over to chapter seven, she has the stature of a palm tree (Eph. 4:13), a symbol of uprightness and victory. Note also that she has a navel; in other words, her umbilical cord has been cut and she can sustain life herself. She is now ready to give birth.

Song 8:5 KJV:

Who is this that cometh up from the wilderness, leaning upon her beloved? I raised thee up under the apple tree: there thy mother brought thee forth: there she brought thee forth that bare thee.

The word "this" used here is in the feminine gender. Who is this woman that cometh up from the wilderness? The same woman of Rev. 12. But to whom is she speaking? The son to whom she has given birth! Bill Britton was a good friend of mine. He pioneered the writing of the sonship message, a truth that has been slandered and misrepresented. I know how he felt. But I prophesy that the very ones who have despised this message are going to lean on it in these days. I can't help that there flaky people preaching sonship. There was a brother running around in Luther's day claiming to be Elijah. I've seen error and excess in every realm. The Shulamite addresses the son, telling him that she raised him up under the apple tree. The manchild had to learn to submit. But who is the apple tree? In chapter two we see that it is Jesus Christ. We could say more, but that is enough to give you a taste of this wonderful Song.

I wrote an extensive introduction to my study of the Song of Solomon. First, I wanted to know everything the book said about Him, the Lord Jesus, the Bridegroom. He is called "Beloved" thirty-three times, one time for each year that He dwelled among us! I studied all his symbols and names in the Song. Next, I wrote down His actions, or everything that He did. I repeated this whole process for the Shulamite, the Bride. Did you know that "Solomon" means "peaceful" — compare it with the word "shalom." She is called the "Shulamite" in 6:13, which is the feminine form of Solomon! It's the same Hebrew word for "restoration" used in Joel 2:25 and other places! It speaks of that which is complete or finished. A Greek equivalent could be "teleios," the adjective for "perfect." He is the Prince of Peace. The Shulamite is the Princess of Peace! He's the Restorer. She's the restored one! He is the Author and the Finisher of our faith. We are the ones that He authored and we are the ones that He will finish! Jesus and His Church have the same name, which denotes the same nature, character, and authority. This reveals a people who are to share His more excellent ministry. Two become one.

As I continued my analysis of the Song of Solomon, I noticed something about their relationship. After having written down what belonged to Him and to her, I was struck by what belonged to "them"! We are joint-heirs with Him of the grace of life. By looking up the word "our," I discovered seven things that we share with Him.

1. Our bed — His rest (1:16).
2. Our house — His dwelling-place (1:17).
3. Our rafters — His strength and support (1:17).
4. Our land — His inheritance (2:12).
5. Our vines — His life (2:15).
6. Our gates — His ministry (7:13).
7. Our sister — His responsibility (8:8).

These same seven principles are mentioned below and linked with the seven-fold promise to the overcoming Church of Rev. 2-3. As heirs together of the grace of life, and joint-heirs of His more excellent ministry, we enjoy:

1. His peace (Rev. 2:7).
2. His protection (Rev. 2:11).
3. His provision (Rev. 3:12).
4. His property (Rev. 2:17).
5. His power (Rev. 3:5).
6. His purpose (Rev. 3:2).
7. His privilege (Rev. 2:26-28).

The Song of Songs contrasts the vanity of vanities of the book of Ecclesiastes. There we see the pursuit of all things under the sun. Here we see the pursuit of all things in Christ. The first thing they share together is found in Song 1:16 where she says, "Our bed is green." This is honorable, because this is the book of wedded love (Heb. 13:4). Secondly, they share "our house" (1:17), because they need a place to put this bed. This house has some support, so they share "our rafters." Then we have to put this house on some land, which is shared in 2:12 — "our land." "Our vines" are mentioned in 2:15; "our gates" are in 7:13; and "our sister" in 8:8.

To illustrate this, consider "our bed." The Psalmist declared in chapter 23 that the Lord makes us lie down in "green" pastures. Green is the color of life. We're heirs together of the grace of life. That's His rest or His peace. All through the Old Testament, God warned us about polluting His sabbaths. Whenever we fret, we defile His bed. His grace is sufficient for us. "You're not enough for me, Jesus. I'm going to look for another." When we get sick, we run to the doctor (I'm not against doctors). When we need money, we run to the bank (I'm not against banks). Why can't we run to Him? I've already shown you the story of the woman at the well (Jn. 4) who wasn't satisfied until she had met the Seventh Man. There is no satisfaction, or fulfillment, or contentment outside of Jesus Christ. There is no peace outside of Him. Whenever we worry, we commit spiritual adultery. We try to join ourselves to another source of strength. That's one reason why I'm not trigger-happy to point a bony, Pharisaical finger at folks who have messed up their lives in the natural realm. I've seen so many more spiritual whoremongers in church, and, whenever I have moved out of His rest, I have been one of them. If we don't make Him our Source, we are going to get thrown into another bed and go into great tribulation (Rev. 2:22).

After we share His rest, we share His house or dwelling-place, which is the place of His protection. Then we share His rafters, or His strength, which bear the stress and the strain of the house. The joy of the Lord is your strength (Neh. 8:10). Do you remember the corner boards of the Tabernacle of Moses and the two huge pillars in Solomon's Temple? He is the Corner and the Overcomer (Rev. 3:12). His strength is His provision. Then we move this house onto some land, which is His inheritance or property (Psa. 2:8;

Matt. 5:5). Somebody has died and left us something! This Word is His last will and testament, and, as the Testator, He died. But then He rose again to become the Administrator of His own will! We are heirs together of the grace of life! Our bed, our house, our rafters, our land ... next come our vines, which speak of His life (Jn. 15:1-7). This is His power, for the more excellent ministry after the order of Melchisedec is energized by the power of an endless life. And we share that ministry, for we share His gates. He has set before us an open door.

Song 8:8 KJV:

We have a little sister, and she hath no breasts: what shall we do for our sister in the day when she shall be spoken for?

I Thess. 5:8 KJV:

But let us, who are of the day, be sober, putting on the breastplate of faith and love; and for an helmet, the hope of salvation.

The breasts speak of faith and love. We could also mention the breastplate of righteousness and judgment. The "little sister" comprises all those believers whose faith and love, or whose righteousness and judgment, are undeveloped and immature (Heb. 5:11-6:3). These folks are part of our nation, but just come from a different tribe. Some of these people can't even live right. What shall we do for "our sister" in the day when she shall be spoken for? This is the day which the Lord hath made. Will we kick her in the teeth and send her to hell and say, "We're the sons of God. We're better than you"? This principle of "our sister" speaks of His responsibility to the rest of the family, and that is His privilege. It's not an inconvenience to minister to these who have never heard. It is an honor to flow in a ministry without walls.

He Standeth Behind Our Wall

Song 2:9 KJV:

My beloved is like a roe or a young hart: behold, he standeth behind our wall, he looketh forth at the windows, shewing himself through the lattice.

When the Shulamite spoke these words, she was standing in the Holy Place, in the Feast of Pentecost. She needs to move out of that realm and into the Most Holy Place, the realm of the more excellent ministry. Let me share my notes on this verse from my book on the Song of Solomon: "There were seven things that the King and His Bride could share, as seen in the word 'our' — but this was not 'our wall.' He had nothing to do with it. This was her wall, for it speaks to us of the veil separating the Holy Place from God's living room and love-seat. Jesus took down the middle wall of partition. This veil of flesh is her own blinded mind; it is her image of herself, and an idol that must be dealt with. She wants Him to remain a roe or young hart, and stay in the realm of Pentecost, or adolescence. He is very near to her, but her vision of His glory is obscured as she is bound in the earthly house of her tabernacle. When there is a real wall between the Lord and us, it is our wall, for we have built it. He hides Himself at times to quicken our faith. He reveals Himself little by little through the light we receive in blessing and affliction. He longs as He looks from within. This veil is the wall of a prison, and the lattice ('network') a net which must be broken. Although He always beholds her, she does not always see Him. This wall was in her mind and was her attempt to shut herself in with Him (only for herself). But there is not only sweetness of communion, but also power for service and spiritual warfare. His desire is to move and lead His love to new scenes beyond the bounds of the enclosure of her own reasonings. The king could not be held (1:13), and He would not be held now. His voice may well be heard, but its meaning was not comprehended.''

I can almost hear the conversation between the Shulamite and the King: "Lord, You're standing behind our wall. We share all these other things and we share this, too." He replies, "No, my dear. The wall isn't ours. It's yours." She is startled. "But, Lord, I want to share it with You. I want You to give honor and respect to my wall." "No, darling," He gently speaks. "It's your wall. I just stand. I just stand."

What stability! What continuity! Everything is falling apart and the Rock, Jesus Christ, just stands. He is looking and waiting, expecting till all His enemies are made His footstool (Heb. 10:12-13), till she wakes up and realizes that the wall isn't real. The weapons of our warfare are not carnal, but they are mighty through God to the pulling down of strongholds. So many things have bugged me. I have been harrassed, intimidated, and disgusted with the wall that I created. Thank God I have learned that these things are lying vanities because they are outside and separate from the Christ nature within. These things belong to a realm that is passing and not permanent. At this point, the soul says, "What in the world are you preaching?" The spirit says, "That's right! That's right!"

II Cor. 4:17-18 NIV:

For our light and momentary troubles are achieving for us an eternal glory that far outweighs them all.

So we fix our eyes not on what is seen, but on what is unseen. For what is seen is temporary, but what is unseen is eternal.

The Authorized Version says that we "look not at the things which are seen"; that is, we don't stare at it. We've not focused or riveted on the passing. We're gazing at the permanent, the eternal. The walls are not real. They are only real to the carnal mind. God's mind doesn't have any walls. He thinks without limitations. When he looks at this little ball of earth and sees these five billion people, tell me He sees these silly little things we call walls. Does God get up in the morning and start wringing His hands? "Devil, you're tearing up my creation!" No. He looks and says, "The earth is the Lord's, and the fulness thereof; the world, and they that dwell therein. For he hath founded it upon the seas, and established it upon the floods" (Psa. 24:1, 2 KJV).

Somebody says, "Varner, you've got to be a realist." I'm not saying that if we will imagine that the wall is not there, it will go away. But I am telling you that the things which have limited us and held us captive are coming down. These walls are the walls of a prison house which we have made. If we created it, then we can destroy it! This is the Year of Jubilee. I can't preach a message and tear the walls down, because they're already down!

Don't blame God. It's not His fault because it's not His wall. It's our wall. We had this baby, nursed it, and watched it grow. It started small, but now it's a Goliath parading back and forth in our thinking. The giant was a bully and a tyrant. He probably never fought a battle a day in his life. He was just a bluff. We've sold ourselves for nothing. We shall be redeemed without money (Isa. 55:1-3).

II Tim. 1:7 KJV:

> *For God hath not given us the spirit of fear; but of power, and of love, and of a sound mind.*

God's Prophets And The Wall

God has dealt with the wall. He is going to teach us how to appropriate His victory. Every wall is coming down, and it's coming down by the Word of the Lord. God sends a prophet when He wants to knock down a wall. There is a progression in how He deals with the walls:

1. The prophet Daniel and the wall.
2. The prophet Ezekiel and the wall.
3. The prophetic army of Joel and the wall.
4. The prophet David and the wall.
5. The prophet Joshua and the wall.

Dan. 5:5 KJV:

> *In the same hour came forth fingers of a man's hand, and wrote over against the candlestick upon the plaster of the wall of the king's palace: and the king saw the part of the hand that wrote.*

That's what God is doing in the earth now. He's saying, "Get ready, saints. I'm going to do something about the walls." God wrote on the wall. Daniel was promoted that night, but who wants to be the third ruler in a kingdom that is about to fall? God is writing on the wall. Perhaps He may use this little book to do some of that warning.

Ezek. 8:7-10 KJV:

> *And he brought me to the door of the court; and when I looked, behold a hole in the wall.*
> *Then said he unto me, Son of man, dig now in the wall: and when I had digged in the wall, behold a door.*
> *And he said unto me, Go in, and behold the wicked abominations that they do here.*
> *So I went in and saw; and behold every form of creeping things, and abominable beasts, and all the idols of the house of Israel, portrayed upon the wall round about.*

Daniel wrote on the wall. Ezekiel dug through the wall. God showed his prophet all the idolatry that was going on inside the house of the Lord, the things that men do in the darkness of their soul. The Word of God is sharp, and it's digging us now.

Joel 2:7-11 KJV:

> *They shall run like mighty men; they shall climb the wall like men of war; and they shall march every one on his ways, and they shall not break their ranks:*
>
> *Neither shall one thrust another; they shall walk every one in his path: and when they fall upon the sword, they shall not be wounded.*
>
> *They shall run to and fro in the city; they shall run upon the wall, they shall climb up upon the houses; they shall enter in at the windows like a thief.*
>
> *The earth shall quake before them; the heavens shall tremble: the sun and the moon shall be dark, and the stars shall withdraw their shining:*
>
> *And the Lord shall utter his voice before his army: for his camp is very great: for he is strong that executeth his word: for the day of the Lord is great and very terrible; and who can abide it?*

Daniel wrote on the wall and Ezekiel dug through it. Joel's army climbed all over it. Do you see the progressive, relentless intent of the Lord to bring down the wall by the mouth of His servants the prophets? You won't be able to hide from the word of the Lord.

Psa. 18:29 KJV:

> *For by thee I have run through a troop; and by my God have I leaped over a wall.*

Psalm 18 is a grand and glorious testimony of the faithfulness of God in David's life. Daniel wrote on the wall. Ezekiel dug through it and Joel's army climbed all over it. But David got happy in the Lord and leaped over it! There's not a wall too high. Retreat all you want. The prophet of the Lord will find you and jump over your fence. There's no obstacle that God's sons can't surmount.

Josh. 6:20 KJV:

So the people shouted when the priests blew with the trumpets: and it came to pass, when the people heard the sound of the trumpet, and the people shouted with a great shout, that the wall fell down flat, so that the people went up into the city, every man straight before him, and they took the city.

Joshua didn't write on the wall or dig through the wall. He didn't climb on it or jump over it. He just shouted and it fell! Joshua had gone out one evening to look at the double-walled city of Jericho. Like a lot of preachers, he was looking for a good idea. Then the Captain of the Lord's host appeared and said, "Let's do business. Take your shoes off, and walk softly in warfare. What I am going to tell you makes no sense, but those walls aren't real. I see all things, you know. I see the end from the beginning, and I'm telling you that there's no city there!" This was only a Christophanie. Jesus had yet to be born of the virgin and die on the cross. He had yet to say, "It is finished!" He finished every wall. But the faith of God was at work. The heavenly Visitor continued, "Joshua, if you'll hold steady and just listen to what I tell you, you'll see the victory. I'm going to give you a formula, a strategy, a word of wisdom, an answer. I'm about to work the greatest miracle to be recorded in the book you will write. I'm going to show you how to get three million people to walk in the same direction with their mouths shut until it's time to shout!"

The Shout Of Faith

Joshua and his band had a shout of faith. You and I can do the same! We're not going to shout the walls down. We can't do that because Jesus has already destroyed the walls. The shout of faith is not to pull the walls down. The shout of faith is to celebrate His victory for already doing it! All they had in Josh. 6 was a celebration. Let us praise Him. Let us exalt the victory of the ascended, risen, overcoming, victorious King of kings and Lord of lords! He is our peace (Eph. 2:14). He has broken down, destroyed, loosed, disintegrated, and dissolved the middle wall of partition. The veil was completely rent from the top to the bottom, never to be a wall again! It's only real to the immature who stand in their adolescence and lack of understanding. The tune of the Shulamite will change. She won't say "our wall" for long. He will begin to perfect and prove her. Her speech will graduate from "He is mine" to "I am His." Then she will mature and declare, "His desire is towards me."

Song. 8:10 KJV:

I am a wall, and my breasts like towers: then was I in his eyes as one that found favour.

Isa. 60:18 KJV:

Violence shall no more be heard in thy land, wasting nor destruction within thy borders; but thou shalt call thy walls Salvation, and thy gates Praise.

This is her final testimony. She has become His salvation in the earth. She has learned that God tears down a wall so He can build a wall (Jer. 1:10; Matt. 16:18). He tears down the old so He can build the new.

There are no walls in the more excellent ministry. The victory of Jesus Christ is so perfect, so permanent, so binding, so lasting! We can only celebrate the victory that He already won. In the book of Joshua, Jesus is also typified by the Ark of the Covenant of the Lord of all the earth. The Ark came against the greatest wall of all, the Jordan, a symbol for death. In Josh. 3-4, the Jordan was at flood stage. But when the priesthood took the step of faith, the walls of that water backed up ... it backed up through the Minor Prophets and the Major Prophets ... it backed up through all the kings of Judah and Israel ... it backed up through the Judges and the patriarchs ... it backed clear up to a place called Adam! Can't you see it? A royal priesthood upholding the Ark, and a nation following just 2,000 cubits behind. The application is obvious. Jesus Christ, the Ark of the Covenant, defeated death, hell, and the grave, and cut off every hindrance clear back to Adam! Then 2,000 cubits ... 2,000 years later, a holy nation follows their Head through the rent veil into the promise of God. The rending of the Jordan is the same principle as the rending of the veil. Every wall, every barrier, every limitation was cut off ... if there is still a curse, it's between our ears (Gal. 3:13-14)! If there are limitations, they are in our mind. They are only illusions. They're not real! Hear the Word of the Lord, "The wall is gone. It is not there! Look again. He nailed it to His cross. He nailed it! Can you hear it? Listen to the nails. He abolished it. It's gone!"

The men of Beth-shemesh learned this lesson the hard way (I Sam. 6:19). When you lift the lid of the Ark, only death and hell can come out. I refuse to uncover what His blood has covered. I refuse to give consent to the walls. Speak to me no more of circumstances and hindrances. I refuse to tread underfoot and do despite to the blood of His Covenant. I love Him too much. We're heirs together of the grace of life. I will no longer stand in obstinance, rebellion, and unbelief to say, "It's our wall."

The king-priest ministry of Jesus is a ministry without prejudice and without walls. Folks in eastern North Carolina ask, "Do you preach in black churches?" All the time. "Brother Varner, you've been to college. You can't preach the Kingdom." Don't tell me that now. "Varner, don't you know that fat people aren't going to make it in?" No more walls. No tight squeeze. I can walk through that. What will the world do when it stands face to face with a ministry that flows from the Mercy-seat? A ministry without traditions, without boundary lines, without walls. A ministry without jealousy and competition. What's the world going to do? The world is going to get delivered! Amen!

Note: At this point in the message preached at the House of Prayer in Springfield, the Word of the Lord came forth. Here is a copy of that prophecy.

"This night, O house of God, is a Jubilee unto thee. If thou shall allow the faith of thy spirit man to arise unto the reality of My Word, I shall do for thee this night what thou cannot or ever do thyself. I shall dissolve bondages, bodies shall be healed, and minds shall be restored. I shall cause great healing to sweep across thee and deliverance shall be thy portion. O house of the Lord, fret not over this and say no longer, 'I sit in a prison house.' I say unto thee, not only is the door open, but the walls are knocked flat. It is not there, and thou sittest in a prison house of thine own imagination. I say unto thee this night, look unto My Word and thou wilt read that the veil is rent. It is finished, and now thou canst only praise Me, saith the Lord, and celebrate, rejoice, and exalt the victory that I have already won for thee. Thou shalt not need to fight in this battle in thy human genius and thy human strength. That would fall before the onslaught of thine enemies. But I say unto thee, thou hast no enemies. He is defeated, yea, even under thy feet. Say no longer, 'One day I shall do this.' Settle it, and settle it this night. He is under thy feet and he is defeated. And this night thou shalt lift up thy voice and thou shalt shout with a resounding shout, and thou shalt celebrate the victory of thy king. For He hath died for thee, and risen again for thy justification, and thou shalt be saved by His life."

Saints, there is a shout of faith. The king of Jericho is satan, the prince of this world system. He is fearful. The demons, the inhabitants of Jericho, are trembling. They've heard about you. They've heard how the Lord opened up the Red Sea and brought you through. They watched while you walked across the Jordan in the time of harvest. And now you are encamped at the door of their city and you're about to walk around their walls. Can you hear the trumpets? Can you see the priests?

Note: At this point in the service, I asked the people to shout. What followed was a most amazing demonstration of the power of God. For a full ten minutes, the whole congregation shouted at the top of their voices. As the last of that awesome sound trailed off, I said these words:

"Now listen. Just listen ... You just heard what it sounds like for 400 to shout. Just listen. What was it like? What was it like when 3,000,000 shouted? And I believe, somehow, through the Spirit of God, we have experienced some of the reality of what took place that day. However long that shout lasted, I believe there swept across the valley, along with the billows of smoke and dust of a city that had just fallen ... I believe there swept an eerie silence. I believe a whole nation went on their knees, perhaps on their faces, in worship, in awe, for that thing that had been an insurmountable obstacle was no more. And the king of Jericho ... try to find him. He lies somewhere beneath the rubble. It's not how long or how loud we shout ... I want us to begin, softly, just to magnify and praise and honor Him. For I tell you by the Word of the Lord, whatever your Jericho is, and whatever it is to me, in this moment, it is no more ...''

When Jesus gave His life on the cross, He died with a shout of faith. When He got up on the third morning, He arose with a shout of faith. It was impossible for death to hold Him. His triumphant priesthood flows out of the Most Holy Place without condemnation or prejudice, a ministry without walls, a ministry without retaliation.

Chapter Five

A Ministry
Without Retaliation

There's a Man in the throne with a ministry. A ministry without condemnation, prejudice, or walls. Now we come to another facet of the Christ nature. There's no fight in this new creation Man. His is a ministry without retaliation, without a spirit of revenge. He is a Man of peace and not a Man of war. He is a Lover and not a Fighter. All the fight has been knocked out of Him. He's not defending God. God is defending Him.

I Kg. 5:1-5 KJV:

> And Hiram king of Tyre sent his servants unto Solomon; for he had heard that they had anointed him king in the room of his father: for Hiram was ever a lover of David.
> And Solomon sent to Hiram, saying,
> Thou knowest how that David my father could not build an house unto the name of the Lord his God for the wars which were about him on every

*side, until the Lord put them under the soles of his
feet.*

*But now the Lord my God hath given me rest
on every side, so that there is neither adversary
nor evil occurrent.*

*And, behold, I purpose to build an house unto
the name of the Lord my God, as the Lord spake
unto David my father, saying, Thy son, whom I
will set upon thy throne in thy room, he shall
build an house unto my name.*

David could not build the house of the Lord because
he was a man of war. The man of war has to perish so
that the man of peace, Solomon the lover, can come
forth and build the Temple. There remains a rest on
every side for the people of God.

Rom. 16:20 NIV:

*The God of peace will soon crush satan under
your feet. The grace of our Lord Jesus be with
you.*

What is the spirit of revenge? Webster defines
"retaliate" to mean "to repay (as an injury) in kind; to
return like for like; to get revenge." The primary
Hebrew word for "vengeance" (#5358 in *Strong's*)
means "to grudge, avenge, or punish." The classical
passage is given below.

Deut. 32:35 KJV:

*To me belongeth vengeance, and recompence;
their foot shall slide in due time: for the day of
their calamity is at hand, and the things that shall
come upon them make haste.*

Moving to the New Testament, the Greek word for
"vengeance" is "ekdikesis" (#1557) which means "vin-
dication, retribution." It comes from two other Greek
words:

1. "ek," meaning "out of."
2. "dike" meaning "right (as self-evident); justice (the principle, a decision, or its execution)."

The vengeance of God flows out of His righteousness. This word and principle is found nine times in the New Testament, in Lk. 18:7-8; 21:22; Acts 7:24; Rom. 12:19; II Cor. 7:11; II Thess. 1:8; Heb. 10:30; and I Pet. 2:14.

Rom. 12:19 KJV:

Dearly beloved, avenge not yourselves, but rather give place unto wrath: for it is written, Vengeance is mine; I will repay, saith the Lord.

Heb. 10:30 KJV:

For we know him that hath said, Vengeance belongeth unto me, I will recompense, saith the Lord. And again, The Lord shall judge his people.

There's a Man in the throne with a ministry without retaliation. The patriarch Joseph was such a man. His first problem was that he told his dreams to the wrong people, his half-brothers. They had the same daddy but a different momma (Gal. 4:21-31). Joseph had a vision of the throne of grace from his youth. He was predestined to be a ruler. Once his brethren sold him into slavery, he was unjustly accused in the house of Potiphar in Egypt and put into prison. He could have complained. He could have gotten angry with God. But he stayed sweet in the prison house and became king over the prisoners. He stayed sensitive to the voice of the Lord, and the word that flowed from his lips meant life for some and death for others. In due season, he was brought out of prison to reign.

This man of patience was stripped three times. He was first stripped by his jealous brethren. They attacked him and spoiled his coat of many colors, the birthright coat. Before honor is humility (Prov. 15:33).

Secondly, Joseph was stripped in Egypt by Potiphar's wife. He had refused to lay with the harlot and paid the price. In the Outer Court and the Holy Place, others strip you, but in the Most Holy Place, you strip yourself (I Pet. 5:5)! After spending years in prison, Joseph removed his prison garment and shaved his face, removing the covering or veil from his countenance. God deals with a man and breaks him down in the first two realms. The Holy Place, the Feast of Pentecost, the realm of adolescence, is the place where most of the fight takes place. Being a realm of duality and mixture, it tends to produce insecurity and therefore frustration. When you're fourteen going on twenty, you're no longer a child but not quite a man. It's an awkward time. Once you get through it, and stand on the threshold of the Most Holy Place with its baptism of fire, you begin to sense that the Lord is going to deal with you differently. When you were a child and youth, He did most of it for you. As you become a man, He puts the ball in your yard. He has trained us and told us what to do. Then He has backed off and waited for our response. "Have your way, Jesus," we used to pray. We beat our heads against the chair and begged God to come and do it. Now that we have walked with Him and talked with Him, we know what He wants, and we do it with Him. Some of you are waiting for God to have your baby. He wants you to taste the pain and travail of that birth for yourself. He will help you, but you have to start. I sense that I am talking to some preacher who is fearful and afraid. Rise up, my brother, and do what God has told you to do. Do it now!

Gen. 50:20 KJV:

But as for you, ye thought evil against me; but God meant it unto good, to bring to pass, as it is this day, to save much people alive.

This was the testimony of value from the lips of Joseph. He had committed his cause to the protection and the intercession of the Lord. Commit your works unto the Lord, and your thoughts shall be established (Prov. 16:3).

Another good example of this is David in his youth. Though he later was known as a man of war, David was still a man after God's own heart, and there were times in his earlier life when he exemplified the ministry without retaliation. Like Joseph, he was picked out to be picked on. Anointed while yet in his teens by the prophet Samuel, David discovered the weight of that oil to be heavier than the crown he would one day wear. With the first anointing, he killed a bear, a lion, and a giant. That was preparation for his relationship with Saul, first king over Israel. Day by day the rage and jealousy of Saul intensified toward this sweet psalmist. It finally drove young David from the king's court into the place of waiting on his ministry. With the death of the Dead Sea on his right hand, and the desolation of the wilderness of Judea on his left, David discovered the secret of Engedi, which means "fount of the kid." In the wilderness of his adolescence, he tapped a leaping fountain of the Spirit within as God spread a table for him in the presence of his enemies.

On two occasions, in I Sam. 24 and 26, God delivered Saul into David's hands to test his servant. Just one whack of the sword and all his problems would have been over! After all, the nation really loved him, and were just waiting for Saul to die. It would have been so easy to give the people what they wanted. Just one whack of the sword ...

I have been there. Have you? "Just let me tell them, God. I'll be nice, but just this once, let me defend myself. Let me get him for you, Jesus!" Don't do it, David. Saul is mad, but he's still God's anointed. Don't listen to Abishai or any of the younger warriors. They

love you, the king-to-be, more than the principles of
the Kingdom. You can't circumvent the cross, David.
You must fellowship His sufferings. You must make
yourself of no reputation and become obedient to the
death of everything you think, feel, and want. A
crucified man can only face in one direction. Don't
blow it now, David. If you kill Saul, we'll just have to
endure another administration of madness. Don't you
see, David? The Saul in you must die ... God's way. Go
back to the cave, the hold, for a while longer, David.
Pick up your instrument in the darkness of your
loneliness and begin to sing.

Psa. 27:1-6 NIV:

*The Lord is my light and my salvation — whom
shall I fear? The Lord is the stronghold of my life
— of whom shall I be afraid?*

*When evil men advance against me to devour
my flesh, when my enemies and my foes attack
me, they will stumble and fall.*

*Though an army besiege me, my heart will not
fear; though war break out against me, even then
will I be confident.*

*One thing I ask of the Lord, this is what I seek:
that I may dwell in the house of the Lord all the
days of my life, to gaze upon the beauty of the
Lord and to seek him in his temple.*

*For in the day of trouble he will keep me safe in
his dwelling; he will hide me in the shelter of his
tabernacle and set me high upon a rock.*

*Then my head will be exalted above the
enemies who surround me; at his tabernacle will I
sacrifice with shouts of joy; I will sing and make
music to the Lord.*

And what of the great Apostle Paul? Few men have
known suffering as this servant of the Lord (II Cor.
11:23-32). Because of the abundance of revelation, he

had qualified for a thorn. What that "thorn in the flesh" was — the relentless effort of legalistic Judaizers who came in to tear up everything the Apostle tried to build, or his own personal devil sent to buffet him — I don't know. But I know that Paul had reason to fight. His apostolic burden caused him to spend, and be spent. His weariness was more than physical. He could have used the rod of his apostleship more than once, but didn't. Where did he get such meekness and patience? He told us himself.

II Cor. 12:1-4 KJV:

> *It is not expedient for me doubtless to glory. I will come to visions and revelations of the Lord.*
> *I knew a man in Christ above fourteen years ago, (whether in the body, I cannot tell; or whether out of the body, I cannot tell: God knoweth;) such an one caught up to the third heaven.*
> *And I knew such a man, (whether in the body, or out of the body, I cannot tell: God knoweth;)*
> *How that he was caught up into paradise, and heard unspeakable words, which it is not lawful for a man to utter.*

Paul had an experience in the Most Holy Place, the third heaven. There he was a partaker of the divine nature at the Mercy-seat. He would later write about it in the epistle to the Hebrews. He had a vision of the Man in the throne with a ministry without retaliation. He soon got to walk in what he saw.

On his first missionary journey with Barnabas (Acts 13-14), he established the Galatian churches at Antioch of Pisidia, Iconium, Lystra, and Derbe. It was at Lystra that he was stoned and perhaps killed, left for dead. If you know the geography of that region, you see that it would have so easy for Paul to skip on home to Tarsus and chuck the ministry. He could have gone back home mad at God and at everybody else, but the lover in Paul swallowed up the fighter. He retraced his steps and went back to the very people who had tortured him. He was well rewarded for his faith, for young Timothy of Lystra (Acts 16:1) was a witness to the more excellent ministry working in Paul's life. He would later become one of the Apostle's most faithful co-laborers.

Joseph, David, Paul, Jesus Himself ... these are examples of the ministry without retaliation. The sons of God are going to be the instruments of His vengeance. The Church is going to judge the world and the angels (I Cor. 6:1-3). Before a man is fit to minister like that, he must be placed in situation after situation where he is justified to lash back at something or somebody but doesn't. You can't be freed from a spirit of revenge until you have had ample opportunity to hit back, but refuse because of the enabling of Him who lives within. Only then can you be an able minister of the wrath of the Lamb. God's judgments are unto victory. Get off your soapbox, preacher, and get on your knees. Make doubly sure that you are a watchman and not a watchdog. Understand that the deeper the call of God upon your life, the deeper the dealings of the Father to prepare and equip yourself for that ministry. When you have run out of gas and hot air, and have no more points to make, then God will send you forth to speak for Him and as Him.

Jesus Didn't Turn The Other Cheek

The Sermon on the Mount is the Constitution to the Kingdom of God. The Beatitudes, the blessed attitudes, are the Preamble, and are not just isolated character traits from which we can pick and choose. All of them are operative in the life of every believer, for they contain a pattern for receiving and releasing the life of the King.

Matt. 5:3-6 KJV:

> *Blessed are the poor in spirit: for theirs is the kingdom of heaven.*
>
> *Blessed are they that mourn: for they shall be comforted.*
>
> *Blessed are the meek: for they shall inherit the earth.*
>
> *Blessed are they which do hunger and thirst after righteousness: for they shall be filled.*

To receive the life of the King, you first have to be needy; in other words, you must see your need of Him. Then you mourn, or repent. This allows you to be comforted, for the Holy Ghost is the Comforter. He changes our heart and we are born from above. Meekness is thus a divine attribute, for it is not natural for man to be humble. This humility creates a hunger and thirst so that we be filled with the Spirit.

Matt. 5:7-9 KJV:

> *Blessed are the merciful: for they shall obtain mercy.*
>
> *Blessed are the pure in heart: for they shall see God.*
>
> *Blessed are the peacemakers: for they shall be called the children of God.*

Here we see the release of the life of the King. This is the heart-beat of the Kingdom, receiving His life and releasing His life. Mercy, purity, and peace flow out of His nature from within. The result of this is a clash with the kingdom of darkness, as we see in the rest of the Preamble.

Matt. 5:10-12 KJV:

> *Blessed are they which are persecuted for righteousness' sake: for theirs is the kingdom of heaven.*

> *Blessed are ye, when men shall revile you, and
> persecute you, and shall say all manner of evil
> against you falsely, for my sake.*
>
> *Rejoice, and be exceeding glad: for great is your
> reward in heaven: for so persecuted they the
> prophets which were before you.*

The remainder of Matt. 5, along with chapters six
and seven (compare these with Lk. 6) are filled with
the laws of the Kingdom, each of which issues from the
nature of the King. It is essential that we understand
that a Christian does not go out and "try" to live right
according to this discourse. The old Puritan writers
said, "The lifestyle that Jesus sets forth in the Sermon
on the Mount is not difficult ... it's impossible!" Each of
the principles governing Kingdom living must have
their source in the energy of His light and life. One of
these principles is the Law of Action and Reaction.

Matt. 5:38-42 KJV:

> *Ye have heard that it hath been said, An eye for
> an eye, and a tooth for a tooth:*
>
> *But I say unto you, That ye resist not evil: but
> whosoever shall smite thee on thy right cheek,
> turn to him the other also.*
>
> *And if any man will sue thee at the law, and
> take away thy coat, let him have thy cloak also.*
>
> *And whosoever shall compel thee to go a mile,
> go with him twain.*
>
> *Give to him that asketh thee, and from him that
> would borrow of thee turn not thou away.*

The law of sin and death reacts (Ex. 21:24; Lev. 24:20;
Deut. 19:21). The law of the Spirit of life in Christ Jesus
acts. Here is a classic example of a principle that has
been taught from the letter and not the Spirit. Jesus
was dealing here with the spirit of revenge! While it is

true that Matt. 5:38 has been called "lex talionis," or "the law of retaliation," and was introduced as a principle of legal punishment as a safeguard to insure adequate and not excessive punishment, we are dealing here with something higher in principle. Some feel that once we turn the cheek, we are free to strike the other fellow. No! The key to this whole passage is the word "compel" in v. 41. Taken from ancient Persian custom, the Romans "compelled" the Jews to carry their packs for one mile. Why the need for compulsion? Because the Jews hated the Romans! That's the issue! The hate. The desire for revenge. What do you really sense from within when you are smitten? If you get uptight the first time you are slapped, then turn the other cheek and get slapped again. If you still want to hit back, turn the cheek again and again until that ungodly attitude is purged from your life. One reason why some folks get slapped around all their lives is because they haven't gotten over the first time they were slapped ... and everybody gets slapped the first time.

Are you hesitant to give in to the other party? Do you want to fight for your rights like the world system? Men everywhere are seeking a cause. Some spend all their energies fighting for or against some doctrine or teaching. To those who are against everything, I would ask, "What are you for?" I see this fighting occurring in three different worlds:

1. The individual world.
2. The domestic world.
3. The church world.

Individuals fight for their rights and opinions. Individuals hold grudges, refusing to forgive themselves and others. Most people are walking around with a civil war on the inside. Everyone is screaming for his or her rights. One reason that the Gospel of the

Kingdom is making such a stir right now is because it comes against that kind of mentality. Jesus is our Saviour and He is becoming our Lord. We are no longer our own. We have been bought with a price. We have surrendered our rights to the King!

In the home, folks fight for their rights and opinions. In the home, folks hold grudges, refusing to show any mercy. Husbands won't speak to wives. Wives run home to momma. Parents play children off their mate. Children pit parent against parent. The greatest problem in married life is that one or both still want to live like a single. Everyone demands his own space. Family feud is a way of life in far too many homes. Divorce is rampant. Relatives are taking one another to court. All because each is demanding his or her rights.

In the local church, the saints fight for their rights and opinions. In the local church, Christians hold grudges and won't forgive each other. Sadder still, preachers are fighters. Some would rather fight than switch. Change is interpreted as compromise. Men boast that they have fought for the same message for thirty years. Others are a one-man crusade against certain doctrines. Some are just angry with everybody else. The nation and the whole world has seen men of God square off against each other. All the while His children are squabbling, the Father patiently waits for the precious fruit of the earth, a people in the image of Jesus. Peacemakers and reconcilers, men who refuse to fight over doctrine or argue about the Scriptures. Men who, without apology or explanation, simply bear witness unto the truth.

God will sacrifice our externals to deal with the internal. Outward chastening cleanses the inward parts. The Lord has knocked the fire out of more than one preacher. Jacob discovered that reality one lonely night. You can let the hills of your pride flow down at

His presence, or you can let the wind blow them over. One way or the other, they are coming down. God isn't concerned about your stance or position. He is only interested in Himself and His purposes in the earth. Because men are ignorant of the purposes of the Lord, they invent one cause after another upon which to squander their time and money. Will we ever learn? God is saying something now to His people. Can you hear what He is saying? The greatest blessing in your walk with Christ is that you can still hear (Ruth 2:8). The Lord is calling forth a company of peace-creators who impart the wisdom that is from above (Jas. 3:16-17). Jesus wants us to be free from a spirit of revenge and holding grudges. He wants to remove that reactionary spirit which wants to fight back with words or acts.

Prov. 20:30 KJV:

The blueness of a wound cleanseth away evil: so do stripes the inward parts of the belly.

Jn. 18:36 KJV:

Jesus answered, My kingdom is not of this world: if my kingdom were of this world, then would my servants fight, that I should not be delivered to the Jews: but now is my kingdom not from hence.

We turn the cheek, give up the cloak, or walk the second mile only if we have the wrong spirit of retaliation. Otherwise, we will turn the other cheek, give our wardrobe, or walk with the burden until we have learned this lesson (Heb. 5:8-9) and principle ... until the blueness of the wound cleanses the inward parts. Then mercy and forgiveness can flow from the throne of grace. Jesus didn't turn the other cheek. He didn't have to. In His humilation His justice was taken away, but there was nothing in Him that wanted to fight back (Jn. 14:30). He was led like a Lamb to the slaughter, yet He opened not His mouth. The old song says, "He could have called ten thousand angels, but He died alone for you and me." He is the Man in the throne with a ministry, a ministry without retaliation.

Jn. 18:19-23 NIV:

Meanwhile, the high priest questioned Jesus about his disciples and his teaching.

"I have spoken openly to the world," Jesus replied. "I always taught in synagogues or at the temple, where all the Jews come together. I said nothing in secret.

Why question me? Ask those who heard me. Surely they know what I said."

When Jesus said this, one of the officials nearby struck him in the face.

"Is this the way you answer the high priest?" he demanded.

"If I said something wrong," Jesus replied, "testify as to what is wrong. But if I spoke the truth, why did you strike me?"

Better Things Than That Of Abel

We have already learned that the more excellent ministry is a ministry of forgiveness and blessing. It doesn't keep inventory or score. It goes about loosing the creation by forgiving it and blessing it out of Zion in the name of the Lord.

Heb. 12:22-24 KJV:

But ye are come unto mount Sion, and unto the city of the living God, the heavenly Jerusalem, and to an innumerable company of angels,

To the general assembly and church of the firstborn, which are written in heaven, and to God the Judge of all, and to the spirits of just men made perfect,

And to Jesus the mediator of the new covenant, and to the blood of sprinkling, that speaketh better things than that of Abel.

Gen. 4:8-10 KJV:

And Cain talked with Abel his brother: and it came to pass, when they were in the field, that Cain rose up against Abel his brother, and slew him.

And the Lord said unto Cain, Where is Abel thy brother? And he said, I know not: Am I my brother's keeper?

And he said, What hast thou done? the voice of thy brother's blood crieth unto me from the ground.

... whose message is nobler than Abel's ... (Moffatt).

... which graciously forgives instead of crying out for vengeance as the blood of Abel did (Living Bible).

Blood has a voice. Throughout the epistle to the Hebrews, the key word is "better." As noted, this word means "nobler, stronger." The blood of the New Covenant is the blood of Jesus, which is better blood. It speaks better things than that of the blood of Abel.

What did the blood of Abel speak? It cried for vengeance! It called out for revenge! "It doesn't matter how You get him, God ... just get him." I think that all of us have prayed some imprecatory prayers. When we did, we didn't know what spirit we were of (Lk. 9:51-55). Then where did the blood of Abel cry from? From the ground, the realm of the dust. The first man, Adam, was a man of dust. Dust is the serpent's meat. The dust realm is the Adamic realm. From the lower plane of man's reason and logic, the blood of Abel cries out for retaliation.

The blood of Jesus Christ is better blood. It does not cry from the dust. It cries from the heavens, from the

Most Holy Place, from the love-seat! It does not cry out for vengeance. It pleads for mercy! That precious blood anoints the Mercy-seat, the throne of grace, and sprinkles the man who sits there. This sprinkling welds him to the law of the Spirit of life in Christ Jesus and a ministry free from the spirit of revenge. A ministry that doesn't hold grudges because it forgives and then forgets, a ministry that doesn't fight back because the battle was fought and won before we got here, a ministry without retaliation. Because we kept ourselves clean from this spirit of anger, we have not opened our mouths to speak things which we would later regret. The Melchisedec priesthood is swift to hear and slow to speak because is it also a ministry without profanity.

Chapter Six

A Ministry Without Profanity

The more excellent ministry is the ministry of Jesus Christ. It is the ministry of the Ascended Christ. It flows to all men without condemnation, without prejudice, without walls, and without retaliation. The key or catalyst which works all these principles is the tongue. The creative, spoken word operates the Mercy-seat ministry. The tongue is a creative force. The secret to life and health is a mouth filled with words of life. Our lips and our speech must be in agreement with His Word and Spirit (Amos 3:3).

Prov. 10:11 KJV:

The mouth of a righteous man is a well of life: but violence covereth the mouth of the wicked.

Prov. 12:19 KJV:

The lip of truth shall be established for ever: but a lying tongue is but for a moment.

Prov. 15:1-4 KJV:

A soft answer turneth away wrath: but grievous words stir up anger.

*The tongue of the wise useth knowledge aright:
but the mouth of fools poureth out foolishness.*

*The eyes of the Lord are in every place,
beholding the evil and the good.*

*A wholesome tongue is a tree of life: but
perverseness therein is a breach in the spirit.*

Psa. 50:23 KJV:

*Whoso offereth praise glorifieth me: and to him
that ordereth his conversation aright will I shew
the salvation of God.*

Rom. 8:31 NIV:

*What, then, shall we say in response to this? If
God is for us, who can be against us?*

In Rom. 8, we saw that there is no condemnation, no
fear, no comparison, and no separation. What shall be
our response to all these wonderful benefits of the
New Covenant? Let us put away the lie, and speak
every man truth with His neighbor. What we say, and
how we say it, is very important. Every word that we
speak is an ambassador of life or death. Conceived in
the womb of the mind, our words are delivered
through the mouth. The law of sowing and reaping is
ever working while we speak (Gal. 6:7-8), for we are
reaping as we sow. It's a matter of life and death. The
river of life-giving words that flow out of the love-seat
in the living room is pure. There is no condemnation,
prejudice, walls, retaliation, or profanity in the words
of Jesus and His brethren.

Profanity is any speech that comes out of our mouth
that is not in agreement with the letter and the Spirit
of the Word of God ... words that are not in agreement
with the Christ nature. Anything else we speak is a
lying vanity, an idol (a "nothing") that is not even real.
Profanity is that which disagrees with the Word of
truth (I Jn. 2:27). The only killer we have to watch for is

the tongue, full of deadly poison (Jas. 3:1-8).

Webster says that "profane" means "to treat something sacred with abuse, irreverence, or contempt; desecrate; violate; to debase by a wrong, unworthy, or vulgar use; not holy because unconsecrated, impure, or defiled; unsanctified; serving to debase or defile what is holy; irreverent." It adds that "profanity" is "the quality of state of being profane; the use of profane language; profane language."

The Hebrew word for "profane" is "khaw-lal" (#2490 in *Strong's*) and means "to bore, by implication, to wound (fatally), pierce, or dissolve; to profane (a person, place, or thing); to break (one's word); to begin (as if by an opening wedge); to play (the flute)." The root and its derivatives are used eighty-three times in the Old Testament. Note the Messianic passage of Isa. 53:5 where He was "wounded for our transgressions" ("tormented" — KJV margin; "pierced through" — *Jerusalem Bible*). The root "hll" is used to mark the act of doing violence to the established law of God (Zeph. 3:4), breaking the Covenant (Psa. 55:21) or the divine statutes (Psa. 89:31). Thus to profane is to misuse the name of God (Lev. 18:21), the sabbath (Ex. 31:14), or the holy place, and so desecrate it.

In the New Testament, the word for "profane" is "bebelos" (#952) and means "accessible (by crossing the doorway); crossing the threshold as a heathen or wicked man and thus to profane the holy place; to profane or desecrate." It is taken from two other Greek words:

1. "baino," which means "to go, walk."
2. "belos," which means "a threshold."

The verb "bebeloo," meaning "to desecrate," is used in the Septuagint (LXX). There the idea is "what may be used freely," suggesting the principle of license. Its uses in the Greek Old Testament concern the profaning of:

1. God (Ezek. 13:19).
2. His name (Lev. 18:21).
3. His day (Neh. 13:17-18).
4. His land (Jer. 16:18).
5. His covenant (Psa. 55:20).
6. The name of His priest (Lev. 21:9).

The word "profane" means "to cross the threshold." The heathen would cross the threshold of the Temple and thus defile it. Don't let the heathen in the door! We profane the temple of the individual, the home, and the local church when we cross the threshold of these areas and speak words which minister death and not life. Let us keep our foot when we go to the house of God (Eccl. 5:1-2). Let us not be rash with our mouths. Determine to talk right the minute you cross the threshold of your home or church! And when another brother or sister allows you entrance to their heart or spirit, walk and talk reverently as you enter their temple. The adjective ("bebelos") and the verb forms ("bebeloo") of "profane" are used seven times in the New Testament:

I Tim. 1:9 KJV:

Knowing this, that the law is not made for a righteous man, but for the lawless and disobedient, for the ungodly and for sinners, for unholy and profane, for murderers of fathers and murderers of mothers, for manslayers,

I Tim. 4:7 KJV:

But refuse profane and old wives' fables, and exercise thyself rather unto godliness.

I Tim. 6:20 KJV:

O Timothy, keep that which is committed to thy

trust, avoiding profane and vain babblings, and oppositions of science falsely so called:

II Tim. 2:16 KJV:

But shun profane and vain babblings: for they will increase unto more ungodliness.

Heb. 12:16 KJV:

Lest there be any fornicator, or profane person, as Esau, who for one morsel of meat sold his birthright.

Matt. 12:5 KJV:

Or have ye not read in the law, how that on the sabbath days the priests in the temple profane the sabbath, and are blameless?

Acts 24:6 KJV:

Who also hath gone about to profane the temple: whom we took, and would have judged according to our law.

If we sow corruption and death with our words, we will reap the same. The Greek word for "corruption" is "sapros" (#4550) and means "rotten, worthless (literally or morally); degenerated from the original virtue." It is rendered as "bad, corrupt" in the King James. It is akin to "sepo" which means "to putrify or perish; rot or decay." The early Church fathers used the word in their writings to describe the decaying fruit of the vine, the rotting of flesh, and the uselessness of stones. It is found eight times in the New Testament, in Matt. 7:17-18; 12:33; 13:48; Lk. 6:43; and Eph. 4:29.

Eph. 4:29-32 NIV:

Do not let any unwholesome talk come out of your mouths, but only what is helpful for building others up according to their needs, that it may benefit those who listen.

And do not grieve the Holy Spirit of God, with whom you were sealed for the day of redemption.

Get rid of all bitterness, rage and anger, brawling and slander, along with every form of malice.

Be kind and compassionate to one another, forgiving each other, just as in Christ God forgave you.

The Tongue Of The Learned

Isa. 50:4 NIV:

The Sovereign Lord has given me an instructed tongue, to know the word that sustains the weary. He wakens me morning by morning, wakens my ear to listen like one being taught.

I wrote a book in 1980 called *The Tongue of the Learned*. It is a handbook of 336 Bible terms with their definitions under nine practical headings. Pastor J. L. Dutton of Hartsville, South Carolina, co-authored the book and wrote a tremendous introduction which is still timely:

"We are in the midst of a great move of the Spirit of God for these last days. The Lord is helping us to take and possess the Kingdom as in Dan. 7:18. As we do this, we are learning the pure language of the Kingdom. As we had to learn how to talk in the natural realm, so now we are learning how to talk as we come into the Kingdom. How we talk will reveal to others where we are in God, for your speech betrays you (Matt. 26:73). There is a beautiful story in the Old Testament that reveals the value of knowing how to talk. It is found in the ministry of Jephthah (Judg. 12:1-6). Jephthah was leading the Gileadites into victorious battle against the Ephraimites. Some of these Ephraimites escaped and the Gileadites 'took the passage of Jordan' before them to overtake and catch them as they would later try to cross the Jordan. In case any of the Ephraimites would attempt to cross over Jordan by disguise, the Gileadites would have them say the word 'shibboleth' to see if they could 'frame' or pronounce it right. You see, this people of Ephraim could not say 'shibboleth' but could only say 'sibboleth'. They didn't know how to talk the language of the people of God.

"'Sibboleth' doesn't mean anything, but 'shibboleth' means 'flowing like a river or stream', and 'there is a river, the streams whereof shall make glad the city of God, the holy place of the tabernacles of the Most High (Psa. 46:4)'. As we flow with this river, as we cross Jordan, let us learn how to talk. Those who are not moving with what God is doing in the earth today have not learned the language of the Kingdom. Like the Ephraimites, they will be destroyed for lack of knowledge (Hos. 4:6). Our experience, our growth, our knowledge in God will change our speech as we are ever understanding how to speak with 'the tongue of the learned'. Our desire is that the book before you will be a help and a blessing to many who are crossing their Jordan and who are moving into the land of their inheritance and promise in God. Learn to talk in faith with a positive speech and a right confession of real Kingdom language.''

Isa 50:4 KJV:

> *The Lord God hath given me the tongue of the learned, that I should know how to speak a word in season to him that is weary: he wakeneth morning by morning, he wakeneth mine ear to hear as the learned.*

God is giving His people the "tongue of the learned" that we may know:

1. How to speak.
2. What to speak ("a word").
3. When to speak ("in season").
4. To whom to speak ("to him that is weary").

You are an influential person. Your words are powerful, whether you know it or not. The teaching on our having a "positive confession" has been taken to extremes, but what hasn't? It's still true that most folks are living on the level of their confession, walking in the world created by their words. What the extremes of the faith message missed was that the word of faith was in two places, the heart and the mouth (Rom. 10:6-10). Faith is a gift. It is imparted as well as imputed. Do you remember the times in prayer when God really spoke and you knew it? Nothing could move you from what He said. That was an impartation of His own faith. Once that faith is in the heart, then you can speak it with your mouth. The classic volume *The Real Faith* by Charles Price will help you to understand this truth. Otherwise, men will have faith either in the heart or the mouth. If faith is just in the heart, the result is silent faith. If faith is just in the mouth, the fruit of the lips will be empty words! These are "idle" (literally, "barren") words!

Prov. 18:21 KJV:

Death and life are in the power of the tongue: and they that love it shall eat the fruit thereof.

Matt. 12:34-36 KJV:

O generation of vipers, how can ye, being evil, speak good things? for out of the abundance of the heart the mouth speaketh.
A good man out of the good treasure of the heart bringeth forth good things: and an evil man out of the evil treasure bringeth forth evil things.
But I say unto you, That every idle word that

men shall speak, they shall give account thereof in the day of judgment.

The more excellent ministry speaks the truth in love. God wants to deliver His people that they might no longer blaspheme. The Greek word for "blaspheme" is "blasphemeo" (#987) which means "to vilify, to speak impiously." It is from two other words:

1. "blapto," which means "to injure, harm."
2. "pheme," which means "speech".

Blasphemy is slander. We blaspheme God whenever we resist what He has done for us or do not agree with what He has said about us in His Word. The Melchisedec priesthood is a ministry without profanity. Whenever we fail to agree with the Father, we bring harm to His working in our lives. Like Paul, I used to be a blasphemer. I frustrated the grace of God. I was filled with condemnation and fear. Out of that death came words of death. I praise Him for changing me and allowing me to have a vision of His Mercy-seat. My tongue was once an instrument or weapon of unrighteousness, but now it flows with the sword of the Spirit!

I Tim. 1:12-14 NIV:

I thank Christ Jesus our Lord, who has given me strength, that he considered me faithful, appointing me to his service.

Even though I was once a blasphemer and a persecutor and a violent man, I was shown mercy because I acted in ignorance and unbelief.

The grace of our Lord was poured out on me abundantly, along with the faith and love that are in Christ Jesus.

Don't take the name of the Lord in vain (Ex. 20:7). That verse not only warns us about using vulgar language and foolish jesting, but also alludes to water baptism in the Name of the Lord Jesus Christ for the remission of our sins and the circumcision of our hearts. His wonderful Name was invoked over you in baptism. Don't let this marriage fail. Don't take His Name in vain. Walk with Him, and talk like Him! Don't rebel. Don't let the Holy Ghost become your enemy and then torment you until you walk right and talk right!

Psa. 139:20 KJV:

For they speak against thee wickedly, and thine enemies take thy name in vain.

Isa. 63:10 KJV:

But they rebelled, and vexed his holy spirit: therefore he was turned to be their enemy, and he fought against them

Isa. 45:9 KJV:

Woe unto him that striveth with his Maker! Let the potsherd strive with the potsherds of the earth. Shall the clay say to him that fashioneth it, What makest thou? or thy work, He hath no hands?

Mal. 3:13 KJV:

Your words have been stout against me, saith the Lord. Yet ye say, What have we spoken so much against thee?

Prov. 4:23 KJV:

Keep thy heart with all diligence; for out of it are the issues of life.

Matt. 15:18-19 KJV:

But those things which proceed out of the mouth come forth from the heart; and they defile the man.

For out of the heart proceed evil thoughts, murders, adulteries, fornications, thefts, false witness, blasphemies:

Col. 3:8-9 KJV:

But now ye also put off all these: anger, wrath, malice, blasphemy, filthy communication out of your mouth.

Lie not one to another, seeing that ye have put off the old man with his deeds;

Jas. 3:10 KJV:

Out of the same mouth proceedeth blessing and cursing. My brethren, these things ought not so to be.

Study these verses. Pray these verses. Ask the Lord to help you with your speech. All of us need help in this area, especially parents and pastors. Be careful what you say in front of the kids. Children hear every word you say.

Swear Not At All

Matt. 5:33-37 KJV:

Again, ye have heard that it hath been said by them of old time, Thou shalt not forswear thyself, but shalt perform unto the Lord thine oaths:

But I say unto you, Swear not at all; neither by heaven; for it is God's throne:

Nor by the earth; for it is his footstool: neither by Jerusalem; for it is the city of the great King.

Neither shalt thou swear by thy head, because thou canst not make one hair white or black.

But let your communication be, Yea, yea; Nay, nay: for whatsoever is more than these cometh of evil.

Let me share with you some insights from my manual on *The Sermon on the Mount*. This principle could be called the Law of Truthfulness because it shows us how to speak, and the more excellent ministry is a ministry without profanity. The orientals of Jesus' day were profuse in their vulgarity and swearing. Some may take verse 34 by the letter in an extreme sense and not swear on the Bible in court, but let us look at the spirit of what Jesus is teaching. All four things mentioned here (heaven, earth, Jerusalem, and the head) were sacred to the Jewish mind. The Jew in Bible days emphasized that he was speaking the truth by giving an oath. Contemporary examples of such exaggerations would be:

1. "I swear this on a a stack of Bibles!"
2. "I swear this on my mother's grave!"
3. "Cross my heart and hope to die!"
4. "This is the God's honest truth I am telling you!"

Such oaths are and were necessary in the lives of those who have a reputation of being dishonest with their words. The king-priest ministry is open and honest, a ministry of integrity, a trustworthy or faithful priesthood. It is a ministry without profanity, for dishonest words are profane words. But the words which flow out of Zion are His words, full of grace and truth. In the Kingdom of God, Jesus' subjects have a reputation for speaking the truth in love. We tell it like it is. We speak the truth consistently; thus, our consistency and not our oath is the evidence of truthfulness. Jesus the King is the Truth (Jn. 14:6). His nature is within us. A man is no better than his word. His name hinges upon His Word and His consistent faithfulness in keeping that Word. Truth is an attribute of our Heavenly Father. We can stake our lives upon His

Word! If the Word of the God or the man can be trusted, then the God or the man can be trusted. If the word of the man is unreliable, then the man and his name (nature) is unreliable.

To balance this, we must note that, in man's case, there can be interjected the human element of circumstances which sometimes simply happen to prevent a man from keeping his word. However, God is not a man that He can lie (Num. 23:19). If we speak falsely consistently, it will be difficult for others to trust us (Matt. 21:28-32). If we are ever using profanity, we will be an unprofitable servant. "I'll be home at four o'clock." "Are you sure?" we ask. "I promise ... I really mean it." Sound familiar? When some folks say that they will see you Sunday at the 10:00 a.m. service, they really mean the 10:20 service! It is sad that we tend to classify or stereotype people into two categories: those who speak the truth and those who do not, those who are dependable and those who are not. A man has one of two reputations, and he has no one to blame but himself. "Where's brother and sister _____ this morning?" somebody asks. "Oh, you know ..."

Preachers don't help this problem in the Body of Christ one bit when they exaggerate their ministry and its "results." These spiritual "fish stories" mystically cause the number in attendance or the amount in the plate to double or triple! Face it, preacher, every meeting is not a "great" meeting. I hit a real dud every now and again. "Well, what kind of preacher are you, Varner?" I'm trying to be an honest one. "God really moved," we are told. He started "moving" in Gen. 1 and hasn't stopped since! "God really blessed!" another enthusiastically reports. I'd like to know when He stopped. The saints will never stop using profanity until they have an example. Anyway, it is a sad commentary that we have added the words "evangelastically speaking" to our vocabulary.

Jas. 5:12:

Above all, my brothers, do not swear — not by heaven or by earth or by anything else. Let your 'Yes' be yes, and your 'No,' no, or you will be condemned.

Above all things ... pledges of money, service, making deals with God ... I think you understand. This principle is so important because the more excellent ministry is to be released through the spoken word. God will have a prophetic people who will stand up in the earth and proclaim His Word. This many-membered voice is going to shake heaven and earth (Heb. 12:25-29). When the Lord speaks, we can rest that there will be a performance of what he said. The same is true with those under His rule and dominion, who sit with Him in the Mercy-seat.

Eph. 4:15 KJV:

But speaking the truth in love, may grow up into him in all things, which is the head, even Christ.

Eph. 4:25 KJV:

Wherefore putting away lying, speak every man truth with his neighbour: for we are members one of another.

Gossip

Gossip is profanity.

Satan knows the power of the spoken word. The only way he can stir up trouble in the home or local church is with the tongues of men. In the passage below, note how many of these verses have to do with the tongue and the words which we speak:

Prov. 6:16-19 NIV:

There are six things the Lord hates, seven that are detestable to him:
Haughty eyes, a lying tongue, hands that shed innocent blood,
A heart that devises wicked schemes, feet that are quick to rush into evil,
A false witness who pours out lies and a man who stirs up dissension among brothers.

It is interesting to contrast these seven principles with the seven spirits of God as seen in Isa. 11:1-2 and Rev. 1-5. Six is the number of man. Note the progression. First, the eyes are mentioned, then the tongue, the hands, the heart, the feet, and then the whole man. Compare this with the image of Dan. 2. Could it be that this passage in Proverbs describes the man of sin and the son of perdition in his full stature? A completely developed abomination, the beast or the spirit of antichrist in fullness. God's answer to this monster is a new-creation man who is a peacemaker, deliverer, healer, curer, lover, reconciler, mediator, and unifier ... the Man in the throne with a ministry!

This more excellent ministry is concerned with the glory of the Lord among men. He knows that trouble distracts. Slander is speech that injures another, whether true or false (Psa. 101:5; Prov. 10:18; 11:9). A peacemaker gives no ear to slander (Prov. 26:20; I Pet. 3:10-11). There are three practical ways of being a peacemaker:

1. Learn when not to speak. Before you begin, always ask yourself these three questions:

    a. "Is it true?"
    b. "Is it kind?"
    c. "Is it necessary?"

2. Don't repeat something when you know it will

harm others. Some folks feel that they have to always know what is going on. Burn the grapevine in your church!

3. Think in the context of the Word of God. Put the cause of the Kingdom above your own feelings. Ask yourself, "What would Jesus do or say?"

The talebearer or busybody is one who travels about carrying or peddling tales. He is a slanderer and a whisperer, just like the serpent of Gen. 3. The book of Proverbs has much to say about this subject. Perhaps you may want to pursue it further. Study Prov. 10:12; 13:10; 15:17-18; 16:27-30; 17:1, 9, 14, 19; 18:8, 19; 20:3, 19; 22:10; 25:8-10; 25:23; 26:17, 20-22; 28:25; and 29:22.

The talebearer himself has deep problems. He belittles others to exalt himself. He makes a short man tall by cutting a tall man's legs off. He is often under tremendous condemnation. Because he is so critical with God and himself, it is easy for him to be critical of others. It doesn't help when he also has the tenth gift of the spirit: suspicion!

Here are four practical ways to stop a talebearer, especially when he peddles his wares under the guise of bringing something to you to "pray" about. This is particularly true with some sisters who have a matriarchal spirit. They want to "mother" their husbands and the pastor. When confronted by genuine authority in the Spirit realm, they back off and look for ways to undermine that authority. Under the guise of being an "intercessor," these prey upon the weaker saints who can't tell the difference. Worse yet is a so-called "prophetess" who has a hair-trigger on her prophecy gun. She has a "word" for everybody. Please understand that I am not sexually prejudiced. Remember? I'm not against women or men. I'm against gossip. Better said, I am for the glory of God in the midst of His people. Because women open up to God and the realm of the Spirit more readily than men, they also tend to open up to the other kingdom as well. The mark of a real intercessor is that he has his own life together. He has to, because he does not focus upon himself or his own needs in prayer. His emphasis is prayer in the behalf of others. Whether male or female, does this person who comes with some news to "pray" about have his own life and family in order? More often than not, those areas have been neglected as he has pursued his "ministry." If you don't have the courage to tell these kind of people the truth, then look them in the eye and say:

1. "Please write that down and sign it."
2. "Let's go together and pray for the brother."
3. "Please ... I don't want to hear it. My ears are not slopbuckets!."
4. "Let's go the leadership of the church."

Matt. 18:15-17 NIV:

> *If your brother sins against you, go and show him his fault, just between the two of you. If he listens to you, you have won your brother over.*
>
> *But if he will not listen, take one or two others along, so that "every matter may be established by the testimony of two or three witnesses."*
>
> *If he refuses to listen to them, tell it to the church; and if he refuses to listen even to the church, treat him as you would a pagan or a tax collector.*

In dealing with a talebearer, one must follow Jesus' teaching in the above passage. If the person still persists after all has been done, he must be marked and the saints are to separate from his company (I Cor. 5:11; II Thess. 3:11-14).

Ten Common Curse-words

To illustrate this principle of a ministry without

profanity, I will mention some of the more familiar words and phrases that people use as they take His name in vain. Please excuse me, for I am a gentleman, and I don't relish using these "cuss-words" in front of some of you ladies. You may just want to proceed to the next chapter.

Amos 3:3 NIV:

Do two walk together unless they have agreed to do so?

I Cor. 1:10 NIV:

I appeal to you, brothers, in the name of our Lord Jesus Christ, that all of you agree with one another so that there may be no divisions among you and that you may be perfectly united in mind and thought.

Col. 3:9, 10 NIV:

Do not lie to each other, since you have taken off your old self with its practices
And have put on the new self, which is being renewed in knowledge in the image of its Creator.

As we note these varied forms of profanity, remember that behind every excuse is a lack of desire. None of this mess is in the mouth of the overcomer. It has nothing to do with the more excellent ministry.

"That is just my nature," or "I'm only human." Which nature? You are a spirit being of which God is the Father (Heb. 12:9)! There is no fear or any other negative aspect in the new nature, which is the Christ nature. Folks have hewed themselves out a human ... a mentality of what they think they are. People who are just "naturally" nervous or anything else need to understand that the soul-life is in the blood and we got that from Adam. Our only problem has been bad blood. We are a new creature that never existed before. Now that we have been given a new heart, there is a new life coursing through our beings.

II Cor. 5:17 NIV:

Therefore, if anyone is in Christ, he is a new creation; the old has gone, the new has come!

"One of these days ..." Too long we have served the god of "gonna" ... I'm gonna do better. You just wait and see! Today is the Day of the Lord. Today is always the Day of the Lord, the day of salvation. The Old Covenant message was, "He's coming ..." The New Covenant reality is that He has come and He is here (Heb. 1:1)! He is speaking now. Good intentions are not good enough. God wants us to press in to do His will now. Don't live in the past or the future. There's no future in the past, and the devil, who is a procrastinator, doesn't care what you believe, as long as it is in the future. Flow with the God of the present and the God of the now. He's a Mighty-Right-Now God!

II Cor. 6:1-2 NIV:

As God's fellow workers we urge you not to receive God's grace in vain.
For he says, "In the time of my favor I heard you, and in the day of salvation I helped you." I tell you, now is the time of God's favor, now is the day of salvation.

"What if?" This curse-word is motivated by the spirit of fear, and fear is not of God. Faith is a spiritual force and comes by meditating on the Word of God. Fear is a spiritual force and comes by meditating on the word of the devil. All of us have crossed bridges before we got to them. Folks who use this curse-word are smart enough to be dumb. They know that the hardest thing to do is to start. If you are constantly afraid of the future, you never have to step out and put your neck on the line. These kind of people love to have you pray for them and prophesy over them all the time. Go ahead and pray and prophesy, but show them the rent veil and then encourage them to believe God. They need to know that He will answer their prayer. Fear is perverted faith. The Lord has not given us that spirit, but rather the spirit of love, power, and a sound mind.

Matt. 6:33-34 NIV:

> *But seek first his kingdom and his righteousness, and all these things will be given to you as well.*
>
> *Therefore do not worry about tomorrow, for tomorrow will worry about itself. Each day has enough trouble of its own.*

"But ..." When we use this word of profanity, we erase everything that we said prior to the use of the word. This is a curse-word of unbelief, and unbelief is unfaith. This word changes everything that precedes it. Only "goats" use this word. Their stubbornness is as iniquity and idolatry. If you have experienced some things that got your "goat," then rejoice. You are the sheep of His pasture. His people believe every word of God. Don't look at the giants or the walled cities from the realm of the dust. Get into the heavenlies where you belong, look down on the same circumstances, and say with Caleb, "They are bread for us!"

Matt. 4:4 NIV:

> *Jesus answered, "It is written: Man does not live on bread alone, but on every word that comes from the mouth of God."*

"Nobody understands me." I know. Nobody loves you, everybody hates you, so you're going to go and eat worms! Isn't that silly? This is self-pity, the devil's baby-sitter free of charge. There are too many like Naomi in the book of Ruth who are bitter against God and others. Don't be introverted and withdrawn.

Open up to God and His people. Lift up your eyes to new horizons and get a fresh vision. Focus on the needs of others and you won't have to bother with this curse-word. This is a very selfish excuse, and flows out of folks who have their eyes on the dealings of God rather than the God who is doing the dealing. They want you to feel like nobody has suffered quite like them. The martyr complex. Because they tell you that you can't understand the depth of their "suffering," they don't have to open up, get some real help, and change!

I Cor. 10:13 NIV:

> *No temptation has seized you except what is common to man. And God is faithful; he will not let you be tempted beyond what you can bear. But when you are tempted, he will also provide a way out so that you can stand up under it.*

"I can't!" Be a man about it. The truth is, you won't! How will you know if you never try? We can do all things through Christ. Without Him we can do nothing, but with God all things are possible. Like David, we can kill the bear, the ferociousness of the world. We can slay the lion, our adversary the devil. Now let us arise and slay the uncircumcised giant of self and self-sufficiency that is between our ears. The carnal mind. The word "defeat" is not in God's dictionary. Our walk in God is like walking up a pair of steps. First the riser, then the tread. Don't be afraid to step out into new territory.

Phil. 4:13 NIV:

> *I can do everything through him who gives me strength.*

"You don't love me," or "You need to show more love." This curse-word flows from a wrong response to the chastening or training of the Lord. Too many have a perverted notion of what love is. Love is a Person. He is described in I Cor. 13:4-8 as a full-grown Son. His name is Jesus. This One who is real love will not let you have your way. Love rejoices in fellowship with the truth, so if somebody tells you the truth and has a right spirit, that's love! God does love me and, because of it, He will purge out of my life those things which hurt me. The person who swears like this has never been confronted or challenged.

Jer. 31:3 NIV:

The Lord appeared to us in the past, saying: "I have loved you with an everlasting love; I have drawn you with loving-kindness."

"Maybe ..." This is a word of uncertainty and double-mindedness (James 1:8). It is a word of duality, and God hates a mixture. This word is often heard when we are about to create another "Ishmael" (Gen. 16:2). When we bring forth that which is a product of human wisdom and human strength, it will never be quite enough to do the job. There's always a question mark. The Hebrew word for faith is "aman" and means that which is "certain"; the Greek word "pistis" means "persuasion or conviction; to rely by an inward certainty." The outer realm of circumstances has nothing to do with the faith of God. Folks who speak this way like to throw out fleeces. Don't get fleeced. If you must, then at least do what Gideon did ... make it doubly impossible.

Phil. 1:6 NIV:

Being confident of this, that he who began a good work in you will carry it on to completion until the day of Christ Jesus.

"We've always done it this way before." So that makes it right? When we follow the traditions of the fathers, we will always end up "cussing." The old order is governed by the law of sin and death. The move of God in the earth today is energized by the law of the spirit of life in Christ Jesus. Man's traditions rob the Word of its power (Mk. 7:13). Spiritual growth denotes change after change after change. We are being changed from strength to strength, from faith to faith, and from glory to glory. If not, then we are drawing back unto perdition and are being changed from evil to evil (Jer. 9:3). You can't use a Model-T message in a jet age. The cloud is moving. Move with the cloud.

Isa. 43:19 NIV:

See, I am doing a new thing! Now it springs up; do you not perceive it? I am making a way in the desert and streams in the wasteland.

"I'm afraid of what people will think or say about me." If it's any consolation, don't believe the preachers when they say that what others think or say doesn't matter. Sure it matters. But whether we are cursed or praised, it doesn't move us one way or the other. I have already showed you that Heb. 11 faith is "good report" faith, which is bound by polls and public opinion. Heb. 12 faith is "no reputation" faith, so we're not afraid of people. There is no fear in Him, and God is love. The majority is not always right (Num. 13-14). Somebody has to stand up. Get out of the boat, Peter. Go before the king, Esther. Preach the Word, Timothy. If I please men, I cannot be the servant of Christ. All I need to know is what He thinks and says about me, and His thoughts toward me are thoughts of peace!

I Jn. 4:17-18 NIV:

In this way, love is made complete among us so that we will have confidence on the day of judgment, because in this world we are like him.

*There is no fear in love. But perfect love drives
out fear, because fear has to do with punishment.
The one who fears is not made perfect in love.*

We certainly have not exhausted the excuses that
people make. If you want to hear some more, start
pastoring a church and preaching Covenant commitment and the lordship of Jesus Christ. But whatever
our reason for not moving on in God, there is a strong
verse somewhere in the Bible to help us to renew our
minds and go with God. You may want to remember
the song we teach our children: "Be careful, little eyes,
what you see. Be careful, little ears, what you hear. Be
careful, little mouth, what you say ...''

Psa. 19:14 NIV:

*May the words of my mouth and the meditation
of my heart be pleasing in your sight, O Lord, my
Rock and my Redeemer.*

Jas. 1:26 NIV:

*If anyone considers himself religious and yet
does not keep a tight rein on his tongue, he
deceives himself and his religion is worthless.*

Jas. 3:1, 2 NIV:

*Not many of you should presume to be teachers,
my brothers, because you know that we who
teach will be judged more strictly.*
*We all stumble in many ways. If anyone is
never at fault in what he says, he is a perfect man,
able to keep his whole body in check.*

The more excellent ministry is a ministry without
profanity. The Son only speaks what the Father says.
There is no other word, no other calling, no other love.
Our eyes are focused on our glorious Head. There is no
other image but His in our vision. The other gods and
concepts have perished for those called to the more
excellent ministry, a ministry without idolatry.

Chapter Seven

A Ministry Without Idolatry

The more excellent ministry is a vast subject. Keep in mind that we have only discussed one of the nine principles which summarize His king-priest ministry as detailed in the seventh chapter of Hebrews — the ministry of Jesus is universal, reaching out to forgive and bless all men:

1. Without condemnation.
2. Without prejudice.
3. Without walls.
4. Without retaliation.
5. Without profanity.

We must understand that His ministry is being imitated. The spirit of antichrist and religious humanism has set forth a cheap counterfeit in every generation. So we come to our final principle. The more excellent ministry of Jesus Christ after the order of Melchisedec is a ministry without idolatry.

Do you remember that the Christ within (Col. 1:27), the Anointed One, is a prophet, priest, and king? And that the kingdom which is within you (Luke 17:20-21) is righteousness, peace, and joy?

The Christ nature produces the Kingdom of God.

The prophet produces righteousness.

The priest produces peace.

The king produces joy.

There are seven things that are being ministered by the Spirit of Christ, the ox nature which is characterized by patience, humility, and the strength of God:

1. Reconciliation (II Cor. 5:17-21).
2. Forgiveness (Eph. 4:29-32).
3. Healing (Matt. 10:8).
4. Life (II Cor. 2:16).
5. Liberty (Lk. 4:18).
6. Sweet water (Jas. 3:8-18).
7. Love (Rom. 5:5).

Now consider the flip side or the counterfeit to these truths. The more excellent ministry is a ministry without idolatry.

The antichrist nature produces the kingdom of self.

The false prophet produces unrighteousness.

The false priest produces turmoil and unrest.

The false king produces sorrow and sighing.

Here are some real guidelines for discerning true ministry. A true prophet declares God unto men. A false prophet declares himself. A true priest brings men unto God. A false priest brings men unto himself. A true king rules in the power of God's name. A false king rules by the power of his own reputation.

There are seven things that are being ministered by the spirit of antichrist, the wild ass nature which is characterized by impatience, arrogance, and the weakness of his own strength:

1. Division (Jn. 7:40-43).
2. Resentment (Jn. 4:20).
3. Disease (I Cor. 11:28-30).
4. Death (II Cor. 3:7).
5. Bondage (Gal. 5:1, 13-16, 25-26).
6. Bitter water (Jas. 3:11; Heb. 12:14-15).
7. Hate (Acts 9:1-2).

Man has always made attempts throughout the Bible to imitate and thus counterfeit the moving of the Spirit of God. At the tower of Babel, man wanted to make a name for himself (Gen. 11). Ichabod was an imitation of the manchild Samuel (I Sam. 1-4). Michal made a goat-hair dummy to imitate the sweet psalmist (I Sam. 19:13-17). And did you know that there is a counterfeit five-fold ministry in the land?

In II Sam. 6 David brought the Ark of the Covenant back to Zion. In I Sam. 6 the Philistines sent the Ark back to its people. There's a lesson there: in a real move of God, men get involved; they don't just send, they bring. David copied the "new cart" method of the Philistines in his first attempt to restore the Ark (I Chron. 13), and breached the due order. We won't solve a spiritual problem with a worldly or natural answer. A cart has wheels which go in circles and make ruts. Uzza ("strength") and Ahio ("brotherly") drove this denominational machine, whipping the oxen as they went. These preacher's kids had grown up with the Ark in their home, and knew nothing of reverence or the fear of the Lord. When God broke up this "revival," and killed "strength" when he put his hand to the Ark, David went home and had a Bible study. There he discovered that only a God-ordained priest separated by blood and oil could carry the love-seat.

So we see a counterfeit restoration. But what of the imitation five-fold ministry? Going back to I Sam. 6, we see that the Philistines had filled the "new cart" with five golden emerods and five golden mice for a trespass offering (they had stolen the Ark). God had plagued their pentapolis with mice and emerods, destroying their fish-god Dagon. I won't describe a golden emerod, but the five golden mice represent a counterfeit of Eph. 4:11.

1. The mice were idols and false images.
2. The mice were cold and lifeless.
3. The mice were golden — representing the love of money.
4. The mice were unclean (Lev. 11:29).
5. The mice left their droppings everywhere.

Christ Is The Image Of God

II Cor. 4:1-4 NIV:

Therefore, since through God's mercy we have this ministry, we do not lose heart.

Rather, we have renounced secret and shameful ways; we do not use deception, nor do we distort the word of God. On the contrary, by setting forth the truth plainly we commend ourselves to every man's conscience in the sight of God.

And even if our gospel is veiled, it is veiled to those who are perishing.

The god of this age has blinded the minds of unbelievers, so that they cannot see the light of the gospel of the glory of Christ, who is the image of God.

Now we see satan's strategy. If you don't know who you are, how can you know what you have? The serpent keeps nipping at our heel (Gen. 3:15) to distract us and keep us off balance lest we get established in the truth. His sole objective is to keep you from the light or understanding of the more excellent ministry. He wants to blind your mind to your destiny. Now learn a basic principle:

Christ is the image of God.

Antichrist is any other image, an idol.

The Greek word for "antichrist" is a transliteration of "antichristos" (#500 in *Strong's*) and means "an opponent of the Messiah." It is taken from two other words:

1. "anti" (#473), which means "opposite, instead of."
2. "christos" (#5547), which means "anointed, Messiah"; from "chrio," which means "to rub or stroke with oil."

The term carries the first meaning of "instead of Christ" and then "against Christ," combining both. This word is used five times in the New Testament:

I Jn. 2:18 KJV:

Little children, it is the last time: and as ye have heard that antichrist shall come, even now are there many antichrists; whereby we know that it is the last time.

I Jn. 2:22 KJV:

Who is a liar but he that denieth that Jesus is the Christ? He is antichrist, that denieth the Father and the Son.

I Jn. 4:3 KJV:

And every spirit that confesseth not that Jesus Christ is come in the flesh is not of God: and this is that spirit of antichrist, whereof ye have heard that it should come; and even now already is it in the world.

II Jn. 1:7 KJV:

*For many deceivers are entered into the world,
who confess not that Jesus Christ is come in the
flesh. This is a deceiver and an antichrist.*

The indwelling Christ is a prophet, priest, and king.
The biggest problem in the Church is that we don't
know our identity in Christ. Consequently, our imagination invents the other images of ourselves, which are a
product of the carnal mind, and to be carnally minded
is death (Rom. 8:1-6). Do you see the simplicity of this?
These other images are idols which need to be destroyed. Learn to agree with the Father (Amos 3:3). It
doesn't matter if the more excellent ministry is without
condemnation, or prejudice, or walls, or retaliation, or
profanity. If these idolatrous concepts of yourself are
still your gods, you'll not know the joy of sitting with
Him in the Mercy-seat.

One other word must be noted in our study about
the spirit of antichrist. The word "pseudochristos"
(#5580) means "a spurious Messiah" and is rendered as
"false Christs" in Matt. 24:24 and Mk. 13:22. An obvious
application of this would be someone today who has
deluded himself and others into thinking that he is
some kind of Messiah. However, knowing that the
"beast" of Gen. 3 was more subtle and cunning than
any beast of the field, we also note that there are "false
anointings," or a wisdom that is perverted.

But let us return to the Christ nature. Christ in and
among all of you, the hope of glory. It is my fervent
prayer that you become aware of the greatness of the
One who lives in your heart. I want you to receive a
progressive vision of Him as He is, and as He is in you
and through you (Prov. 29:18)!

1. As He is, the Exalted One.
2. As He is in you, the Greater One.
3. As He is through you, the Ministering One.

The first principle speaks of our worship. The second of our warfare in the heavenlies. And the third of our welfare to others as we release the Christ from within. No longer a garden inclosed and spring shut up and a fountain sealed, we allow the spices of His grace and truth to flow out to the creation.

Phile. 1:6 KJV:

That the communication of thy faith may become effectual by the acknowledging of every good thing which is in you in Christ Jesus.

The issue is that there are two images of you:

1. Christ, which is His image of you.
2. Antichrist, which is your image of you.

The image we have of ourselves is the one we believe "instead of" the one who is real. A word of caution here: this is not metaphysics, which is lifeless and bloodless, an endless, empty pursuit through mental gymnastics. What I am preaching is only available through the Person and finished work of the Lord Jesus Christ. I am proclaiming the good news of the New Covenant in His blood. I am telling you who you are in Him, not what you can be in yourself. You will have to be put to death so that you can be replaced by Him!

Two Images, Two Covenants

The Bible is divided into two covenants, the Old Testament and the New Testament. While these parts have a historical setting and meaning, it is more important to realize that they embody spiritual principles. Thus the Old Testament speaks of the old nature, the New Testament of the new nature. In light of this teaching on spiritual idolatry, the Old Testament carries the spirit of your image of you, while the New Testament projects the spirit of His image for you,

Christ who is the image of God. Consider Paul's allegory as an example of this.

Gal. 4:21-31 KJV:

Tell me, ye that desire to be under the law, do ye not hear the law?

For it is written, that Abraham had two sons, the one by a bondmaid, the other by a freewoman.

But he who was of the bondwoman was born after the flesh; but he of the freewoman was by promise.

Which things are an allegory: for these are the two covenants; the one from the mount Sinai, which gendereth to bondage, which is Agar.

For this Agar is mount Sinai in Arabia, and answereth to Jerusalem which now is, and is in bondage with her children.

But Jerusalem which is above is free, which is the mother of us all.

For it is written, Rejoice, thou barren that bearest not; break forth and cry, thou that travailest not: for the desolate hath many more children than she which hath an husband.

Now we, brethren, as Isaac was, are the children of promise.

But as then he that was born after the flesh persecuted him that was born after the Spirit, even so it is now.

Nevertheless what saith the scripture? Cast out the bondwoman and her son: for the son of the bondwoman shall not be heir with the son of the freewoman.

So then, brethren, we are not children of the bondwoman, but of the free.

THE OLD COVENANT	THE NEW COVENANT
Bondwoman	Freewoman
Hagar	Sarah
Ishmael	Isaac
Human effort	Sabbath rest
Sweat (dust)	No sweat
Born of the flesh	Born of the Spirit
Son of the flesh	Son of promise
Not the heir	The heir, God's chosen
From Mount Sinai	From Mount Zion
Earthly Jerusalem	Heavenly Jerusalem
Natural Jew	Spiritual Jew
Natural Israel	Spiritual Israel
Natural land	Spiritual land
Natural temple	Spiritual temple
From beneath	From above
In bondage	Free

There is too much to teach here, but I'm sure you can see the pattern. In the Old Testament, there was a Levitical priesthood, as we have mentioned. The New Testament priesthood is after the similitude of Melchisedec, and is the more excellent ministry of Jesus. There was an old priesthood, and there is a new priesthood. The first was energized by the law of sin and death, the second by the law of the Spirit of life in Christ Jesus. As I am endeavoring to summarize and tie together all that I have taught you in this volume, I want to share three other charts with you. A separate book could be written for each of them. They are filled with "seed thoughts" for your further consideration of the more excellent ministry. The first is taken from II Cor. 3-4 and needs to be referred to again when we discuss the "Genesis face" of Jas. 1. This rich Pauline study listed below not only sheds more light on the ministry without idolatry, but also brings to your remembrance much of what I have previously showed you about the other aspects of the more excellent ministry. The second chart, below, parallels the first as well as Paul's allegory above; it is a contrast of God and mammon taken from Matt. 6:19-34. The third chart, on the next page, parallels all the others from yet another perspective, and is taken from I Cor. 15:40-49. Its emphasis on the "image" principle also illustrates the truth of our being conformed to the Christ, the image of God.

Read II Cor. 3:1-18 and find these principles:

THE FACE OF MOSES	THE FACE OF JESUS
Epistle of antichrist	Epistle of Christ
Written with ink	Written with the Spirit
Tables of stone	Tables of the heart
Incompetent ministry	Able ministry
Of the letter	Of the Spirit
Kills	Gives life
Ministration of death	Ministration of life
Glorious	More glorious
Fading glory	Permanent, excelling glory
Through glory	In glory
Ministry of condemnation	Ministry of no condemnation
Unrighteous ministry	Righteous ministry
Levi	Melchisedec
In part	Perfect, complete
Done away	Remains
No hope	Hope
Dark sentences	Great plainness of speech
Veil untaken away	Veil done away with
Veiled face	Open, unveiled face
Veiled heaven	Open heaven
Old Testament	New Testament
Old man	New-creation man
Antichrist	Christ
Law	End of the law
Still active	Abolished
Blinded minds	Opened, enlightened minds
Blinded heart	Open heart
Bondage	Liberty

| Glory of man | Glory of the Lord |
| A different image | The same image |

Read II Cor. 4:1-18 and find these principles:

NO MERCY	RECEIVED MERCY
Faint	Faint not
Veiled Gospel	Unveiled Gospel
Believe not	Believe
Another image	Image of God
Image of the beast	Image of the beauty
Preach ourselves	Preach Christ Jesus
No treasure	Treasure
No power	Power
Outward man perishes	Inward man renewed
Light affliction	Weight of glory
For a moment (temporal)	Eternal
Things seen	Things not seen
Sight	Faith

As you can see, this is a broad study. Now turn to the Sermon on the Mount and Matt. 6. There we see yet another way of saying the same thing. In Matt. 6:19-34 we have the Law of Reduced Interests; that is, our interests are reduced as we walk with the King. The realm of the Spirit takes priority over anything in the realm of the natural. As His Lordship increases, other interests will fade. Men today fear this lonely place of surrender, favoring the crowded place of a "social" and often undisciplined atmosphere. This passage brings to light yet another key of understanding the ministry without idolatry:

Duality is idolatry.

Again, we will discuss this principle below in the section on the "Genesis face." We must have a clear, uncluttered, single eye (Matt. 6:22), not being double-minded (Jas. 1:8), ever looking unto Jesus (Heb. 12:1-2).

What is "mammon"? It is a transliteration of the

Greek "mamonas" (#3126 in *Strong's*) which means "confidence, wealth, avarice deified." This is the common Aramaic word for "riches." It is akin to the Hebrew word "aw-man," the word for "faith; that which is firm, steadfast." Gesenius refers it back to "treasure" in Gen. 43:23. The word actually means, "that in which one trusts." The rich man puts his trust in his money. Mammon is that in which I place my confidence or trust. This idea links mammon to any idolatrous image that I have of myself. The word does not occur in the Old Testament, but is used in Jewish writings in the senses of "resources," "gain" (especially dishonest), "compensation," "ransom," or "bribe." Luke noted that mammon is "unrighteous" and that it shall "fail" (Lk. 16:9-11). In a very practical sense, mammon is the self-sufficiency of man's way. We cannot serve God and mammon. Read the passage below and parallel Lk. 12:22-34. Note as you read that Jesus was also teaching here about life and immortality, the key words being "arrayed," "clothe," and "body."

Matt. 6:19-34 KJV:

Lay not up for yourselves treasures upon earth, where moth and rust doth corrupt, and where thieves break through and steal:

But lay up for yourselves treasures in heaven, where neither moth nor rust doth corrupt, and where thieves do not break through nor steal:

For where your treasure is, there will your heart be also.

The light of the body is the eye: if therefore thine eye be single, thy whole body shall be full of light.

But if thine eye be evil, thy whole body shall be full of darkness. If therefore the light that is in thee be darkness, how great is that darkness!

No man can serve two masters: for either he

will hate the one, and love the other; or else he will hold to the one, and despise the other. Ye cannot serve God and mammon.

Therefore I say unto you, Take no thought for your life, what ye shall eat, or what ye shall drink; nor yet for your body, what ye shall put on. Is not the life more than meat, and the body than raiment?

Behold the fowls of the air: for they sow not, neither do they reap, nor gather into barns; yet your heavenly Father feedeth them. Are ye not much better than they?

Which of you by taking thought can add one cubit unto his stature?

And why take ye thought for raiment? Consider the lilies of the field, how they grow; they toil not, neither do they spin:

And yet I say unto you, That even Solomon in all his glory was not arrayed like one of these.

Wherefore, if God so clothe the grass of the field, which to day is, and to morrow is cast into the oven, shall he not much more clothe you, O ye of little faith?

Therefore take no thought, saying, What shall we eat? or, What shall we drink? or, Wherewithal shall we be clothed?

(For after all these things do the Gentiles seek:) for your heavenly Father knoweth that ye have need of all these things.

But seek ye first the kingdom of God, and his righteousness; and all these things shall be added unto you.

Take therefore no thought for the morrow: for the morrow shall take thought for the things of itself. Sufficient unto the day is the evil thereof.

MAMMON	GOD
Natural realm	Spiritual realm
Rich man	Poor (needy) man
Self-sufficient	Daily sufficiency from God
Treasures upon earth	Treasures in heaven
Corruption	No corruption
Thief enters	Thief cannot enter
Earthly heart	Heavenly heart (after God's)
Evil eye	Single eye
Double vision	Looking unto Jesus
Cluttered eye	Uncluttered eye
The way I see Him	The way He sees Himself
The way I see me	The way He sees me
The way I see others	The way He sees others
Seeing falsely	Seeing truly
Body full of darkness	Body full of light
Body full of death	Body full of life
Taking thought	Seeking first
The passing	The permanent
Temporal	Eternal
Unstable kingdom	Stable Kingdom

Our third and final chart is found in I Cor. 15:40-49, the resurrection chapter of the Bible. The examples there and in each study above show us again and again that there are two images, which we now understand to be the principle of two covenants.

I Cor. 15:40-49 KJV:

There are also celestial bodies, and bodies terrestrial: but the glory of the celestial is one, and the glory of the terrestrial is another.

There is one glory of the sun, and another glory of the moon, and another glory of the stars: for one star differeth from another star in glory.

So also is the resurrection of the dead. It is sown in corruption; it is raised in incorruption:

It is sown in dishonour; it is raised in glory: it is sown in weakness; it is raised in power:

It is sown a natural body; it is raised a spiritual body. There is a natural body, and there is a spiritual body.

And so it is written, The first man Adam was made a living soul; the last Adam was made a quickening spirit.

Howbeit that was not first which is spiritual, but that which is natural; and afterward that which is spiritual.

The first man is of the earth, earthy: the second man is the Lord from heaven.

As is the earthy, such are they also that are earthy: and as is the heavenly, such are they also that are heavenly.

And as we have borne the image of the earthy, we shall also bear the image of the heavenly.

IMAGE OF THE EARTHY	IMAGE OF THE HEAVENLY
Terrestrial bodies	Celestial bodies
Sown in corruption	Raised in incorruption
Perishable	Imperishable
Sown in weakness	Raised in power
Natural body	Spiritual body
The first Adam	The Last Adam
A living soul	A life-giving spirit
First man	Second man
The man out of earth	The Lord out of heaven
Earthy man	Heavenly man
Earthly minded	Heavenly minded
Man of dust	Man of spirit
Jacob	Israel

The principle of resurrection is past, presently progressive, and future in its scope. Our bodies shall be changed, but we are to put on Christ now. Christ in you will become Christ on you. Thus the literal rendering of I Cor. 15:49 is, "So let us now put on and wear as a garment or a piece of armor the image of the heavenly!" Are you seeing the right image?

The Man In The Mirror

Christ is the image of God, the way the Father sees you. Antichirst is any other image, the way that you or others may see youself. From the beginning, God has wanted a man in His image. The problem is that man has resisted the wisdom of God and has exchanged God's plan for one which Adam has invented.

Gen. 1:26 KJV:

And God said, Let us make man in our image, after our likeness: and let them have dominion over the fish of the sea, and over the fowl of the air, and over the cattle, and over all the earth, and over every creeping thing that creepeth upon the earth.

Rom. 1:21-25 KJV:

Because that, when they knew God, they glorified him not as God, neither were thankful; but became vain in their imaginations, and their foolish heart was darkened.

Professing themselves to be wise, they became fools,

And changed the glory of the uncorruptible God into an image made like to corruptible man, and to birds, and fourfooted beasts, and creeping things.

Wherefore God also gave them up to uncleanness through the lusts of their own hearts, to dishonour their own bodies between themselves:

Who changed the truth of God into a lie, and worshipped and served the creature more than the Creator, who is blessed for ever. Amen.

Where is God? He was in Christ, reconciling the world unto Himself. And where is Christ? Christ is in you. God is in us, but when we fail to recognize and acknowledge His presence, problems develop. The first thing that happens is that we are not thankful. The downward degenerative process of Rom. 1 begins in a man's life with his not being thankful! Then his imagination runs wild with one vain thought after another. Ignorance fills the heart. Darkness is presumed to be light. It's one thing to be wrong. It's another thing to be wrong and not know it. Finally, he changes ("exchanges") the image of the uncorruptible God, the image of Jesus Christ, for an image made like corruptible man. This is true in all three dimensions or feasts:

1. Creeping things — Outer Court — Passover.
2. Four-footed beasts — Holy Place — Pentecost.
3. Birds — Most Holy Place — Tabernacles.

The corruptible image of the Outer Court is a humanity that crawls on its belly and sucks dust. The antichrist of the Holy Place is a humanity on all fours, not knowing which end is up. The false image of the Most Holy Place is a counterfeit eagle, a dirty bird, one that leaves its mess everywhere. Baptist images, Pentecostal images, pseudo-Kingdom images. Bodies, families, churches have been dishonored because of these images. By not believing His Word, we have changed ("exchanged" — intensified form) the truth for the lie and worshipped and served the creature (Adam) more than the Creator (Christ).

This idolatry is seen in the Old Testament as well. Do you remember the man of sin who sat in the "naos," the inner sanctuary? God took the prophet Ezekiel into the Temple and showed him the same thing. There was an image of jealousy in the entrance.

Ezek. 8:3 KJV:

And he put forth the form of an hand, and took me by a lock of mine head; and the spirit lifted me up between the earth and the heaven, and brought me in the visions of God to Jerusalem, to the door of the inner gate that looketh toward the north; where was the seat of the image of jealousy, which provoketh to jealousy.

Ezek. 8:12 KJV:

Then said he unto me, Son of man, hast thou seen what the ancients of the house of Israel do in the dark, every man in the chambers of his imagery? for they say, The Lord seeth us not; the Lord hath forsaken the earth.

The awfulness of this scene is magnified by the observation that this idol was seated at the "gate of the altar" (Ezek. 8:5). This was the Brazen Altar, a type of the cross of Jesus Christ and thus His finished work. Where that should have been, there stood an image of jealousy, the very spirit of antichrist with its humanistic substitutes and alternatives for the plan and ways of God! There the prophet watched as men practiced idolatry in the darkness of their souls, in the chambers of their imaginations. He wept as He saw portrayed on the inward walls of the Temple the abomination of condemnation, man's blatant refusal to be accepted in the Beloved.

Dan. 2:31 KJV:

Thou, O king, sawest, and behold a great image. This great image, whose brightness was excellent, stood before thee; and the form thereof was terrible.

Dan. 3:1 KJV:

Nebuchadnezzar the king made an image of

gold, whose height was threescore cubits, and the breadth thereof six cubits: he set it up in the plain of Dura, in the province of Babylon.

The prophet Daniel was also aware of the image that makes God jealous. Nebuchadnezzar's dream was Adam's dream all over again. He not only saw the Gentile nations stretched out over the history of the world, but he saw a horrible composite of the philosophy and beastly mentality of each of those civilizations. From another perspective, he saw the ungodly mixture of doctrinal and moral thought which fills the present Church world, from the golden head of Kingdom/sonship theology down to the feet and toes of Roman Catholicism. One awful-looking, mixed-up man, the present condition of the wounded Body of Christ. The image that was later constructed and set up in the plain of Dura had the number six, the number of man, all over it!

Rev. 9:20 KJV:

And the rest of the men which were not killed by these plagues yet repented not of the works of their hands, that they should not worship devils, and idols of gold, and silver, and brass, and stone, and of wood: which neither can see, nor hear, nor walk:

Compare this with Psa. 115:4-8. I have met so many Christians over the years who go to church every Sunday and are good people. But they cannot see, they are not hearing, and they are not walking in what God is saying to the Church today. All because of idols ... false images invented by the carnal mind. Settle it, child of God. There is dwelling in you a new nature, Christ in you the hope of glory, Christ who is the image of God. You are a new creation that never existed before. His image of you is the only healthy one. Any other image is an antichrist and a false teacher.

Hab. 2:18 NIV:

Of what value is an idol, since a man has carved it? Or an image that teaches lies? For he who makes it trusts in his own creation; he makes idols that cannot speak.

Christ is the image of God. Anything less misses the mark. What niche are you trying to carve for yourself? Is it a "good old boy" image? An uptown or downtown image? A white or black image? A macho image? A sexy image? An intellectual image? A famous preacher image? Any image of ourselves that is not in agreement with the Word and Spirit is a false teacher. One problem with these images is that they tend to change with the whims of the beast, running after fads and fashions which are in today and out tomorrow. "Brother Varner, I can see what you are saying. But what can I do about it?" That's easy. You created the idol with words of fear. Prophesy its destruction with words of faith. I know that won't be easy, because men take years to create a certain image. They don't want to change because the false teacher will let you get away with a lot. He will also keep you out of the city of the living God.

Tit. 2:11-12 NIV:

For the grace of God that brings salvation has appeared to all men.
It teaches us to say "No" to ungodliness and worldly passions, and to live self-controlled, upright and godly lives in this present age,

Rev. 22:14-15 NIV:

Blessed are those who wash their robes, that they may have the right to the tree of life and may go through the gates into the city.
Outside are the dogs, those who practice magic arts, the sexually immoral, the murderers, the

*idolaters and everyone who loves and practices
falsehood.*

Christ is the image of God. We must keep our eyes
on Jesus. He is the Pattern Son and our Example. He
must be our First Love. Why settle for second best?
You are called to the top of the mountain. You are
called to be the best, so if you're only good, that makes
you fair. You'll never be happy until you are satisfied
in Him. He is the Goal. His life is the prize. We are
called to be like Him! He is the image of God.

Rom. 8:29 KJV:

*For whom he did foreknow, he also did predes-
tinate to be conformed to the image of his Son,
that he might be the firstborn among many
brethren.*

Col. 1:15 KJV:

*Who is the image of the invisible God, the
firstborn of every creature:*

Heb. 1:3 KJV:

*Who being the brightness of his glory, and the
express image of his person, and upholding all
things by the word of his power, when he had by
himself purged our sins, sat down on the right
hand of the Majesty on high;*

We must see Him! We must look to Him! I want to
show you how to destroy the false image and lay hold
of Him. Let me share with you a revelation that
changed my mind about my relationship with God.
Let me show you the man in the mirror.

Jas. 1:5-8 NIV:

*If any of you lacks wisdom, he should ask God,
who gives generously to all without finding fault,
and it will be given to him.*

> *But when he asks, he must believe and not doubt, because he who doubts is like a wave of the sea, blown and tossed by the wind.*
> *That man should not think he will receive anything from the Lord;*
> *He is a double-minded man, unstable in all he does.*

Duality is idolatry. God hates a mixture. To be "double-minded" is to be, literally, "double-souled." *Weymouth's* translation says that such a one is "a man of two minds, undecided in every step he takes." Beck said that he is "half-hearted" and the *Amplified Bible* says that he is "hesitating, dubious, irresolute; he is unstable and unreliable and uncertain about everything he thinks, feels, decides." His problem is the way he thinks. I also call the land of double-mindedness the "twilight zone"! Not day, not night ... twilight (Zech. 14:6-7). Did you know that God's day begins in the evening and ends in the morning (Gen. 1)? The thing that is bugging everybody now is that nobody has a full handle on what the Lord is doing and how and when He is going to do it. The dawn is approaching and things are becoming increasingly more clear. Shadow is giving way to substance. But our dilemma is that He is commanding us to get up and go forward while it's yet dark, when we don't have all the answers. Thank God that somebody is going to arise in the "twilight" and find a place where there is no enemy, just a table spread (II Kg. 7)!

Jas. 1:16-18 NIV:

> *Don't be deceived, my dear brothers.*
> *Every good and perfect gift is from above, coming down from the Father of the heavenly lights, who does not change like shifting shadows.*
> *He chose to give us birth through the word of truth, that we might be a kind of firstfruits of all he created.*

Here is contrasted the nature of God. We are the lights of which He is Father (Matt. 5:13-16; Heb. 12:9). The Father is not double-minded and neither is His seed. The word for "kind" is "tis" which means "a certain kind." A Kingdom species, if you will. A Kingdom people who will remain (Heb. 12:25-29). Note that there is a birth here in verse 18. That's very important to remember.

Jas. 1:19-25 KJV:

> *Wherefore, my beloved brethren, let every man be swift to hear, slow to speak, slow to wrath:*
>
> *For the wrath of man worketh not the righteousness of God.*
>
> *Wherefore lay apart all filthiness and superfluity of naughtiness, and receive with meekness the engrafted word, which is able to save your souls.*
>
> *But be ye doers of the word, and not hearers only, deceiving your own selves.*
>
> *For if any be a hearer of the word, and not a doer, he is like unto a man beholding his natural face in a glass:*
>
> *For he beholdeth himself, and goeth his way, and straightway forgetteth what manner of man he was.*
>
> *But whoso looketh into the perfect law of liberty, and continueth therein, he being not a forgetful hearer, but a doer of the work, this man shall be blessed in his deed.*

The word for "beholding" means to "contemplate or gaze." What are we looking at? Our "natural face." Who is the man in the glass? Who is the man in the mirror? When we think of the Brazen Laver of the Tabernacle of Moses, we understand that the mirror represents the Word of God. In the old order, we would come to church and look into the mirror to behold our sinfulness. There is an application of truth to that, but I want to show you something better. In this new day, we come looking into the Word of God to behold His righteousness!

What is this "natural face"? It is the key to our understanding this entire chapter. The word for "natural" face is "genesis" (#1078 in *Strong's*) and means "nativity; nature." It is from "genea" (#1074) which means "a generation; an age." It is used here in Jas. 1:23 and again in Jas. 3:6 as "nature." It is the word for "generation" in Matt. 1:1. It is rendered literally here as "the face of his birth." What birth? The one in verse 18! The man in the mirror is the new man! And he has one eye ... a single eye (Matt. 6:22-24)! We are beholding our natural face ... the face of a new nature ... His nature!

II Cor. 3:18 KJV:

> *But we all, with open face beholding as in a glass the glory of the Lord, are changed into the same image from glory to glory, even as by the Spirit of the Lord.*

In Jas. 3, we behold our "natural face," the face of our birth. Here we are looking at the same thing, but termed as "the glory of the Lord!" Add one more verse and the picture is clear.

II Cor. 4:6 KJV:

> *For God, who commanded the light to shine out of darkness, hath shined in our hearts, to give the light of the knowledge of the glory of God in the face of Jesus Christ.*

Where is the glory of God? In the face of Jesus Christ! The man in the mirror is the new man ... it is His face! Our gaze is not focused on our weakness, our fear, our sorrow, our limitation ... it is looking unto

Jesus, and His strength, His faith, His joy, and His ministry! Keep looking, child of God. Then begin to understand that you are becoming like the man in the mirror. You are becoming what you worship. You are being changed into that same image ... His image ... His face!

I Cor. 6:17 NIV:

But he who unites himself with the Lord is one with him in spirit.

Somebody says, "Varner, I just can't see it." That's right, you can't. I am going to show you why you can't see His face. We have been taught that when we die and go to heaven, we will see His face. I believe in heaven, but I can see His face now! There are glories to come in ages yet to be explored, but I can be changed now!

Ex. 20:3-4 KJV:

Thou shalt have no other gods before me.
Thou shalt not make unto thee any graven image, or any likeness of any thing that is in heaven above, or that is in the earth beneath, or that is in the water under the earth:

This is the first commandment in the Decalogue. It warns against false images. The margin of verse 3 reads, "Thou shalt have no other gods before My face"! Why can't some folks see the glory of the Lord revealed in the face of Jesus Christ? All they see is darkness, disease, death, and damnation. What is blinding me? My face is in the way of His face. My image of me stands between me and His image of me. Antichrist stands in the way of Christ. Antichrist is any other image. What is holding me back and keeping me defeated and confused? It's the lie that satan and his ministers have peddled to me all of my life. It is a veil that must be rent, an alabaster box that must be broken, a wall of Jericho that must come down.

James cautioned us to continue looking into the law of liberty. If not, we will go our own way (Isa. 53:6) and forget what manner of man we were in the mirror. As you have read and studied this message, have you seen the Glorified Christ? Like the young prophet Elisha, have you seen Him in His ascension? Have you peered through the rent veil to see a new Man in the throne with a ministry? Set your face like a flint, Abraham. Before you is Bethel, "the house of God." Behind you in the direction of Ur of the Chaldees, the place of your past, is Ai, "a heap of ruins." In that pile of rubble are some of my favorite previous teachings. In that heap are some concepts that you used to believe before you read this message. Don't look back now. Fix your vision on the One who is the Author and the Finisher. If you must have an idol, then idolize Him, our Role Model and Ruler!

Rom. 1:1 KJV:

Paul, a servant of Jesus Christ, called to be an apostle, separated unto the gospel of God,

Rom. 1:9 KJV:

For God is my witness, whom I serve with my spirit in the gospel of his Son, that without ceasing I make mention of you always in my prayers;

Rom 1:16 KJV:

For I am not ashamed of the gospel of Christ: for it is the power of God unto salvation to every one that believeth; to the Jew first, and also to the Greek.

The "Gospel of God" is the judgment written. This is the Bible, the Scriptures, the infallible and inerrant Word of God. The "Gospel of His Son" is the judgment personified. Jesus Christ was the Word made flesh (Jn. 1:14-18). "The Gospel of the Christ" is the execution of the judgment which He is! The Church is going to judge the world. The word for "judgment" is "krisis," from which we derive the English "crisis" and "criterion." The nature and the life of Jesus Christ is the standard by which all men are to be judged! His life, His image, His stature, His name ... He is the fulfillment of the law ... He is all that is right, for He is all-righteous.

The Mark Of The Beast Is A Present Reality

Christ is the image of God. Antichrist is any other image. There is a Man in the throne with a ministry, a ministry without idolatry, a ministry without two images. In the Most Holy Place, the emphasis and focus is not God and the devil, just God ... not the new man and the old man, just the new man. His Word is becoming flesh in our lives.

I Jn. 4:1-3 KJV:

Beloved, believe not every spirit, but try the spirits whether they are of God: because many false prophets are gone out into the world.

Hereby know ye the Spirit of God: Every spirit that confesseth that Jesus Christ is come in the flesh is of God:

And every spirit that confesseth not that Jesus Christ is come in the flesh is not of God: and this is that spirit of antichrist, whereof ye have heard that it should come; and even now already is it in the world.

This doesn't read "did come" in the flesh, or "will come" in the flesh ... He did and He will ... but "is come" in the flesh. That's the shocker. Note as well that this passage does not mention one who denies that He is come in the flesh. It says that the spirit of antichrist will not "confess" it. Our confession is our profession. Confession is a lifestyle. You can memorize this book and every Scripture in it, but if you don't speak out by the way you live every day that these truths are for the Church today, you have been taken by the spirit of error. I know that's strong, but this is the Day of the Lord. The party is over. Somebody says, "I still don't understand what you mean. All this is so new to my thinking." Then consider these verses.

Jn. 6:51 KJV:

I am the living bread which came down from heaven: if any man eat of this bread, he shall live for ever: and the bread that I will give is my flesh, which I will give for the life of the world.

Eph. 5:30 KJV:

For we are members of his body, of his flesh, and of his bones.

His bread is His flesh. His bread is His body. His body is His flesh. His Church is His body, His flesh, His bread. You are somebody's bread. The Church is the ongoing incarnation of Christ. The spirit of antichrist will not confess that He is come in His flesh, His body. In particular, that He has come in the flesh of His hand, the five-fold ministry. He who divided the five loaves divided Himself into five loaves, and He is speaking through His flesh.

Eph. 4:11 KJV:

And he gave some, apostles; and some, prophets; and some, evangelists; and some, pastors and teachers;

All through this section we have dealt with two images, Christ and antichrist. The right image and the wrong image. The way that the Father sees you and the way you see yourself. That is clear. But what about the "image of the beast" in the book of Revelation?

Rev. 13:13-18 KJV:

And he doeth great wonders, so that he maketh fire come down from heaven on the earth in the sight of men,

And deceiveth them that dwell on the earth by the means of those miracles which he had power to do in the sight of the beast; saying to them that dwell on the earth, that they should make an image to the beast, which had the wound by a sword, and did live.

And he had power to give life unto the image of the beast, that the image of the beast should both speak, and cause that as many as would not worship the image of the beast should be killed.

And he causeth all, both small and great, rich and poor, free and bond, to receive a mark in their right hand, or in their foreheads:

And that no man might buy or sell, save he that had the mark, or the name of the beast, or the number of his name.

Here is wisdom. Let him that hath understanding count the number of the beast: for it is the number of a man; and his number is six hundred threescore and six.

Rev. 14:9-11 KJV:

And the third angel followed them, saying with a loud voice, If any man worship the beast and his image, and receive his mark in his forehead, or in his hand,

The same shall drink of the wine of the wrath of God, which is poured out without mixture into the cup of his indignation; and he shall be tormented with fire and brimstone in the presence of the holy angels, and in the presence of the Lamb:

And the smoke of their torment ascendeth up for ever and ever: and they have no rest day nor night, who worship the beast and his image, and whosoever receiveth the mark of his name.

Rev. 15:2 KJV:

And I saw as it were a sea of glass mingled with fire: and them that had gotten the victory over the beast, and over his image, and over his mark, and over the number of his name, stand on the sea of glass, having the harps of God.

Rev. 16:2 KJV:

And the first went, and poured out his vial upon the earth; and there fell a noisome and grievous sore upon the men which had the mark of the beast, and upon them which worshipped his image.

Rev. 19:20 KJV:

And the beast was taken, and with him the false prophet that wrought miracles before him, with which he deceived them that had received the mark of the beast, and them that worshipped his image. These both were cast alive into a lake of fire burning with brimstone.

Rev. 20:4 KJV:

And I saw thrones, and they sat upon them, and judgment was given unto them: and I saw the souls of them that were beheaded for the witness of Jesus, and for the word of God, and which had not worshipped the beast, neither his image, neither had received his mark upon their foreheads, or in their hands; and they lived and reigned with Christ a thousand years.

These are the eight times that "charagma" or "mark" is used in the book of Revelation. The exegesis of all these verses is beyond the scope of this writing.

Taken as a whole, however, there is one principle in all of them that you must understand:

The mark of the beast is a present reality!

I'm not necessarily doing away with a future application to the mark of the beast. That will remain to be seen. But I want something that is relevant and practical. The word for "beast" in Rev. 13 is "therion," which means "a wild beast". Compare this with the wild man Ishmael. "Therion" is different from the word "beast" in the opening chapters describing the throne room; there the word means "living creatures." The word for "mark" in chapter 13 is "charagma" (#5480 in *Strong's*) which means "a scratch or etching; stamp (as a badge of servitude); sculptured figure (statue)." The underlying verb "charasso" means "to cut to a point, to inscribe." It is a mark, stamp, brand, or impress. Compare it with the word "charakter" of Heb. 1:3 where Jesus is the "express image" or "character" of God.

There is only one other place in the New Testament where "charagma" is used. It is interesting that this word is mentioned a total of nine times. Nine is the number of finality. Jesus said, "It is finished!" at the ninth hour. He dealt the death blow to the beast and its mark.

Acts 17:29 KJV:

> *Forasmuch then as we are the offspring of God, we ought not to think that the Godhead is like unto gold, or silver, or stone, graven by art and man's device.*

When Paul went to Athens, he saw the city wholly given to idolatry. It is interesting that some feel that the reason that this was the only city that the Apostle visited where he did not establish a New Testament church is because he appealed to his education and the philosophy of the Greeks. I hope that's not educational prejudice. One thing I do know: the more excellent ministry is a ministry without idolatry. It will not worship or show respect to any other image except Christ, in itself or in others. In the midst of this Athenian ignorance, an altar had been erected to the "unknown God." Paul had found his way to Mars Hill. Mars was the god of war. The "Mars Hill" of the Bible is Mount Sinai. There the law of sin and death energizes a Levitical order of ministry that can bring nothing to conclusion. All it can do is fight for the doctrine of its particular nation. Every idol on that hill was the product of man's mind and man's hand. Man imagined it, and then man fashioned what he had imagined. The word for "graven" here is "charagma," the same word describing the "mark" of the beast. Something characterized these idols.

Where was the mark of the beast? In the right hand and the forehead. The word for "art" in Acts 17:29 is "techne" and speaks of that which is made by "hand" ... handicraft. Consider the English derivatives "technology," "technician," "technical." The word for "man's device" is literally "man's inner reasoning." Man's wisdom and man's strength. Anything that has the mark of man's wisdom and man's strength, man's mind and man's hand, has the mark of the beast. Beastly wisdom and beastly strength ... all of it is wild. The irony is that the pre-tribulation rapture theory and all its trappings teaches that the Church will be gone and won't have to worry about the mark of the beast ... man's mind imagined that and man's hand is pushing it. That whole systematic deception has Adam's brand on it! The old man is a beast. The beast nature is the old nature. The beast nature is the Ishmael nature.

Gen. 16:1-4 KJV:

Now Sarai Abram's wife bare him no children: and she had an handmaid, an Egyptian, whose name was Hagar.

And Sarai said unto Abram, Behold now, the Lord hath restrained me from bearing: I pray thee, go in unto my maid; it may be that I may obtain children by her. And Abram hearkened to the voice of Sarai.

And Sarai Abram's wife took Hagar her maid the Egyptian, after Abram had dwelt ten years in the land of Canaan, and gave her to her husband Abram to be his wife.

And he went in unto Hagar, and she conceived: and when she saw that she had conceived, her mistress was despised in her eyes.

Ishmael was a product of Sarah's head and Abraham's loins ... human wisdom and human strength, just like the mark of the beast. Ishmael was a wild man who persecuted the son of promise, and still does. King Saul stood head and shoulders above his peers, illustrating the same principle. Ishmael was a good idea. "Maybe" it will work, Abraham. Throw out a fleece. Sarah, human wisdom, said, "Old man, if you can get Hagar pregnant, we'll know it's God!" What if I told you that God worked a miracle so that Abraham could produce the works of the flesh? When Hagar conceived, I can see Abraham strutting around the camp. "Look what I've done, everybody," he probably thought. Well, look what you've done, Abraham. You are the proud father of a wild ass! It looks like you, Abraham, but it has an Egyptian heart like its mother. The day will come when you will have to get rid of it, and what produced it.

Corporations hire men to sit in think tanks and come up with a "good idea." I wonder how many preachers are looking for a good idea? Brother, the last thing you need right now is a good idea! You need to hear from God. Cast out the bondwoman and her son. The time will come when every "good idea" will fail. Maybe that day is here. Men have run out of answers. Whoever is elected president this year will inherit, as one prophet said during the previous election, an office of confusion. What is the answer?

II Chron. 7:14 KJV:

> *If my people, which are called by my name, shall humble themselves, and pray, and seek my face, and turn from their wicked ways; then will I hear from heaven, and will forgive their sin, and will heal their land.*

Do you remember Nebuchadnezzar, king of Babylon, in the book of Daniel? He was a man who became a beast, and then was restored to sanity. What a panorama of the cycle of restoration and redemption as God brings man back to his senses through the cross of Christ.

Too long we have sought His hand, His power, what He can do. Now let us seek His face, His nature, who He is! The mark of the beast is stamped on everything that is a product of man's wisdom and strength. The mark of the beast is a present reality. But wait! There is another mind and another hand ... His! God has a plan. God is a Thinker. One day the Thinker thought, and then the Thinker spoke, and the Word was made flesh and tabernacled among us. God has imagined something. He has a dream and a vision. He has fashioned a masterpiece in His mind's eye ... a new Man in the throne with a ministry! A people just like Jesus! And what the mind of God has purposed, the hand of God (Eph. 4:11) is building! His technicians, working with the technology of the Holy Ghost, are laborers together with Him. Wise masterbuilders, or architects, who look at the Pattern and then create the masterpiece in His likeness and image. When the masterpiece is finished (Eph. 4:13), each will be a piece of the Master, the fullness of Him that filleth all in all!

Chapter Eight

A Groan From The Throne

God lives in a three-room house. The third room is the living room. The Mercy-seat is the love-seat. Out of that throne of grace flows a river of forgiveness and blessing. The more excellent ministry of the Lord Jesus Christ after the order of Melchisedec is:

1. A ministry without condemnation.
2. A ministry without prejudice.
3. A ministry without walls.
4. A ministry without retaliation.
5. A ministry without profanity.
6. A ministry without idolatry.

This is the grandest hour of Church history. There has never been a day like this before. For a young man or woman who will give his life to God, there is no limit to what He will do in you and through you. It's not enough to be hearers of this word of present truth. We must practice it.

I am persuaded that your greatest need is to be able to hear the voice of the Lord. Nothing is going to happen in your life or ministry until you hear Him speak. Everything is screaming at fever pitch in this generation. It is becoming increasingly more difficult to find a quiet place for a sweet hour of prayer. Then the parade starts. The cares of this life. Even the work of the Lord. Just be patient. Every parade I ever watched came to an end if I waited long enough.

Do you really want this ministry? Are you willing to sell out? The cost is dear. A baptism of fire awaits. It's going to take years for God to change you. Can you handle that? The greatest tests are going to come in your home and the local church. Those personal relationships are the key to your transformation.

Have you seen the glory of the Lord? Ezekiel did. He saw the likeness and appearance of a man (Ezek. 1:5). So have we ...

The Still, Small Voice

By now you know that I'm a Jesus preacher. He is the center and the focus of this whole message. In an hour when everyone is so concerned about his own feelings, may we dare ask our Head what might be on His heart?

I Kg. 19:11-12 KJV:

> *And he said, Go forth, and stand upon the mount before the Lord. And, behold, the Lord passed by, and a great and strong wind rent the mountains, and brake in pieces the rocks before the Lord; but the Lord was not in the wind: and after the wind an earthquake; but the Lord was not in the earthquake:*
>
> *And after the earthquake a fire; but the Lord was not in the fire: and after the fire a still small voice.*

I thank the Lord for all the ministers whom I have met and the Word that they proclaimed. Don't make a doctrine out of this, but I see the outpouring of the

Charismatic renewal of the 1960's as "the great and stormy wind." It did some rending and breaking, didn't it? Following that came the "earthquake" of the discipleship movement and the shepherding controversy of the 1970's. Now we are feeling the "fire" of the 1980's as He purges His Church. What awaits in the 1990's and the turning of the century? I believe that it will be His "still, small voice."

I hear something now. I hear it above the blowing of the wind, above the earthquake, and above the roaring of the flames of the fire. I hear Him. I hear a groan from the throne. It's so faint I can hardly hear it. But I do hear it.

The word for "still" here means "to be silent or to wait." One of its derivatives means "to whisper." Somebody said, "Brother Varner, the Lord has blessed you in the knowledge of the Scriptures." Yes, and I am grateful, but multiply what all of us know by one hundred times and then say with me, "I've only heard a whisper of the voice of God!" We've only come to the edges of His ways, to the border of the land called the mind of Christ. We stand on but the threshold of the Most Holy Place. The new day has only begun. What a great day to be alive! And think what our children are going to become!

The still, small voice. The word for "small" is the same word that described the manna as a "small" round thing. It was used to tell of the incense that was beaten very "small," that which was, literally, "crushed, broken, and ground." There is a Zion company. There is a people who have been apprehended for the top of the mountain. The word for "apprehended" in Phil. 3:1-14 is "katalambano," which means "to seize or lay hold of with intensity." The King has laid hold of us. Our Heavenly Husband is gripping us, desiring our love. May we hold Him with the same intensity!

There is a climbing-vine people who won't build their mansion halfway up the hill. The same nature that was in the root out of a dry ground is in them, an ability to find water and grow in the most difficult places. Above all the shouting, all the music, all the squeals of the religious playpens, above all that noise, I hear something. It's not very loud, but it is becoming more and more distinct. It's a voice ... the voice of a Man ... and I do believe that He is weeping ...

"Come Up Hither!"

Song 2:10-13 KJV:

My beloved spake, and said unto me, Rise up, my love, my fair one, and come away.

For, lo, the winter is past, the rain is over and gone;

The flowers appear on the earth; the time of the singing of birds is come, and the voice of the turtle is heard in our land;

The fig tree putteth forth her green figs, and the vines with the tender grape give a good smell. Arise, my love, my fair one, and come away.

Song 4:8 KJV:

Come with me from Lebanon, my spouse, with me from Lebanon: look from the top of Amana, from the top of Shenir and Hermon, from the lions' dens, from the mountains of the leopards.

There's a groan from the throne. There's a call from the top of Zion's hill. It's coming from the lips of One who has already entered into His rest. And now He waits, expecting His enemies to become His footstool. He longs for His Bride. In the Song of Songs, the King invites His Shulamite to "arise ... and come away." Later, He sings another verse, "Come with me ..." That sounds like something we have read in the New Testament.

Rev. 4:1 KJV:

After this I looked, and, behold, a door was opened in heaven: and the first voice which I heard was as it were of a trumpet talking with me; which said, Come up hither, and I will shew thee things which must be hereafter.

Rev. 21:9 KJV:

And there came unto me one of the seven angels which had the seven vials full of the seven last plagues, and talked with me, saying, Come hither, I will shew thee the bride, the Lamb's wife.

"Come up hither!" And once you have ascended into the hill of the Lord, "Come hither!" Covenants changed. The cry didn't. "Come away ... come with Me!" From deep within the Zion of my spirit, I hear the voice of my Beloved wooing His Church. I am often asked, "Where did you hear that? How did you discover that in the Scriptures?" The answer is simple. I heard God say it. As I have written this book, I have heard words and phrases in my spirit. Out of that Zion, I have heard a groan from the throne ... a thirsting ... a crying out ... a longing ...

Come out of the lower realms. Get away from the creeps and the crawlers and get around some climbers and some dreamers. The higher you go, the farther you can see. You will begin to look from the top, from His perspective. Look through the eye of His faith and see the end from the beginning. See with a faith that never stops believing. There is a crying desire from our Lord for someone to rise up and ascend into His same dimension of nature and ministry, to become a part of the more excellent ministry, and sit down with Him in the throne of grace.

The last thing I want this book to be is a good

teaching. I have sensed the power and presence of Jesus while writing this, and there must be a prophetic impartation to your spirit if you are to be changed. You must be anointed to hear just as I must be anointed to write. There's a groan from the throne. I can hear it. Can you? I don't condemn you if you can't. You won't until He pierces your ear. But I have heard it. And I must proclaim it. From deep within, My Saviour and Lord calls, "Son, I long for you. I long to hear your voice. I long to see your countenance. You're in the cleft of the rock ... you're in Christ. You're in the secret places of the stairs ... now that you're in Christ, begin to ascend into Christ."

The Shulamite had seen her blackness in Adam and her beauty in Christ. Only God can show you that. There is a dimension of holiness, dedication, sanctification, and purification that is about to break upon the Church. Like Isaiah in chapter five, we have been pouring out "woes" on everybody else. But when we see the Lord high and lifted up (Isa. 6), we will say, "Woe is me!"

All through this teaching we have seen God's purpose in three dimensions ... excellent things ... three-fold things. The Lord is beckoning us to come all the way up the mountain. Out of the Holy Place into the Most Holy Place. Out of Pentecost into Tabernacles. Out of adolescence and into manhood. From within the rent veil, He beckons us.

Psa. 122:1-3 NIV:

> *I rejoiced with those who said to me, "Let us go to the house of the Lord."*
> *Our feet are standing in your gates, O Jerusalem.*
> *Jerusalem is built like a city that is closely compacted together.*

The King James Version says that Jerusalem is a city that is "compact" or "joined, coupled" together. There were different levels to the city, and there's no one dimension of that city that is any more important than the other. There are three levels in our ascent toward the groan from the throne. All three levels are necessary and interdependent. There are people who live on the lower level, and there are middle-class folks in the Kingdom, and there are those who refuse to settle for anything less than God's best. These three levels were three mountains:

1. Mt. Ophel — the prophet.
2. Mt. Moriah — the priest.
3. Mt. Zion — the king.

The first level is Mt. Ophel, which means "hill, activity." There's a lot going on at that level. It was elevated above the lowlands (Psa. 40:2), revealing the victorious Christian life. We are to walk in victory on the first level! That's not the same as a full-grown overcomer, but there is a difference between victory and deliverance. Then II Chron. 27:3 tells us that King Jotham built much on Mount Ophel. There's building going on there. Finally, there's a spring halfway up the slope of this first mountain that bubbles out and runs down into the Pool of Siloam (Jn. 4:4; 7:38; 9:7), the place where Jesus healed a blind man. That's the place of the beginning of sight. Out of a man's belly shall flow ("rheo," which means "rhetoric") rivers of living water. There's a prophetic flow out of Mt. Ophel, but that's not the ultimate. I don't condemn those who live and stay on that level. I just thank God for those who want to rise above it. These have heard the groan from the throne. I can still hear a sound coming from the top of the mountain. Don't get content in Ophel. Some of you have heard Him say afresh, "Come up hither!"

What's on Mt. Moriah, the second mountain?

"Moriah" means "vision of Jehovah" and you'll begin to see as He sees when you get to this level. He'll open your eyes so that you can behold wondrous things out of His Word. There are only two scriptures in the Bible which mention the second level of our ascent:

Gen. 22:2 KJV:

And he said, Take now thy son, thine only son Isaac, whom thou lovest, and get thee into the land of Moriah; and offer him there for a burnt offering upon one of the mountains which I will tell thee of.

II Chron. 3:1 KJV:

Then Solomon began to build the house of the Lord at Jerusalem in mount Moriah, where the Lord appeared unto David his father, in the place that David had prepared in the threshingfloor of Ornan the Jebusite.

Both these verses reveal the principle of Body life and ministry. You'll have to lay down everything, for Isaac was a burnt offering, or "ascending offering," and God got 100% of that! Compare Rom. 12:1-2. Dedication and consecration are not exampled by those who return from a backslidden condition, bawling all over the altar, and crying, "Lord, help me! Help me!" Then the same fellow comes back next week and gets "saved" all over again. That's not rededication, that's repentance. Real dedication takes place when a people who are already holy, already committed, and already set apart hear an upward call ... the high calling ... and say, "Speak, Lord. Here I am." Do you want to be a burnt offering? Do you want Him to set fire to your head, your reasonings? Your inward parts, the affections will be washed with pure water on the mountain of sacrifice. Your legs, your ability to stand in Him, will be cleansed on Moriah. You will learn the meaning of worship there. Worship is sacrifice.

Second, Solomon built a Temple on Mt. Moriah. The man of peace built a sanctuary on the second level. There's a price to "come up hither." What is your Isaac? You'll have to put the axe to your ministry. After Abraham made six separations, he made number seven ... He separated from Isaac. God had promised a son, an heir. The promise was now a reality. Abraham had held his son in his arms, had felt his warmth and heard him breathe. Now God said, "Give him back! Now that I've fulfilled your ministry and have made good My Word and promises to you, give it all back to Me." Do we love the promise or the God of the promise? Are you content just to be one of the stones in the Temple at the second level? There are no famous preachers on Mt. Moriah. Instead, there is a merging of ministry, a baptizing of one's ministry into the Body of Christ. We see the ministry of the priest on this second level. A love that lays down its life for the brethren. A place where you begin to lose your individuality for the Kingdom of God. Men can't be bought at this level. Praise them or curse them, it won't move them. It doesn't matter. Men aren't calling you to the top ... a still, small voice is! After the Baptism in the Holy Ghost, you get what you pay for. Many will settle down in Moriah. But the voice is getting louder. From the top He beckons, "Come up hither!"

Mt. Ophel ... Mt. Moriah ... Mt. Zion. Prophet, priest, and king. "Zion" means "mountain of light." Somebody is going to stand with Him and then sit with Him in the throne (Psa. 15; 24; Rev. 14:1-5). There's a groan from the throne. The thrones of the kings are in Zion, speaking of His life. The tombs of the kings are in Zion, speaking of His death. As we ascend the hill of the Lord, we are not leaving behind the prophetic and the priestly dimensions. The greater always swallows up the lesser. The Apostle Paul noted that some have the fragrance of death about them (II Cor. 2:14-16). The cross has begun its work but then men draw a line. Others who have relinquished the luxury of their own rights have the sentence of death in them (II Cor. 1:8-9). These overcomers are the prisoners of the Lord, His bond-slaves. They only and always face one direction. Their hands and feet are tied. These are crucified men, helpless and defenseless. These have the resemblance of a Slain Lamb. These won't fight back ... they can't. They have become deaf to every other sound but one ... a groan from the throne.

Jn. 11:33 KJV:

> *When Jesus therefore saw her weeping, and the Jews also weeping which came with her, he groaned in the spirit, and was troubled,*

Jn. 11:38 KJV:

> *Jesus therefore again groaning in himself cometh to the grave. It was a cave, and a stone lay upon it.*

Jesus groaned the first time. But then He groaned again. The Head groaned. But He is groaning again through His Body (Gal. 4:4-7). The eighth chapter of Romans tells us that the "whole creation" is groaning together, and Rev. 3:14 lets us know that He is the "beginning" of the new creation man. He's still the King of kings and the Lord of lords, but He condescends to my spirit and groans with me! He travails with me! He is groaning. Are you groaning with us? Lord, let me learn the secret of the still, small voice. A voice that has been crushed and broken and wounded. A voice of no reputation. A voice that is completely unselfish. I can still hear Him. From the top of Zion, out of the Mercy-seat, the throne of grace, I can hear Jesus pray ...

Jn. 17:20-24 KJV:

Neither pray I for these alone, but for them also which shall believe on me through their word;

That they all may be one; as thou, Father, art in me, and I in thee, that they also may be one in us: that the world may believe that thou hast sent me.

And the glory which thou gavest me I have given them; that they may be one, even as we are one:

I in them, and thou in me, that they may be made perfect in one; and that the world may know that thou hast sent me, and hast loved them, as thou hast loved me.

Father, I will that they also, whom thou hast given me, be with me where I am; that they may behold my glory, which thou hast given me: for thou lovedst me before the foundation of the world.

"I Thirst!"

There is a powerful study in the Old Testament that illustrates the groan from the throne. It is taken from the life and ministry of David, a type of King Jesus.

II Sam. 23:13-17 KJV:

And three of the thirty chief went down, and came to David in the harvest time unto the cave of Adullam: and the troop of the Philistines pitched in the valley of Rephaim.

And David was then in an hold, and the garrison of the Philistines was then in Bethlehem.

And David longed, and said, Oh that one would give me drink of the water of the well of Bethlehem, which is by the gate!

And the three mighty men brake through the host of the Philistines, and drew water out of the well of Bethlehem, that was by the gate, and took it, and brought it to David: nevertheless he would not drink thereof, but poured it out unto the Lord.

And he said, Be it far from me, O Lord, that I should do this: is not this the blood of the men that went in jeopardy of their lives? therefore he would not drink it. These things did these three mighty men.

"And David longed ..." Do you see that? This deep desire of David illustrates the deep desire of Jesus for men to see the more excellent ministry, to hear the intercession of the Man in the throne with a ministry, and to draw near with full assurance of faith.

"... and said, 'Oh ...' " There it is. The groan from the throne. A groan so deep that it cannot be articulated. Can you feel the weight of His emotions? He took the cup in the garden and drank it on the cross. He settled the conflict in the olive-press. Jesus loves all men with an everlasting love. He is able to save us to the uttermost through His intercession.

"... that one ..." Not just any one, but a choice one. A prepared one. A sanctified one. A holy one. One that has been called to go to the top of the mountain.

Song 6:8-9 KJV:

There are threescore queens, and fourscore concubines, and virgins without number.

My dove, my undefiled is but one; she is the only one of her mother, she is the choice one of her that bare her. The daughters saw her, and blessed her; yea, the queens and the concubines, and they praised her.

"... would give me to drink ..." This truth is so foreign to the average Christian. If you are a parent, you can relate. If you are a pastor, you long to be ministered to. All of us have sung, "Fill my cup, Lord." But have you realized that He wants ministry, too? We are the water He wants. Two verses reveal this truth so powerfully:

Jn. 4:7 KJV:

There cometh a woman of Samaria to draw water: Jesus saith unto her, Give me to drink.

Jn. 19:28 KJV:

After this, Jesus knowing that all things were now accomplished, that the scripture might be fulfilled, saith, I thirst.

That is awesome! It's one thing to let God supply your daily bread. It's another thing to be the bread of God. It's one thing to drink of Him. It's another thing for Him to drink of you. In the Song of Solomon, the Bridegroom fed among the lilies, that which was fragile, holy, and pure. On the cross, He was God thirsting for man and man thirsting for God.

"... of the water of the well of Bethlehem ..." Not just any water will do. David longed for a drink of water from the old home place, the place of familiar surroundings. Bethlehem means "house of bread" and speaks of the Body of Christ. Jesus longs for the drink that He saw when these predetermined purposes were set forth by the Father. He saw the joy that was set before Him, a people in His image. We are His cup. With wisdom He planned the design of that cup. With passion He will drink from that people!

"... which is by the gate ..." Gates speak of praise (Isa. 60:18). He longs to hear the voice of the Bride calling unto Him in worship so that He can answer and show her great and mighty things which she has not considered. Gates also speak of counsel and might. There is a wisdom that cannot be resisted, reserved for the overcomer.

"... And the three mighty men brake through the host ..." There is coming a Divine breakthrough into the unlimited! There shall be a three-fold breaking through...spirit, soul, and body. Somebody is going to arise and walk in what He died for. Somebody is going to put his "life" or "soul" in jeopardy to see this breakthrough become a reality. Somebody is going to pay the price to meet the need of the King. How these men must have loved their leader!

Rev. 3:21-22 KJV:

To him that overcometh will I grant to sit with me in my throne, even as I also overcame, and am set down with my Father in his throne.

He that hath an ear, let him hear what the Spirit saith unto the churches.

Somebody is going to step out and be part of a firstfruits company. Somebody is going to be a pioneer and a trailblazer. Somebody is going to pour out his life so that others can enter in. Somebody is going to become just like Jesus, the Man in the throne with a ministry.

From the top of Zion's hill, there goes forth a still, small voice. It's a groan from the throne. Some will only hear it as thunder. Others can't hear it above the voice of their angel, or messenger. But there is an anointed people who know "this voice" to be His voice ...

Jn. 12:28-30 KJV:

Father, glorify thy name. Then came there a voice from heaven, saying, I have both glorified it, and will glorify it again.

The people therefore, that stood by, and heard it, said that it thundered: others said, An angel spake to him.

Jesus answered and said, This voice came not because of me, but for your sakes.

The veil is rent. The way is made. The path is soaked with blood. All is now ready. Nothing is held back. The

King in Zion awaits. The invitations have been sent. It's time to arise and ascend. He waits for our response ...

Rev. 22:17 KJV:

And the Spirit and the bride say, Come. And let him that heareth say, Come. And let him that is athirst come. And whosoever will, let him take the water of life freely.

Turn Your Face Into The Wind

This is a prophetic word given to the Church through God's servant, David Minor, April 6, 1987 (quoted by permission). It speaks of the Day of Atonement and the cleansing of the Church. Hear the Word of the Lord:

"The Spirit of God would say to you that the Wind of the Holy Spirit is blowing through the land. The Church, however, is incapable of fully recognizing this Wind. Just as your nation has given names to hurricanes, so I have put My Name on this Wind. This Wind shall be named HOLINESS UNTO THE LORD.

"Because of a lack of understanding, some of My people will try to find shelter from the Wind, but in so doing, they shall miss My work. For this Wind has been sent to blow through every institution that has been raised in My Name. In those institutions that have substituted their name for Mine, they shall fall by the impact of My Wind. Those institutions shall fall like cardboard shacks in a gale. Ministries that have not walked in uprightness before Me shall be broken and fall.

"For this reason, man will be tempted to brand this as a work of satan, but do not be misled. This is My Wind. I cannot tolerate My Church in its present form, nor will I tolerate it. Ministries and organizations will shake and fall in the face of this Wind, and even though some will seek to hide from that Wind, they shall not escape. It shall blow against your lives and all around you will appear crumbling, and so it shall.

"But never forget this is My Wind, saith the Lord. With tornado force it will come and appear to leave devastation, but the Wind of the Lord comes and says, 'Turn your face into the Wind and let it blow.' For only that which is not of Me shall be devasted. You must see this as necessary.

"Be not dismayed. For after this, My Wind shall blow again. Have you not read how My breath blew on the valley of dry bones? So it shall breathe on you. The Wind will come in equal force as the first Wind. This Wind, too, will have a name. It shall be called THE KINGDOM OF GOD.

"It shall bring My government and order. Along with that it shall bring My power. The supernatural shall come in that Wind. The world will laugh at you because of the devastation of that first Wind, but they will laugh no more. For this Wind will come with force and power that will produce the miraculous among My people, and the fear of the Lord shall fall on the nation.

"My people will be willing in the day of My power, saith the Lord. In My first Wind that is upon you now, I will blow out pride, lust, greed, competition, and jealousy, and you will feel devastated, but haven't you read, 'Blessed are the poor in spirit, for theirs is the Kingdom of Heaven?' So out of your poverty of spirit I will establish My Kingdom. Have you not read, 'The Kingdom of God is in the Holy Ghost?' So by My Spirit, My Kingdom will be established and made manifest.

"Know this also, there will be those who shall seek to hide from this present Wind and they will try to flow with the second Wind. But again, they will be blown away by it. Only those who have turned their faces into the present Wind shall be allowed to be propelled by the second Wind.

"You have longed for revival and a return of the miraculous and the supernatural. You and your generation shall see it, but it shall only come by My process, saith the Lord. The Church of this nation cannot contain My power in its present form. But as it turns to the Wind of the Holiness of God, it shall be purged and changed to contain My glory. This is judgment that has begun to the house of God, but it is not the end. When the second Wind has come and brought in My harvest, then shall the end come."

Books By Kelley Varner

How To Order

The cost of each book listed below is given along with the number of cassette tapes which accompany the book. We ask for an offering for the tapes at the following rates:

1 tape — $2.00

4 tapes in an album — $10.00

8 tapes in an album — $20.00

12 tapes in an album — $25.00

16 tapes in an album — $30.00

Your offering for the books and tapes is used to purchase supplies, purchase and maintain equipment, and, most importantly, to send literature and tapes to ministries and saints in other nations for whom nothing has been prepared (Neh. 8:10). We do not actually sell these books, but request these nominal donations to cover our cost.

PREVAIL: A HANDBOOK FOR THE OVERCOMER
— published by Revival Press. Now in its 3rd reprinting since 1982. 170 pages. Three major principles: Jesus is Priest and King, Salvation Is Progressive, and Pressing through Tribulation. What is the balance to the "faith" message? What is the transformation of the soul? How are our minds being renewed? Does God want to take us out or bring us through? This book will provide a much needed balance of the presentation of the foundational truths of the Kingdom of God, and will tear down many traditional strongholds. After the Baptism of the Holy Ghost, then what? —$6.00 (16 tapes available)

PRINCIPLES OF PRESENT TRUTH FROM GENESIS — 76 fullsized pages (4 tapes). What is the Garden of Eden? What is the spiritual significance of Noah's Ark? What are the seven separations of Abraham? What is the Joseph Company? This book is a chapter-by-chapter analysis with an emphasis upon Gen. 1-2 and the life of Abraham. It is the seed-plot of the whole Bible. — $3.00

PRINCIPLES OF PRESENT TRUTH FROM EXODUS-DEUTERONOMY — 152 fullsized pages (4 tapes). What are the three dimensions of the Passover principle? What are five ways to teach the Tabernacle of Moses? What is the significance of the seven Feasts of the Lord? What is the typology of the five major Offerings? Why should every pastor know about the garments of the High Priest? This book places major emphasis upon the Tabernacle of Moses, the Feasts, the Offerings, and the Priesthood. Many diagrams and charts facilitate these studies. Every Bible teacher has to be versed in this. — $3.00

PRINCIPLES OF PRESENT TRUTH FROM JOSHUA-RUTH — 130 fullsized pages (4 tapes). What are principles for possessing the land? What is the Passover of Conquest? What is the significance of the fall of Jericho? Why are the Judges the forerunners of the Kingdom? How can we see in the book of Ruth a detailed picture of the believer's walk from conception to perfection? This book is a chapter-by-chapter analysis of Joshua and Judges, and a verse-by-verse study from the book of Ruth. The entire text of Ruth, using the Hebrew text and other translations, is included. Many charts and diagrams. — $3.00

PRINCIPLES OF PRESENT TRUTH FROM I-II SAMUEL, I CHRONICLES — 120 fullsized pages (4 tapes). Why is there an existing Eli and a growing Samuel? What is the typology of Saul as the old order and David as the new order? What is the panoramic significance of the story of David and Goliath? Why was Jonathan a picture of the man on the fence? What is the Tabernacle of David? This volume highlights Kingdom typology from these O.T. books, emphasizing the lives and the ministries of Samuel, Saul, David, and Jonathan. Many charts and diagrams. — $3.00

PRINCIPLES OF PRESENT TRUTH FROM I-II KINGS, II CHRONICLES — 130 fullsized pages (4 tapes). What is the typology of Solomon and his Temple? What is the Elijah ministry? What is the significance of the School of the Prophets? This book begins with an in-depth look at Solomon's reign with an emphasis upon the Temple. Each of the subsequent kings of Judah and Israel are analyzed, with an emphasis upon the ministry of the prophets, especially Elijah and Elisha. — $3.00

PRINCIPLES OF PRESENT TRUTH FROM EZRA-ESTHER — 130 fullsized pages (4 tapes). How do these books of restoration parallel the restoration of the Church? What are the twelve gates of Nehemiah? Why does the rebuilding of walls picture the building of the human personality and the transformation of the soul? What is the typology of the book of Esther and what does it have to do with the day of the Lord? Many charts and diagrams. — $3.00

PRINCIPLES OF PRESENT TRUTH FROM JOB — 118 fullsized pages (4 tapes). Pastor Varner considers this volume the most difficult work he has attempted. Why do the righteous suffer? Was God or the devil to blame for Job's plight? Why are Eliphaz, Bildad, and Zophar a picture of the soul of man? Why is Elihu a second-day ministry? Who are Behemoth and Leviathan? Why is Jesus our Heavenly Job? What is the significance of the restoration of Job? This book is a chapter-by-chapter and verse-by-verse study and is a most unique presentation. — $3.00

PRINCIPLES OF PRESENT TRUTH FROM PSALMS 1-72 — 154 fullsized pages (4 tapes). Who wrote the Psalms and how are they categorized? What kinds of musical instruments were used in the Bible? What is the importance of Zion and the Tabernacle of David? This book is a chapter-by-chapter and verse-by-verse study of each of these Psalms. Outlines and background material is included with each chapter. The first 33 pages furnish a most thorough introduction to the whole book of Psalms. A must for minstrels. — $3.00

PRINCIPLES OF PRESENT TRUTH FROM PSALMS 73-150 — 156 fullsized pages (4 tapes). Who was Asaph? What is the significance of Psalms 119? What are the Songs of Degrees and how do they picture the believer's ascent into Zion or the ascent of the soul into union with the spirit? This book is a chapter-by-chapter and a verse-by-verse study of each of the remaining Psalms. A must for minstrels. — $3.00

PRINCIPLES OF PRESENT TRUTH FROM PROVERBS

— 118 fullsized pages (4 tapes). Why is this book a book about sonship? How can we release the wisdom of God? What is the significance of the Strange Woman and the Virtuous Woman and how do these picture two kinds of minds? This volume includes a thorough introduction, a verse-by-verse study of chapters 1-9 and 30-31. It is great for young people, for chapters 10-29 are presented under 40 topical headings, analyzing areas of practical, daily Christian living. — $3.00

PRINCIPLES OF PRESENT TRUTH FROM ECCLESIASTES AND THE SONG OF SOLOMON

— 142 fullsized pages. Why is Ecclesiastes the book of the natural mind? Who is the Preacher? What is life under the sun? Why is Eccl. 12 a picture of an order or age that is dying? Who is the Shulamite? What is the relationship between Brideship and Sonship? How is the Song a picture of the development of the believer from conception to perfection? What are seven ways to teach the Song of Solomon? This book gives a thorough introduction to each of these neglected O.T. books. Many fresh insights are opened from Ecclesiastes. The Song is done VERSE BY VERSE! It includes the entire text, other translations, key principles, and a continuous story line! (4 tapes on Ecclesiates and 4 tapes on the Song of Solomon) — $3.00

PRINCIPLES OF PRESENT TRUTH FROM ISAIAH 1-39

— 148 fullsized pages (4 tapes). Who was the man Isaiah? What is the Day of the Lord? Who is the Branch? What are the Seven Spirits of God? Who is Lucifer? What is the significance of Zion? This book furnishes a thorough introduction to the whole book of Isaiah. It is presented in a chapter-by-chapter, verse-by-verse format. An overview of all the prophetical books is included. — $3.00

PRINCIPLES OF PRESENT TRUTH FROM ISAIAH 40-66 — 120 fullsized pages (4 tapes). Who is the Servant of Jehovah? Why does the Servant become servants after chapter 53? Who was Cyrus and what is the significant typology pertaining to him? How are Isa. 58-66 an overview of the Feast of Tabernacles? What is the nation born in a day? This book furnishes a chapter-by-chapter and verse-by-verse study of the remaining chapters of Isaiah. A separate 20-tape series on a verse-by-verse study of Isa. 53 also. — $3.00

PRINCIPLES OF PRESENT TRUTH FROM JEREMIAH — 156 fullsized pages (8 tapes). Who was the man Jeremiah? How is he a prophet to the nations? How does this important book supplement the history of Kings and Chronicles? Who is the modern-day "Judah" to whom this message is sent? What is the significance of the potter's wheel? What about false pastors and shepherds? What is the meaning of each message to the various nations? What about the fall of Babylon? This book furnishes a chapter-by-chapter and verse-by-verse study of this important prophecy. — $3.00

PRINCIPLES OF PRESENT TRUTH FROM EZEKIEL — 138 fullsized pages (8 tapes). This volume was co-authored with Bill Britton's notes. Why is this an end-time book? What did Ezekiel see in chapter one? What is the glory of the Lord? What is the eschatological significance of chapters eight and nine? What are the cherubim? How do Ezekiel's prophecies to the nations compare with those of Isaiah and Jeremiah? How does the prophet deal with false ministries in chapter 34? What about the New Covenant of chapter 36? What is the meaning of the vision of the dry bones? Who are Gog and Magog? What temple did Ezekiel see in chapters 40-48? How does this book compare to the book of Revelation? This volume is a chapter-by-chapter and verse-by-verse treatment of the entire text of this neglected prophecy. — $3.00

THE TABERNACLE OF MOSES — 100 fullsized pages (8 or 24 tapes). What are five ways to teach this pattern of heavenly things? Whose mansion is it? What is the significance of the Ark of the Covenant and the Most Holy Place? This book is filled with notes and outlines. This revelation must be mastered to fully understand the Word of God. Many drawings, charts, and outlines. A must for Bible teachers. — $3.00

THE SERMON ON THE MOUNT — 50 fullsized pages (from 8 to 40 tapes). What is the Kingdom of God? How many kingdoms are there? What is the motive and the purpose of the Kingdom? Why is the Church the instrument of the Kingdom? This is an in-depth study about the Kingdom of God. It is a VERSE-BY-VERSE study of Matt. 5-7, emphasizing the Beatitudes (the Preamble) and the principles (laws) of Christian living. This material will help a new believer and also challenge the more serious Bible student. Very practical. For those who want to know the purpose of the Baptism of the Holy Ghost. — $2.00

THE TONGUE OF THE LEARNED — with J. L. Dutton — over 60 fullsized pages (56 tapes to date). What about the preeminence of the Lord Jesus Christ? What does the Bible say about the Kingdom of God? How do we walk with the Lord? What do the Scriptures say about the Father-son relationship? What about the ministry of the Holy Spirit? Are the gifts of the Holy Spirit (a study of spiritual ministry) for us today? What are the Bible principles governing prayer, praise, and worship? What is the importance of the Church? What is the role and purpose of the Local Church? This book gives the definitions of 335 Bible terms under nine practical headings. The vocabulary of the Kingdom, studied from the original languages of the Bible. Excellent for the classroom. Used in many Bible Schools and churches, both here and abroad. If you have just been introduced to the Kingdom message, this volume is what you need. — $2.00

CHOOSE YE THIS DAY: THE CONFLICTS OF JONATHAN — 34 pages (8 tapes). Why is Saul a picture of the old order? Why is Jonathan a hypocrite? What is the significance of the battle between David and Goliath? Is the Church the Seed of David? What does Saul's encounter with the witch of Endor have to do with the rise of the occult today? This book is in sermon form and tells of the life and ministry of the son of King Saul. A study of the old order and the new order from I Sam. 13-31. For the man on the fence. — $1.00

THE HOLY GHOST BAPTISM — 35 pages (16 tapes). Who is the Holy Spirit? What is His ministry in the Old and New Testaments? Is the Holy Ghost Baptism a present reality for the Church? What are three New Testament purposes for speaking with tongues? How to minister and receive this experience. Excuses are answered with Scriptures. More answers are given to the most frequently asked questions. Bible terminology. Every pastor needs this book. — $1.00

THE LAND AND THE THRONE — 44 pages (4 tapes). What is the significance of Jesus being the Seed of Abraham and the Seed of David? What is the inheritance of the believer? Is it a mansion of gold or the multitude of the nations? This book is an in-depth study of the Abrahamic and Davidic Covenants. Jesus has the land and Jesus has the Throne. The Land is the Earth, and the Throne is the right to rule it! A return to Covenant Theology. Keys to eschatology. — $1.00

THE HOUR IS COME — 28 pages (4 tapes). What is the glorification of the son of man? Who is the corn of wheat? Why do we want to go to hell? How low will you go? This book in sermon form is an exegesis of Jn. 12:20-33. A real challenge to world evangelism. The time is NOW! The Day of Atonement. — $1.00

THE TWELVE GATES OF THE CITY — 27 pages (16 tapes). Is the city of Rev. 21 a literal city? What is the Bible truth about heaven? What about the mansions and the golden streets? The gates of pearl? How does the Christ nature progressively unfold from within the believer? How does the city come from heaven to earth, from the invisible to the visible realm? This book of notes is a VERSE-BY-VERSE study of Rev. 21. The old order concept of heaven is examined. The city is a people. A study of Gen. 49 and the sons of Jacob — from Reuben to Benjamin. For teachers. — $1.00

THE POWER OF THE FLAMING SWORD — 21 pages (8 tapes). What is the flaming sword? How powerful are the words which we speak? What does the Bible have to say about the sword? This book in sermon form is a message concerning our speaking the creative Word of the Lord. This is emphasized in the areas of prayer, praise, and prophecy. — $1.00

THE IMPORTANCE OF THE HOME AND FAMILY — 30 pages (1 tape). What is the importance of the home as the basic unit of society? What is the parallel between the home and the Local Church? What are the two institutions that God has ordained and what is the order of authority in each? What is the significance of the home being a wineskin? What connection is there between the Elijah ministry and the home? This book in sermon form is the first of 12. — $1.00

A LAMB FOR A HOUSE — 39 pages (1 tape). What is God's method of bringing a nation out of bondage? What is the Passover of the Kingdom? What are the characteristics of the Lamb? What about spiritual immunity? This book in sermon form is an exegesis of Ex. 12 and is an excellent study about the home and family. Good for pastors and teachers. — $1.00

KINGDOM PRINCIPLES FOR THE HOME — 43 pages (1 tape). What is the principle of love? What is the principle of mutual respect? What is the principle of open communication? This book in sermon form gives a unique study of the Bible definition of love from the New Testament Greek of I Cor. 13:1-13 (plus the use of several other translations). — $1.00

SKYWALKERS — 44 pages (8 tapes). What examples for teenagers are provided in Samuel, David, Esther, Ruth, Joash, Jesus, and others? How can our young people live in the heavenlies today? This study was prepared by Pastor Varner for our teens. He was assisted by Sue Baird. Other local churches are now using this series to teach their young people. This is very practical. This class was taught as part of the curriculum of our Christian School. — $1.00

DARE TO BE DIFFERENT — 30 pages (8 tapes). Another good book for teens, this was presented in our Christian School. There are two kingdoms. We must dare to be different in our attitude, obedience, joy, meditation, dependability, gratefulness, discernment, perception, enthusiasm, kindness, forgiveness, modesty, and boldness. These are characteristics of young people who are walking in the Kingdom of God. These 13 lessons are also excellent Sunday School material. — $1.00

FOUR FOUNDATIONS OF EFFECTUAL PRAYER — 24 pages (8 tapes). There is a tremendous emphasis on prayer at this time. Here is examined a familiar subject from a fresh perspective. We need to understand prayer from God's side of the Covenant. His thanksgiving for us, His righteousness to us, His boldness through us, and His compassion among us are four principles which must be understood. — $1.00

A VISION OF YOUR WORTH — 28 pages (4 tapes). Every Christian must know His worth in Christ. Worthy is the Lamb! What is the worthy portion? What does it mean to be counted worthy? Who is the lambkin? The answers to these questions will help the believer to become all he can in the Lord. — $1.00

SING, O BARREN — 28 pages (4 tapes). God wants every one of us to be fruitful. We can see keys to this by studying the lives of Sarah, Rebekah, Rachel, Manoah's wife, Hannah, Elizabeth, and Mary. We must travail so that the Christ within us can be formed. There are seven powerful truths coming forth from the Body of Christ. — $1.00

PRAISE TABERNACLE CORRESPONDENCE COURSE

UNDERSTANDING THE KING AND HIS KINGDOM — a one-, two-, or three-year study program — "36 Steps Toward Your Understanding the Bible." Certificates will be given for the completion of each of the first two years and a diploma for the completion of the third year.

Additional Available Tape Series

Jesus, Lord of the Home (12 tapes)
Are You Ready for the Third Dimension? (8 tapes)
Israel: God's Chosen People (8 tapes)
The Kingdom of God (8 tapes)
Spiritual Ministry (12 tapes)
Servant Power (8 tapes)
Four-fold Definition of the Local Church (16 tapes)
The New Testament Local Church (32 tapes)
Halloween, Christmas, Easter (8 tapes)
God's Two Greatest Mysteries (8 tapes)

The Coming of the Lord (12 tapes)
Women's Ministry (8 tapes)
The Book of Acts (8 tapes)
Principles of Kingdom Finance (8 tapes)
Bible Patterns of the Kingdom (12 tapes)
The Faith of God (8 tapes)
The Five-fold Ministry (12 tapes)
Life and Immortality (12 tapes)
Water Baptism (8 tapes)
The Day of Atonement (8 tapes)
Principles of Restoration (12 tapes)
The Will of God (8 tapes)
The Songs of Degrees (16 tapes)
The Emerging Christ (12 tapes)
Apostolic Principles (12 tapes)
Romans, Verse-by-verse (from 8 to 30 tapes)
The Feast of Tabernacles (16 tapes)
The More Excellent Ministry (8 tapes) — these are the
original tapes preached at the House of Prayer in 1981

TAPE OF THE MONTH

There is made available each month two cassette
tapes chosen by Pastor Varner. These messages are
ministered by him and others in the five-fold ministry.
You may join this growing list of listeners on a
monthly offering basis.

TAPE CATALOG

Write or call for your copy of the catalog listing over
500 messages preached by Pastor Varner here at
Praise Tabernacle. There are also listed hundreds of
other messages preached by dozens of other brethren.

SEMINARS AND CONVENTIONS

There are annual meetings here in Richlands for the Body of Christ. Please inquire for further information on the next meeting.

There is a team of ministry here at Praise Tabernacle that is available to your local church to teach the principles of restoration and assist in the areas of praise and worship. Please contact Pastor Varner.

WRITE: Praise Tabernacle
P.O. Box 785
Richlands, N.C. 28574-0785

PHONE: (919) 324-5026 or 324-5027

You may photocopy form for re-use

ORDER FORM

For Phone Orders Call:
919-324-5026 or
919-324-5027

Return with your check or M.O. to Praise Tabernacle, P.O. Box 785, Richlands, N.C. 28574-0785

QTY.	DESCRIPTION	UNIT PRICE	TOT. PRICE
		SUBTOTAL	

Name _____
Address _____   LESS DISCOUNT _____
City/State/ZIP _____   SHIPPING _____
Date _____ Phone# _____   TOTAL DUE _____